# "If It Wasn't for the Women . . . "

# "If It Wasn't for the Women . . . "

*Black Women's Experience
and Womanist Culture
in Church and Community*

## Cheryl Townsend Gilkes

ORBIS BOOKS

**Maryknoll, New York 10545**

Second printing, December 2001

The Catholic Foreign Mission Society of America (Maryknoll) recruits and trains people for overseas missionary service. Through Orbis Books, Maryknoll aims to foster the international dialogue that is essential to mission. The books published, however, reflect the opinions of their authors and are not meant to represent the official position of the society.

To obtain more information about Maryknoll and Orbis Books, please visit our website at www.maryknoll.org.

Copyright © 2001 by Cheryl Townsend Gilkes.

Published by Orbis Books, Maryknoll, NY 10545-0308.

For information on publication history, see pages 247-48.

Manufactured in the United States of America

Typesetting by Joan Weber Laflamme

**Library of Congress Cataloging-in-Publication Data**

Gilkes, Cheryl.
    If it wasn't for the women—: Black women's experience and womanist culture in church and community / Cheryl Townsend Gilkes.
        p. cm.
    Includes bibliographical references and index.
    ISBN 1-57075-343-1 (pbk.)
    1. Afro-American women—Religious life. 2. Afro-American women political activists. 3. Womanist theology. I. Title.

BR563.N4 G54 2000
277.3'0082—dc21

                                                                    00-047863

In Loving Memory
of
Gertrude Holmes Gaines
Clorae Hunt Evereteze
and
Glennie Mae Moseley Crawford

Just a few of the women whose lives generated the questions
I keep asking and trying to answer—

# Contents

*vii*

## PART 4
## CRISES, CONFRONTATIONS, AND CONFLICTS

# Introduction

# Community, Churchwork, Culture, and Crisis

## Toward a Sociology of Indispensable Black Women

The denominational bookstore was an absolute treasure trove. When the manager understood my research project, she went into the back room and came out with a rare historical volume that was absolutely essential to my research. "There are only a few of these left and I have been saving them for the right people." As far as she was concerned, I was one of the right people, and the volume would prove invaluable in my later writing on the Sanctified Church. I shopped the bookstore thoroughly because of the many booklets and handbooks important to ministers, evangelists, and other church workers that were in stock. These would serve as important primary sources for later analysis as primary denominational documents. The prominence and importance of black women in the life of this particular denomination were exhibited plainly in these documents full of rules and regulations, and I did not want to miss a page. They were emblems that offered answers to larger questions about black women in their churches and communities and offered compelling evidence of the well-elaborated women's culture that operated as a political and economic force in the life of the church.

Understanding the importance of women to the institutions of African-American life and culture required immersion in the social worlds of black women. It was one such immersion in a world of black women that had brought me to the denominational bookstore that morning. I was especially intrigued by the handbook for the women's department. As I asked the bookstore manager if I had acquired everything I needed to understand the women's department, a male customer shook his head derisively muttering, "The women's department, the women's department, I'm so tired of the women's department." The manager responded forcefully, confidently, calmly, and not hostilely, "If it wasn't for the women, you wouldn't have a church!"

*1*

This kind of confidence and forbearance was nothing like the images of women presented either in the women's movement, which depicted black women as so oppressed that they were unable to cope with life at any level, or in the social-scientific perspectives that pointed to overbearing and castrating matriarchs whose welfare dependency or professional aggression crippled black men and therefore the black community. The bookstore manager's voice echoed a women's history that demanded an understanding in its own right and not as an explanation of deviance, difference, or pathology.

Several years earlier, when teaching my first sociology courses, I had been confronted by my first questions about black women's participation in the women's movement. I was teaching a race relations course, and I was the only black person in the classroom on a suburban campus of a large university. The room was filled with women who were part of those first waves of older women college students in the 1970s, who had raised their children and served their husbands and were now returning to school to pick up the threads of unfinished college educations. The women were white and affluent and usually wrote papers and exams that were comparable to the work of graduate students. There were some men in the class as well; they tended to huddle at the back of the room and remain silent. They were police officers and prison guards who were upgrading their educations in order to receive the additional salaries being offered through the federal grants of that period aimed at producing a law-enforcement community less prone to gratuitous violence and more professional in its overall approach to civil disorder, particularly black civil disorder. These men were neither affluent nor educationally advantaged.

One of the women, a student who lived in one of the most affluent communities in the area, asked, "Why don't black women participate in the women's movement?" It was 1974 and although activist lawyer Pauli Murray, a black woman, was a founder of the National Organization for Women (N.O.W.) and Toni Cade [Bambara] had already published her anthology, *The Black Woman*, which introduced the concept of double jeopardy, later to become triple jeopardy and then multiple jeopardy, black women were not visible in noticeable numbers at the events or among the voices that constituted a largely white and middle-class women's movement. Even though this reality was rather glaring, I had not thought very hard about it until that moment.

I slowly began to describe the reality of black women at that time. The majority of black women, I pointed out, were employed outside the home before the women's movement began. I spent a little bit of time describing the work history of black women, a history that moved through slavery to freedom with 100 percent labor force participation. One of the readings for another class that was going through my mind at the moment was Linda LaRue's essay admonishing black women to "beware of Miss Anne's warmed-over throne."[1] "Miss Anne" was the female equivalent for "Mr. Charlie," African-American colloquialisms for talking about powerful white people, usually employers and others in authority. La Rue's essay alluded to the warmed over food from scrap pans that black women household domestics brought home from their employers' houses and the cast-off clothing that often supplemented meager wages. The lack of respectable and livable wages mirrored the lack of respect for the occupation of household domestic, one of the lowest paid and least prestigious occupations in industrial nations. Until 1965, the majority of black women who were employed outside the home were employed as household domestics. After my description of that occupational reality, I asked pointedly, "Who are their employers?"

What happened next represented one of those explosions of conscious-ness and understandings about gender, race, and class that remains permanently etched in one's memory. The assertive, affluent, and vocal ma-jority of white women responded, "White people." The usually silent minority of working, lower-middle-class white men shouted, "White women!" What I should have done was used the moment to talk about the multidimensional-ity of privilege and disadvantage and the interactive dynamics of gender, race, and class. In 1974, however, this was not the language of sociology. Sociolo-gists were still talking about class stratification, race relations, and sex roles. The intersectionality of gender, race, and class and their simultaneity in con-stituting structured inequality were not part of the social-scientific vocabulary yet. Instead, I left the women staring at me in disbelief when I bluntly asked, "How does one form a liberation movement with one's boss?"

While I do not remember the discussion that followed in class, I do re-member the explosion of consciousness and curiosity about African-American women and their roles in the society at large and in their churches and com-munities that began to dominate my own sociological imagination. Every time white women raised issues about their socialization and experience as women, questions formed in my mind about the differences between their perspectives and mine. In the twenty-five years since that discussion I have probed the social worlds of black women with my presence and my imagina-tion, subconsciously answering questions about differences between black women's and white women's consciousness while consciously asking and answering questions about black women's historical roles and agency. I have conducted oral histories with community activists, social-agency executives, missionaries in the Sanctified Church, and activist professional women. I have spent time sitting in community meetings, church conventions, women's churchwork groups, and church services. I have followed people on their various rounds of activities in revivals and business meetings. Even when the research question was not primarily focused on women, I found that the women's world could not be avoided if I wanted to understand fully some aspect of African-American social organization and group experience in the United States.[2] The paradox of diversity and unity that James Blackwell placed at the heart of his conceptualization of the black community involved both the women and the men, although most researchers at that time did not specifically place the roles of women in the foreground.[3] Unfortunately, when the roles of black women were noticed, they were usually noticed for the wrong reasons. The differences between white and black women were usually interpreted as black women's deviance. Separating the truth of black women's experience from their deviant images required immersion and participation in their worlds. The voices of uncounted and uncountable black women echoed in their various social worlds, insisting, "If it wasn't for the women, you wouldn't have . . . "

### "If It Wasn't for the Women"

Black women community activists and churchwomen have a deep sense of their indispensability to the organizations and institutions in which they participate.[4] The bookstore manager was not the first black woman I had heard make such a statement, and she would not be the last. In church meetings and in conversations in my own Baptist congregation and denomination, black churchwomen quickly responded to criticism and challenges with this same assertion of their importance—a clear understanding of the essential nature of their roles and presence in the church. At that moment in the bookstore, I realized that the manager's quick response was a perspective shared across denominational boundaries and generations. Later I would hear similar statements made in other convocations—usher conventions, choir conventions, retreats, and national women's department meetings. Black churchwomen approach their churches and communities with the understanding that they matter and they are indeed indispensable. When their voices and authority are challenged within their churches, they sometimes respond, "If it wasn't for the women, you wouldn't have a church."

Black women could just as easily make this assertion about other aspects of black community life and others, especially black men, have made such statements for them. Much of the anguish in black churches over the problems of black men is a signification on black women's importance, faithfulness, and indispensability. Even Louis Farrakhan, in his speech at the Million Man March, made it clear that women were indispensable to the life of the mosque; it was not just in the churches that women were holding things together. Countless essays and editorials written by black men have complained about the failures of their brethren in community and church to match the public presence and commitment of their sisters while inadvertently honoring the contributions of black women to the well-being of the *total* community.

This book contains essays that place black women's agency, centrality, importance, and indispensability to their churches and communities in the foreground. The various essays reveal aspects of black women's experiences in church and community with an eye toward explaining and interpreting more fully precisely what it is that women do within and for their communities. Feminist analysis necessarily stresses the discrimination against and oppression of women. When that analysis is turned toward black women, the focus is on the double or triple jeopardy that confronts black women. White women have trouble seeing black women as agents of culture and community; black men do not want to admit that black women are effective agents of culture and community; black women themselves, knowing that their efficacy contradicts the dominant culture's expectations of women, often refuse to acknowledge openly their own ability to make a difference. As Toni Cade [Bambara] perceptively observed in her 1970 volume *The Black Woman*, black women, in the wake of accusations that they were deviant and unwomanly, felt it necessary to justify themselves as women.[5] Therefore, they often hid from their own legacies of activism and achievement. As a result, there has been almost an abject failure to take seriously the legacy of enterprising agency black women have exercised in the worst and best of circumstances, especially in their churches. Yes, black women have been barred from pulpits as preachers at the same time their activism and constructive leadership have often contradicted and countered the forces that would keep them silent and subservient, occasionally opening pulpits to them anyhow.

Over the past twenty years, I have conducted research on black women community workers and on black churches, especially those historically considered the Sanctified Church. My interest in women's roles and community organization moved me from contemporary activist women to the sacred spaces that emerged at specific crisis points in the African-American experience. The essays in this book focus primarily on the roles of women in their churches and communities and the way in which women's presence and sensibilities have contributed to and shaped African-American political and religious culture. My interest began in a very secularist sociological mode. I discovered during my research on community workers that the religious experience was such a taken-for-granted aspect of their lives that the women usually did not mention it. They assumed, since I was a black woman, that I did not need to be told about the importance of religious experience in the context of their oral histories. These oral histories often began with their responses to the question, "Tell me about yourself." Their repeated response to my specific questions about their religious life was to look at me in a way that said, "You have to ask?," "What country are you from?," or "Did your mother raise a fool?" Regardless of their social-class position and their particular church membership, these community activists evinced an appreciation for the full range of African-American spirituality.

Ironically, I did not begin my study of the Sanctified Church with a focus on women. I was interested in the churches and denominations black people created as they urbanized in the South at the end of Reconstruction and later as they began to move North in search of more opportunities. Because of the power and prominence of the community activists I studied, I could not avoid seeing the importance of women in the Sanctified Church and their parallels and connections with women's roles in other segments of African-American Christianity. Simply discovering that Women's Day was almost uniquely a black women's experience generated a powerful set of questions about women in church and community.[6]

## Early Analysis of Religion—Du Bois and Durkheim

W. E. B. Du Bois and Emile Durkheim both underplayed women's experience and gender in their analyses of religion. W. E. B. Du Bois was gaining his first experiences in the religion of black folk around the time that Durkheim was writing his *Elementary Forms of Religious Life*. Durkheim identified several major elements of religious life including the active distinction between the sacred and profane and the communal sharing of ritual. In the course of developing his analysis, almost as a throwaway comment, he observed that "all the men . . . on the one hand, and, on the other, all the women form what amounts to two distinct and even antagonistic societies."[7] In spite of their competition, "these two sexual corporations" saw themselves as mystically joined through a common totem. I have come to the conclusion that Durkheim should have included this gender antagonism as one of the constitutive elements or "elementary forms" of religion.

Even before Durkheim produced his classic work, W. E. B. Du Bois offered an analysis of black religion that identified its constitutive elements as the preacher, the music, and the frenzy. What Du Bois actually identified was a creative tension among distinct but interlocking sets of actors and their voices. Music represented the collective expression, the community's voice, the shared work in what Robert Wuthnow calls the "production" of the sacred.[8] The preacher indicated the leadership that was generated and sustained by the community. Du Bois's preachers entered the canon as a male elite that Angela Davis has gone so far as to label a caste.[9] Because the preacher was so often "he," there was a failure to take seriously all of the effective leadership voices, male and female, that were both performative and strategic. Du Bois's frenzy was the community's expression of its engagement with the holy and the voice Du Bois presented was a woman's. Almost no one has pointed to the gendering of that voice, which represents the community engaged with and under the authority of the Spirit. However, it was a woman's voice that was the soul of the folk: "the gaunt-cheeked brown woman beside me suddenly leaped straight into the air and shrieked like a lost soul, while round about came wail and groan and outcry, and a scene of human passion such as I had never conceived before."[10]

## Gendered Views in Religion

Taking seriously the social fact of gendered antagonism in religion means always addressing the patterns and the processes that women and men construct as they go about the routine of doing sacred work. Black women and men share a religious life but often disagree about how that life should be organized and the relative importance of women's roles to that life. Black men and women agree on the necessity of opposing racial oppression, but they often disagree over the degree to which the patriarchy that is normative in the dominant society should be reproduced in their lives. Economic disadvantage makes it necessary for most black women to work. Although they contribute to individual, family, and community survival, black women's economic roles present a challenge to normative (or hegemonic) patriarchy. The results historically have been a wide variety of expressions of ambivalence, conflict, and cultural tensions surrounding women's experiences and women's roles in church and community. Through it all, black women have remained committed to an institution that exists largely because of their extraordinary investments of time, talent, and economic resources.

Black women have a sense of their own importance in their churches and communities that is perhaps unmatched in the sense of self-importance felt by women in other racial-ethnic communities in the United States. When describing, analyzing, and criticizing the black church, almost every eye tends to be turned toward the pulpits, pastors, and their convocations and conflicts.[11] Unfortunately, while black women's story may be larger and perhaps more important, the perceptions and realities of their importance have been the source of criticism, deviant images, and stereotypes. Black women know how radically dependent their churches and communities are on their presence and actions for both organizational integrity and effective mobilization. When blocked from the most visible leadership positions, women find ways to make their voices heard and their power felt in alternative spaces of their own creation, spaces that often give them limited access to the sacred platforms. While such access affirmed their importance, that affirmation was essentially tokenism.

I have concluded that black women are fundamentally correct in their self-assessment: "If it wasn't for the women," the black community would not have had the churches and other organizations that have fostered the psychic and material survival of individuals and that have mobilized the constituencies that have produced change and progress. At every level of social interaction and cultural production women are present, and at the same time they are conscious of the way the dominant white society disrespects and rejects their presence. Furthermore, white society historically has communicated that disrespect and rejection through a wide variety of stereotypes that have invited shame and exhortations that black women change their behavior. As a result, black women in American society have left a very large literature of self-conscious justification for their roles as workers and leaders in sacred and secular spaces.

## Roles of Black Women

The overwhelming majority of black women who have contributed to building their communities and moving their children and others forward have not left written records of their activism. Yet they are not invisible. They publicly present themselves on the various occasions of public ritual such as Women's Day and awards ceremonies when they can be visible to and appreciated by the beneficiaries of their labors. When their power and effectiveness become too visible for others to bear to acknowledge because, as one male board member told the female founder and director of the agency on whose board she had placed him, "it looks bad for the race," these women will remind us in a variety of ways that "if it wasn't for the women . . . "

Several years ago Jualynne Dodson and I were asked to describe, discuss, and document the role of black Christian women in the twentieth century.[12] Between the two of us we had gathered data on women community activists, women in the African Methodist Episcopal Church, and women in several Pentecostal and Holiness denominations. As churchwomen ourselves, we also brought our own experiences to the tasks. We came to the conclusion that the role of black churchwomen could be described with a theme taken from a hymn by Lucy E. Campbell. Miss Campbell wrote:

> Something within that holdeth the reins,
> Something within that banishes pain,
> Something within that I cannot explain,
> All that I know there is something within.[13]

In every aspect of African-American life and history black women have been a significant force, the "something within." In every organization where they are present, they have been the key actors responsible for the integrity and efficacy of the operations. According to civil rights movement folklore, one famous civil rights leader said that if the women ever left the movement, he was going with the women, because nothing was going to happen without the women. Black women have either been invisible to researchers who have approached the history and social life of black people armed with presumptions of mainstream social science, or these women's visibility has been overlooked as unimportant to the larger questions governing the research. Over the years, as I have lectured and written about community women and churchwomen, white sociologists who have done research in urban black communities have confessed that they saw the women in the churches and community organizations and simply assumed that they were unimportant. If they were women pastoring storefront churches, the presumption was that the women were insignificant and that the churches were marginal sects and cults and were equally unimportant. Researchers who ventured inside these churches often failed to explore the connections of these women and churches to the larger church community and to associations and organizations at regional and national levels. Yet in every national convocation I attended as either researcher or participant, narratives of women's enterprise and activism that had strengthened, shaped, transformed, and sustained the organization were embedded in the organizations' histories.

## The Essays in This Book

The essays that follow were selected from published and unpublished papers that focused on the roles of women in their churches and communities, the implications of those roles for African-American culture, particularly its Afro-Christian dimensions, and the tensions and stereotypes that shape societal responses to these roles. Many times they were responses to questions asked in classrooms; during academic programs and panels; or in the writings of those who sought to advance feminist critiques of religious studies, sociology, and religious organizations and institutions. The questions were variations on the theme laid down by my early students, "Why aren't black women . . . ?" or "Why don't black women . . . ?" Many of the insights that emerged as I conducted research on the Sanctified Church were conditioned by my previous experience gathering the oral histories of women who became publicly prominent as agents of social change and community survival. As I pursued opportunities for interaction with other researchers in the general areas of race, gender, and religion, many of the emerging feminist theoretical frameworks just did not adequately grasp the black experience. Every new puzzle prompted new sets of questions and attempts to answer those questions.

The chapters in Part 1 highlight the community connection that must be understood if one is ever to apprehend the roles and experiences of black women. When my white women students complain that race is more important to black women than gender, they are complaining about black women's allegiances to organizations and institutions that include black men. Since white women's own sense of alienation from a social structure and culture in which they experience unquestioned racial privilege usually masks their own commitments and investments to elements and segments of the white world of their own orientation, they cannot quite grasp the degree to which the black social worlds that exist oppositionally to theirs are the products of women's culture and sensibility. My white students hear the masculinist language and see the male leaders of the civil rights and black power movements and that is all they see. They do not and cannot see the black women who, when seeing a police car pulling someone over, ask pointedly, "Is that a brother over there?"[14] The essays in "The Community Connection" point to the way in which questions about African-American women's roles and experience cannot be answered without first grasping the centrality of women to the community and the centrality of community to black women as they construct their roles in churches and other organizations. One can argue that women's organizational commitments are a central force in African-American history. W. E. B. Du Bois comes close to saying as much when he interprets the historic role of black women as "the intellectual leadership of the race."

Part 2, "Church Women and Their Work," focuses specifically on the roles black women occupy and actualize in their churches. Often when people call women the backbone of the church, that label is interpreted strictly in terms of their lack of access to pulpit, the expectation that they be silent, and their supposed subservience. However, central to the African-American experience is its religious history and black women's activities and commitments form the backbone or indispensable central framework on which every expression of black religion survives. The essays in this section contain specific observations on the financial, ethical, social, political, and theological contributions they make to specific churches and to the black church overall. The biblical injunctions for women's silence have been persistently subverted through the continuities that black women have maintained and asserted over the entire history of their presence in the Americas. It is impossible to resist speculating about African influences. There are too many parallels between the organizations of black women in the United States and some of the gender roles in the pre-colonial and colonial West and Central African cultures from which their African ancestors were taken. These chapters on women's roles offer theories about such possible continuities.

Alice Walker introduced the term *womanist* in 1982 when she sought an alternative word for organizing our thinking about black women's self-definitions, relationships, activities, and history and their meaning for the black experience. To my mind, her dictionary-style definition offered a grounded theory[15] of black women's culture that was constructed out of the dialogues within the fundamental female-female relationship of any culture, mothers and daughters, and the distinctive values ("loves") that she observed in the world of black women. Walker's definition asserts the existence of a black women's culture that values not only women and women's relationships but the men and the "entire community male and female." Walker identifies a fundamental commitment to the "survival and wholeness" of this community as a hallmark of this womanist idea. Walker begins by stating that a womanist is a "black feminist" and, along with other observers of the black female experience who are usually *not* social scientists, she identifies the most laudable dimensions of black women's culture and experience as behavioral feminism in spite of the fact that its practitioners would probably not choose the word *feminist* for themselves.[16] Most black churchwomen would eschew the label feminist and consider themselves simply to be black women who are or are trying to be "good Christians." It is their sensibilities and concerns that shape the larger religious culture in the black experience. While social scientists have trouble conceptualizing their behavior as feminist, African-American women novelists have not—labeling them "dynamite sisters," "behavioral feminists," or, in Walker's term, "womanist." The essays in Part 3, "Womanist Culture," discuss the ways black women and their experiences make and shape the culture and consciousness of the black religious experience. African-American Christianity is not only a product of black women's presence but also of their active and assertive role in shaping the spirituality and ethics of black churches.

Part 4 focuses on confrontations, crises, and conflicts that shape the context in which black women do their church and community work. In the words of African Methodist Episcopal bishop, the Right Rev. Dr. Vashti Murphy McKenzie, black women participate in the leadership hierarchies of the black church, but "not without a struggle."[17] The struggle of black women is not only against the fundamental discrimination against women who seek to become ordained as clergy and pastors in their congregations and denominations, but against a society that has exploited their every human capacity and skill and then called deviant both them and their modes of survival. Black women are not only workers in their churches and communities, but, in a society that defined "ladies" as women confined simply to the domestic sphere, black women have been full-time workers in the labor force since their arrival. W. E. B. Du Bois pointed out that the expansion of democracy was built on the struggles of black people, women, and workers to be fully included in the national polity. Black women, according to Du Bois, embodied all three struggles because their historical role has been the role of worker. Barbara Hilkert Andolsen, in her comparison of the perspectives of black and white women feminists, identified four areas of fundamental disagreement and one of these disagreements centered on the importance and value of work.[18] Where white feminists identified the family as a primary site of oppression, black women, in spite of the troubles that intrude on their family lives, do not. However, the conflicts, confrontations, and crises black women face place undue burdens on them and present an additional locus of struggle they must address, very often without the perception and understanding of the men who benefit from their commitment and work in church and community. Many of their pastors really do believe that black women are economically and educationally better off and have achieved more than black men. Such beliefs have tremendous implications for the problems and issues that get addressed in black women's congregations.

The conflicts and misunderstandings in the area of gender relations represent one of the crises of the African-American experience. C. Eric Lincoln and Lawrence Mamiya pointed to the growing divergence between black Muslim men and black Christian women in the African-American religious experience.[19] In the largest and most vibrant contemporary churches, there is a growing emphasis on ministries to and for men, with the implications that the church may be headed toward an organization based on serving a militant manhood with a "womanist" infrastructure.[20] Black women take their own problems very seriously, but they have historically given primacy to the problems faced by their children—their male and female children. As a result, men's problems have historically benefited from black women's activism. As I have pointed out elsewhere, "The concern that black women evince for the emergencies facing black men . . . is not reciprocated by a similar concern for black women by the male leadership of black churches."[21] The misperception that black women have succeeded against all the odds masks the realities of single parenting, joblessness, and poverty that create unparalleled stress in the lives of black women. In spite of the agency that black women have exercised to construct a culture that resists the destructions of racial oppression, the problems that create crises in their lives and the conflicts that emerge when black women seek to take their rightful places of leadership still stand as what Du Bois called "mighty causes" requiring attention and action.

# PART 1

# THE COMMUNITY CONNECTION

# 1

# "If It Wasn't for the Women . . . "

## Community Work and Social Change

Many sociologists who studied the relationships between dominant and subordinate racial-ethnic groups in the 1960s stress the creative ways in which individuals and groups enable communities to articulate their own needs and challenge oppressive structures in the wider society.[1] Other sociologists such as Stanford Lyman emphasize the historical experience of racial-ethnic groups in the data used for sociological interpretation.[2] The Civil Rights Movement, the Black Power Movement, and the American Indian Movement, along with diverse movements within Asian American, Puerto Rican, and Chicano communities, challenged sociologists to explore historically rooted conflicts over power, labor, economic resources, and the appropriate strategies for achieving social change.[3]

Creative social conflict is inevitable and necessary if racial-ethnic, gender, and class inequities are to be eliminated and social justice achieved. When enterprising, caring members of oppressed communities become involved in public affairs, their actions often contribute to a creative cultural process that is a force for social change. This chapter is about an aspect of that creative cultural process: enterprising women in African-American communities who shape social change through their community work.

Women are vital to the creative cultural process of social change. African-American women and their community work highlight the importance of a group's history and culture to the process of social change. The rise of the women's liberation movement and public concern about African-American women, their families, and their position in the labor force generated a particular interest in their roles in the process of social change.[4] Along with Asian American, Native American, and Latina women, African-American women's work outside the home was recognized as a distinctive component in their family roles. Community work is part of this work outside the home. It is labor these women perform in addition to work in the household and the labor force.[5]

This chapter describes the contemporary expression, historical foundations, and persistent activities of the community work of African-American women. Community work includes a wide range of diverse tasks performed to confront and challenge racism as a total system. This work has historical foundations, and a historical perspective helps to highlight the areas of activity common to the work at different time periods. Community work consists of the women's activities to combat racism and empower their communities to survive, grow, and advance in a hostile society. The totality of their work is an emergent, dynamic, interactive model of social action in which community workers discover and explore oppressive structures, challenge many different structures and practices that keep their communities powerless and disadvantaged, and then build, maintain, and strengthen institutions within their community. These institutions become the basis for the community's political culture. The women generate an alternative organization and a set of commitments to group interests that are the basic elements of "community." They work for the community that they themselves re-create and sustain, a mutually reinforcing process.

During the late 1970s in a Northeastern city I gathered oral histories and observed the community activities of twenty-five African-American women whom other African Americans had identified as those "who have worked hard for a long time for change in the black community."[6] As these women talked about the ways in which they became involved in community work and the different kinds of organizations and activities in which they participated, I learned about the very intricate and diverse ways in which people make social change. I also learned about the many ways in which women experience racial oppression. Their family roles make them acutely conscious not only of their own deprivations but also of the suffering of their children and the men in their lives. Their insightful and enterprising responses to these many kinds of suffering led to their prominence in the community. They were responsible for maintaining a dynamic community life to create social change and an adaptive family system to foster survival in a hostile environment. Through community and family, these women generated a set of values and a social organization that persistently challenged and changed American society.

## Community Work

Women in American society are expected to be good managers. They organize and coordinate diverse schedules and activities within their families, and among the organizations and institutions with which family members are involved. Work outside the home is often added to this responsibility. African-American women usually work, manage their families, and, if they are community workers, participate in the struggles between the communities and the dominant society.

James Blackwell's definition of the African-American community helps us to understand the context of their work. Blackwell argues that the community, although diverse, is held together by both internal and external forces. It is "a highly diversified set of interrelated structures and aggregates of people who are held together by the forces of white oppression and racism. Unity within the black community is a function of the strategies developed to combat white racism and to strengthen black social, economic, and political institutions for group survival and advancement."[7]

Community work consists of all tasks contained in strategies to combat racial oppression and to strengthen African-American social, economic, and political institutions in order to foster group survival, growth, and advancement. Community work is focused on internal development and external challenge, and creates ideas enabling people to think about change. It is the work that opens doors to elected and appointed positions in the political power struggle, and demands and creates jobs in local labor markets and the larger economic system. Community work also focuses on changing ideas, stereotypes, and images that keep a group perpetually stigmatized. Sometimes this is done by demanding different textbooks in the schools or publicly criticizing newspapers and other media. At the same time, community workers may insist, rightly or wrongly, that community members change their behavior to avoid being treated in terms of prevailing stereotypes. Community work is a constant struggle, and it consists of everything that people do to address oppression in their own lives, suffering in the lives of others, and their sense of solidarity or group kinship.

Women participate in every part of a community's experience of racial oppression. Racial oppression is a phenomenon that not only singles out African Americans because of their heritage and color but also places the entire community in a colonial relationship, a relationship of powerlessness and dependency, within a dominant and dominating society. Robert Blauner calls this "internal colonialism,"[8] and it involves the subordination of an entire group of people in order to take away its land, to capture its labor, or to do both. Colonized people must be excluded from the political process and, by law, have few, if any, citizenship rights. Because the primary purpose of the group is to labor unceasingly for someone else, the other dimensions of its cultural life, such as family life, health, education, and religion become difficult, if not impossible, to pursue.

During slavery African Americans had their children and spouses sold away from them. Their family lives were repeatedly disrupted and invaded by the sexual terrorism that was part of slavery. Teaching slaves to read and write in the antebellum South was illegal. During the last decades of slavery, religious worship outside of the supervision of white people was illegal as well. The health of African Americans was constantly threatened by the violence of white slave owners, through beatings and overwork. Because they were legally nonpersons, emancipation left African Americans overwhelmingly landless and still dependent upon white landowners for a livelihood. Political powerlessness through violence and denial of the vote increased that dependence. Racist stereotypes, ideologies, and actions continued to justify the dominant group's actions and the continued subordination of another group.[9] Racial oppression is a total phenomenon that combines cultural humiliation and destruction, political subordination, and economic exploitation to maintain a hierarchy that limits the life chances of a group of people.

The economic needs and organization of the society change. Slavery was abolished in 1865; African Americans moved to northern cities in large numbers during World Wars I and II; the Civil Rights Movement did away with Jim Crow laws. However, the racist hierarchy retained a life and meaning that survived the massive changes in economic, legal, political, and social institutions. Although slavery ended, the society learned to associate low-paying, dirty work with black people and higher-paying, clean work with white people. Contemporary racial stereotypes and media images perpetuated those images rooted in slavery.

Community work confronts this totality. Everett Hughes suggested that an important way to conceptualize "work" is to view it as a "bundle of tasks."[10] Racial oppression takes up more time and creates extra work, or more "bundles of tasks," for members of a victimized group.[11] People working for and with their communities involve themselves in activities surrounding the problems associated with jobs: labor union activities, creating access to jobs, teaching strategies to fight specific problems in work settings, and seeking legislation to protect occupations where group members are concentrated. One community worker had worked for the Urban League early in her career. She described recruiting other African-American women for newly created jobs during World War II by visiting churches and women's clubs. She then organized discussion groups in order to teach these women how to confront the racial harassment they would encounter in unions and factories. Another woman described in great detail the way her women's club of the 1920s and 1930s taught fellow domestic workers how to demand the full wages their white female employers had promised. That same women's club, in the 1960s and 1970s, was involved in administering job training programs for homemakers *at the same time* they were lobbying for protective legislation for household workers. Community workers involved themselves in activities that confronted ideas as well as structures within and outside the community.

Education is a case in point. Issues of self-image and self-esteem are related to educational success at the same time that employment discrimination and racist attitudes in the educational system account for the lack of African-American teachers. Educational failure locks many members of the community out of the economic system at the same time that political powerlessness through gerrymandering accounts for the lack of access to low-skilled but high-paying municipal jobs. One woman who had been quite prominent in challenging the public educational system talked about the importance of self-esteem for African-American students. Another woman, an elected official, displayed publications she used for raising the racial self-esteem of

teenagers and described the workshops she gave for parents in order to re-
duce the sense of intimidation they felt when confronting white teachers.
Each of these problems presents a different "bundle of tasks," yet they are all
manifestations of the totality of racial oppression. Each woman interviewed
described diverse and intricate daily schedules that reflected the complexity
and connectedness of the social, political, and economic problems that pervade everyday life in minority communities. One woman, for example,
described getting a group of adolescent males assigned to early morning jobs,
going to court as a character witness for a teenager, meeting with a board of
directors in another part of the city, and coordinating a public demonstration against the same board of directors before leaving for the meeting. While
levels of confrontation and activity often vary, community work persistently
rejects racial oppression as a normal and natural feature of human experience. Community work, encompassing issues of challenge as well as survival,
is perhaps more complicated than the racial oppression that gives rise to it.

### Historical Foundations

Community workers' expectations and obligations represent a historical
role. These women, through their public participation on so many levels,
claim a prominent place in the community's history. This historical prominence often provides levels of prestige and influence unmatched in the lives
of white women of similar class backgrounds.[12] All of the women were connected in some way to earlier generations of organizations, activists, and
confrontations. What becomes visible to outside observers as "social movements" are the most dramatic dimensions of an intergenerational tradition of
community work. Bernice Johnson Reagon emphasizes this continuity:

> If we understand that we are talking about a struggle that is hundreds
> of years old, then we must acknowledge a continuance: that to be black
> women is to move forward the struggle for the kind of space in this
> society that will make sense for our people. It is different today. Things
> have changed. The search for high levels of humanity and space to be
> who we know we are is the same. And if we can make sense of our
> people in this society, we will go a long way in making sense for the rest
> of the peoples who also live and suffer here.[13]

The historical continuity of community work depends upon an intricate
fit between many kinds of organizations and people. All of the women worked
within traditional and nationally recognized groups, such as churches, the
National Association for the Advancement of Colored People (NAACP), the
Urban League, the Student Non-Violent Coordinating Committee (SNCC),
the Young Women's Christian Association (YWCA), the National Association of Colored Women's Clubs, and the National Council of Negro Women.

At the same time they formed local organizations that specialized in problems of job training, drug addiction, city services, welfare rights, or public education. People in the community actively encouraged these community workers to be leaders and, once the women responded to a community need, they organized whatever was necessary to see an activity through.

Such activities were not possible without intergenerational connections. When interviewing, I asked the women to identify their heroes and heroines. These women identified specific women within the local community as well as such notables as Mary McLeod Bethune. One woman remembered very clearly being impressed when Mrs. Bethune spoke at a local church for the Women's Day service. Several women identified Mrs. Burns,[14] who was also interviewed, as their heroine and local sponsor. One said, "I walked to Mrs. Burns when I was nine months old!" This elderly community worker identified Mrs. Bethune as a coworker in the National Association of Colored Women. Older community workers, as heroines and sponsors, were the critical connection to earlier generations of community workers or "Race" women. These women who remembered Mary McLeod Bethune and Mary Church Terrell, not only as "heroines" but also as living role models in club work and church work, were the links to an unbroken tradition of community work or working for "the Race" that could be traced directly to antebellum communities, both slave and free.

Working for "the Race" began during slavery. Within the slave community, women not only played key roles in the development of family, education, and religion but also developed a women's network that was a foundation of strength, leaders, and mutual aid.[15] Deborah Gray White names midwives, nurses, and religious leaders as critical sources of survival. One religious leader, a prophet named Sinda, preaching the imminent end of the world, precipitated a strike by an entire plantation labor force. African-American women in Northern free communities built churches and developed abolitionist, literary, mutual-aid, and missionary societies that provided poor-relief and insurance benefits for their communities.[16] Women such as Maria Stewart and Frances Ellen Watkins Harper were militant antislavery crusaders and public lecturers. Stewart was the first woman of any race in the United States to lecture publicly and leave manuscripts that are still extant,[17] and Harper was the first female public lecturer that many women, black or white, ever saw and heard.[18]

After emancipation, church women and teachers organized schools and churches throughout the South. Since male ministers also worked as teachers, male and female educators (preachers and teachers) became the vital source of leaders. With the rise of Jim Crow laws, women's public activism outside the church emerged in the form of an anti-lynching movement under the leadership of Ida B. Wells Barnett. This movement was the basis for the formation of the National Association of Colored Women, whose motto was "Lifting as We Climb." That club movement explored and confronted the way in which racism threatened or distorted every aspect of life.

In order to provide the leadership essential for their communities, African-American women insisted upon their organizational autonomy while addressing their efforts to the condition of the entire community. In 1895, Josephine St. Pierre Ruffin wrote:

> Our woman's movement is a woman's movement in that it is led and directed by women for the good of women and men, for the benefit of all humanity. . . . We want, we ask the active interest of our men; . . . we are not alienating or withdrawing, we are only coming to the front, willing to join any others in the same work . . . and inviting . . . others to join us.[19]

The importance of these women's clubs was evident in the interviews with the elderly community workers, who described these organizations as places where they learned to lead and administer, and where they organized to win elections in organizations seemingly dominated by men, such as the NAACP and the Urban League.[20] The oldest surviving national African-American political organizations are women's organizations whose founders and members also participated in organizing the NAACP, the Urban League,[21] the Association for the Study of Afro-American Life and History,[22] and every other national African-American organization. Emerging as one of the prominent leaders during the Depression, Mary McLeod Bethune created the National Council of Negro Women as a lobby for civil rights and working women. The clubs served as training stations for both middle-class and lower-class women leaders.

Several observers in the late nineteenth and early twentieth centuries noted the prestige associated with women's public participation and work for "the Race."[23] In urban communities, mothers' clubs were organized to deal with childbirth at home, housework, and child care. As children grew older, these clubs became scholarship clubs. Clubs for the protection, cultural "uplift," and mutual aid of household workers were formed. Carter Woodson identified the significant role of washerwomen in financing and building associations that developed into the major black insurance companies.[24] He argued that this was one of many examples of the way in which African-American working women not only supported their families but also contributed to the possibility of economic self-sufficiency in the entire community. Through such community work, Maggie Lena Walker became the first woman of any color to be a bank president in the United States.[25]

W. E. B. Du Bois observed that the club movement, lacking money as a resource, made its most substantial contribution through the web of affiliations it built, connecting and empowering black people across class and status lines:

> The women of America who are doing humble but on the whole the most effective work in the social uplift of the lowly, not so much by

money as by personal contact, are the colored women. Little is said or known about it but in thousands of churches and social clubs, in missionary societies and fraternal organizations, in unions like the National Association of Colored Women, these workers are founding and sustaining orphanages and old folk homes; distributing personal charity and relief; visiting prisoners; helping hospitals; teaching children; and ministering to all sorts of needs.[26]

The organizational history of these women is central to African-American protest and survival history. They and their organizations have provided the space where contemporary community workers work as directors, managers, social workers, elected politicians, and advocates.

Because of the efforts of community workers, ideas and strategies change. People reflect on their successes and failures, and as new problems arise, these reflections contribute to new solutions or a change in ideology. Black Power activists, for instance, often accused older members of the community of complacency, accommodationism, and do-nothingness. One community worker described a confrontation in which "young militants" challenged Mrs. Burns concerning what she had done for the community "lately," implying that she was an accommodationist and represented an old and useless style of leadership. Mrs. Burns reportedly replied, "I was out raising scholarship money to send you to college so you could come back here and give me sass!" When interviewed, Mrs. Burns mentioned things that she would have done differently in light of the logic of the Black Power Movement; she named things that she was currently doing differently because of her own reflections on history. She told of one encounter with a black federal official whom she lectured concerning his being used by his agency to steal ideas from her club rather than empowering the club to be the agency's subcontractor to teach the ideas to others. She claimed her feistiness came from her own reflections on a conflict during the 1920s when she accused another activist of "bringing Jim Crow" to her city by campaigning to build a black hospital. Mrs. Burns conceded, in light of the late 1960s and early 1970s arguments for community control, that he had been right and she, although her view had prevailed then, had been wrong.

## Discovery, Challenge, and Development: An Emergent Model of Community Work

The totality of racial oppression and the diversity of African-American communities combine to make the tasks of community work so varied as almost to defy any kind of classification. Community work comprises both responses to and catalysts for change. Successful or not, it is the effort to make things better and to eliminate the problems and structures that make life difficult. Community work is the persistent effort across time to close the gap between black and white life chances. The work is both immediate and long term, and its effects are cumulative. There is, however, an emergent model of action that is present in all of this. It is a model of discovery, challenge, and development that represents a multifaceted model of resistance.

Discovery that there is a problem is the first critical step. Community workers observe, discover, and explore the effects of oppressive practices and structures in their own and others' lives. They are the critical connection between the abrasions of personal experience and the social and political contexts that shape experience. It can be the simple act of sending one's daughter to the mailbox that leads to critical discovery. Describing this as the impetus for her neighborhood association, one worker said, "And simply because we wanted to get together and do things for the community and get the streets cleaned up and the garbage picked up and wanted a mailbox installed on the corner, things like that . . . and then we branched out into other things."

Personal discovery does not lead immediately to community action. The discovery process is complex and involves communicating with others about the reality and nature of community problems. Another worker, a Southern migrant whose community work addressed drug problems and public education, told of her "discovery" of school problems when comparing her son's homework with that of his cousin, who attended school in another, predominantly white, neighborhood. She went on to talk about the problem of transforming personal discovery into collective action, particularly in the North:

> A lot is like shadow boxing. The problem is there, but you can't quite see it. We cover them a lot. But down South everything is out in the open. . . . You knew where you stood and everybody knew where the line was drawn, and actually you could deal with it better than here. First you've got to find the problem, then you've got to pull it out from under the covers, and then if somebody says its a problem. . . . I remember when I came to Hamptonville, I thought there was discrimination in the schools *then* . . . when my kids were in school. . . . We [she and her sister-in-law] were discussing our children's work from school one day, and I looked at my son and his cousin [who were] in the same grade, and the entire curriculum was different. And I said, "What is this!" You know, they were in the same grade, and why is this curriculum so different . . . so when I questioned these things, I was really put down; I was bringing discrimination from the South. So I really kept quiet, but I've been looking at this thing for a long time.

The activity of discovery and exploration often overlaps with challenge, since discovery itself is subversive. The actions that follow from discovery challenge oppressive structures and practices in a variety of ways. Challenge begins when community workers raise questions among their kin and neighbors, and eventually organize some kind of action. In order to do this they must argue, obstruct, organize, teach, lecture, demonstrate, sue, write letters, and so on. They communicate in such a way that they create a critical speech community around the problem—a group of people who share a point of view on a problem, acknowledging that it exists and that it is something on which public action is necessary.

These initial acts of challenge sometimes emerge into full-blown social movement. At other times, discovery and small-scale actions in one area—welfare rights, for instance—will bring a community worker to the attention of others and involve her in a related but quite different social movement. One woman, describing her involvement on the board of directors of a large human services agency outside of her neighborhood and her own community work focus, said, "The director of the program was having some trouble. . . . She knew that I had raised Hell over in [one neighborhood], so she figured that she needed some raised over in [another neighborhood]."

At the same time they are organizing confrontations with oppressive forces outside the community, community workers address needs within their communities that enable people to resist oppression and participate meaningfully in community life. In the struggle for voting rights, for example, civil rights organizations confronted voter registrars throughout the South with demonstrations and registration campaigns at the same time workers like Septima Clark organized schools to teach African Americans how to read and take the tests.[27] This is the task of internal development, the building and maintenance of organizations and institutions indigenous to the community.

One elected official argued that the most important problem African Americans faced was internal control: "The way they can't have control over their lives. Although I am not a separatist, I feel as though until we can get into the mainstream of this society . . . we are going to be third- or fourth-class citizens." Trained in elementary education, she surprised me when she told me that she had no intention of teaching children. "I felt that even though I worked with a parents' group, that because I wasn't a teacher, no one took my words very seriously, and I decided that I was going to become a teacher, not to work in the classroom but to work with parents." For some community workers, internal development was so critical, it became their full-time vocation. They either found jobs in agencies that permitted them to do such work or they organized their own agencies.

In a society in which "integration" has become the dominant theme in the politics of race, internal community development can often be very controversial, implying separatism and inter-racial hostility. Mrs. Burns experienced such a conflict and found herself, fifty years later, an advocate for the kind of community control she had earlier labeled "bringing Jim Crow." Because of the power of the dominant society, failure to build and maintain community institutions is a problem. Carter Woodson labeled it "mis-education" and suggested that it could be solved by building alternative institutions.[28] In my own research, community workers called this activity "building black-oriented institutions."

What has been labeled a "retreat from integration" is actually the discovery of the internal development that was sometimes accomplished in disadvantaged, segregated, Southern schools. Because education was viewed as something akin to a religious mission, African-American teachers, especially after 1915, taught African-American history in Southern schools at least during the month of February.[29] Aware of the aspirations of many fathers and mothers for their daughters' college educations, and also aware of the grim realities that governed women's opportunities, these teachers often insisted that their students learn classical subjects alongside trades and business subjects. In effect they refused to compound limited social opportunities with inflexible educational policies, now called tracking. Since Southern states made it illegal for white teachers to teach black children, those children were inadvertently provided with important role models. Although African-American teachers in segregated schools could be very assimilationist and Anglocentric in their outlook and thinking, their commitment to the community made a real difference. The teachers believed in and supported the students, who, in turn, observed educated African-American women and men in positions of leadership.

The activities of discovery, challenge, and development are interrelated and together represent a tradition of resistance. This model of social action must be seen as dynamic and interactive. The women are agents of this tradition of resistance as both volunteers and professionals. Their persistent refusal to accept the discomfort of racial oppression is the conflicted connection between the individual and the society that contributes to the emergence of a social force for change. Commenting that "revolutions happen in the funniest ways," one worker whose agency specialized in developing women for jobs and finding jobs for women said: "It just started on a physical level. It really just shocked me that I was going to be physically inconvenienced for the simple reason that I was black. There were certain things that I was not going to be able to get physically, that was going to create conditions of security and warmth and feeling good." The diversity of their work again points to the totality of the pressure on African Americans as a group. When one accounts for the full range of the women's work, it becomes apparent that every question raised about the source of community afflictions contains the seeds of rebellion and social change.

## Conclusion: If It Wasn't for the Women . . .

African-American women's community work connects many "small pieces" of community life and contributes to the process of empowerment.[30] The centrality of their work points to the need to examine the importance of women in any community resisting racial oppression. Racial oppression is a complex and interconnected phenomenon that shapes the lives of women and men. Most women of color are trapped in the worst and dirtiest sectors of the female labor market, providing the sole support of their families or supplementing the wages of their husbands, who are similarly trapped in male markets. Their families are not accorded the institutional and ideological supports that benefit white families.[31] Additionally, African American, Asian, Latina, and Native American women also do community work. They find their historical role organized around the nurturance and defense and advancement of an oppressed public family. Women in a variety of community settings now and historically have demonstrated that it is safe to parallel the oft-repeated statement of African-American church women that "If it wasn't for the women, you wouldn't have a church," to say, "If it wasn't for women of color, African-American, Asian, Latino, and Native peoples would have far fewer alternatives and resources to maintain themselves and challenge a hostile social system."

African-American women, and by extension Asian American, Native American, and Latina women, highlight the importance of women and their work for the creation of a just and more equitable society. Women bring three perspectives to community work that make them particularly rebellious. First, their consciousness is shaped by their experience in the society, especially in the labor force. Second, they see men's suffering and feel its effects in their own lives. These women observe and experience the effects of racism on the men of their community along with the effects of that racism in their own lives. The third and perhaps most important source of discontent is the effect of racial oppression in the lives of their children. Combating the damage to their children and attempting to fashion a more inclusive future for them was stated as the most important motivation for involvement. Community workers get involved "through my kids." It is in their roles as the principal caretakers of children that racial-ethnic women pose the largest political threat to the dominant society. Women and their children are the core around which group solidarity is constructed. Community work derives its character from the shared nature of the problems confronting all members of the community. Community workers are, in the words of Sadie Iola Daniel, "women builders."[32] Community work derives its character from the shared nature of the problems confronting all members of the community. The depths and complexities of racial oppression cannot be grasped without a thorough understanding of its expression in the lives of women and their children.

Although perspectives on women's roles are becoming a prominent part of the social science canon, this development has not incorporated the complex historical roles of women in powerless communities. These women must confront a politics that involves more than the politics implied by race or class or gender. When viewing the creative role of women in the simultaneous processes of social change and community survival, one must conclude that if it wasn't for the women, racially oppressed communities would not have the institutions, organizations, strategies, and ethics that enable the group not only to survive or to maintain itself as an integral whole, but also to develop in an alien, hostile, oppressive situation and to challenge it. In spite of their powerlessness, African-American women and women of color generally have a dramatic impact within and beyond their communities. The translation of this historical role into real power and social justice is the ultimate goal of community work.

# 2

# Exploring the Community Connection

## *Race, Class, and Women's Agency*

Many discussions of the African-American experience raise the question: "Is it race or is it class?" The very question misdirects the path of inquiry. Race and class always intersect. The problems inherent in attempts to treat them as distinct and unrelated factors are compounded by a confusion between class and status and an attendant failure to account for the historical role of middle classes and their members.[1] Although there is growing recognition and attention to the complexity of these issues, sociological inquiry has not adopted a language or a perspective adequate to explain fully the position and the experiences of peoples of color in the United States. These problems with prevailing perspectives on social class in the United States become exacerbated when the discussion turns to the African-American community.[2]

The term race-ethnicity may more accurately direct inquiry. Some scholars have found that the term race-ethnicity grasped the colonial dimensions of racial oppression without negating the particular ethnic experiences and communities of very diverse peoples of color in the United States.[3] The term is an important reminder of the ethnic dimensions of the black experience and it counters those who discount the cultural traditions of black people as simply and only a product of racial oppression.

As members of a racial-ethnic group whose color and historical role in the labor force combined to intensify the experience of oppression, African-American women, particularly, have defied analysis from the eurocentric and androcentric perspectives of those who would treat race, class, and gender as discrete and independent entities. Recent attempts by feminist scholars have also fallen short of grasping fully the theoretical dimensions of African-American women's experience. Although stunning in their labor and scope, these works are incomplete. Jacqueline Jones's work is the most comprehensive.[4] Her framework is "women's history" and in building that framework, she castigated black women for their commitment to racial solidarity. In her attempt to integrate the experiences of black and white women across racial lines, Jones almost discounted the importance of the ethnic or community dimensions of experience. Her failure to grasp the centrality of church work and community work, even for the poorest working women, led her to imply that black women's commitments to their community organizations and their churches was a source of their white mistresses' oppression. Describing the problems of post-Civil War era white mistresses "in a patriarchal world," she writes:

> Domestics arrived at work late, left early in the afternoon, or stayed away for days at a time to mark special events and holidays. Communal celebrations in their own neighborhoods took precedence over the needs and expectations of their employers. Revivals periodically inspired sinners to "get religion" and join with others in an ecstasy of newfound salvation. . . . "Excursions"—the chartering of a train for pleasure and fund raising on behalf of a church or benevolent society—proved to be the bane of many a mistress's existence.[5]

Although Jones acknowledged the failure of white power to address the political and economic concerns of black people, at the end of the book she complained:

> Black women's relation to the gender gap remains problematic, for they show little willingness to embrace political candidates endorsed by mainstream white feminist organizations . . . if a black candidate of either sex presents a viable alternative. . . . [B]lack working women tend to filter their political activity through the lenses of black loyalty, a reflection of both the historic an unique impact of racial prejudice on their lives and the lives of their foremothers. . . .[6]

Similar failures can be found in analyses of the civil rights movement that ignore the roles played by women in leadership, organizational integrity, political education, and mobilization. Only recently has there been work available that grapples adequately with the centrality of black women to this movement.[7] In actuality, in order to comprehend the black female experience, one must understand and explore the "community connection." It is black women's relationship with their entire community—both in consciousness and in practice—that facilitates a unique intersection of race-ethnicity and class as a motive force for social change. Indeed, failure to account for the role of black women in their communities has flawed most analyses of social change and the black experience.

This chapter, then, attempts to account for and interpret the interaction among black women across class lines and to account for what seems to be a unique effort to share consciousness and community across the barriers of social class. It is an interpretation of African-American women's history and experience based on data collected on women who achieved prominence as advocates and activists in an urban African-American community;[8] additional observations are taken from field work and interviews for work in progress on African-American churches.[9] Consistent with their historical antecedents in church and politics, black women have been a force for social change through a tradition of activism or "womanist insurgence." This activism has been tied to black women's discovery that communal or group responses to common problems have facilitated women's survival and women's contribution to overall community survival. Such collectivism and traditions of activism have led to the integration of female political leadership across class boundaries and, more recently, has enabled the emergence of a distinct politically conscious occupational mobility[10] in those helping professions which most directly address the problems faced in urban black communities.

## Womanist Insurgence: The Community Connection

Black women have had a distinctive experience, and their response to that experience has been as distinctive. Some of that distinction has been captured by Alice Walker in her introduction and definition of the term "womanist."[11] Although not a systematic sociological concept or theory, Walker suggested certain directions for any one seeking to interpret African-American women's experience from a point of view that is grounded in the black experience or is africentric in its approach while at the same time acknowledging the importance of the critique of culture stemming from women's experience, generally known as feminist. Walker implied that the womanist approach incorporates a broader and more radical critical scope. First of all, her definition grasps some key historical realities that have emerged as models in the consciousness of black women. Regardless of their social class, many black women are able to name a number of women such as Sojourner Truth, Harriet Tubman, Mary Church Terrell, Nannie Helen Burroughs, and Rosa Parks as role models. Activities in their churches involving both middle-class and working-class women provide opportunities for public "remembering" of these heroines' bold behavior. Walker, as part of her definition, alluded to the boldness of these ancestors, stating, "Traditionally capable, as in: 'Mama, I'm walking to Canada and I'm taking you and a bunch of other slaves with me.' Reply: 'It wouldn't be the first time.'"[12] Obviously, Walker is alluding to Harriet Tubman whose heroic activities as a conductor on the Underground Railway and as a scout for the Union Army are legendary. Both Joyce Ladner and Bonnie Thornton Dill pointed to the importance of strength, self-reliance, and autonomy as elements in a role model that black women view as normative.[13] Ladner's work is crucial because that model is incorporated into the world view of lower-class black girls as well as working women. Dill's observations point to the way in which such a role model contradicts and contrasts with what has been considered normative for white women.

Walker's definition of womanist also contains an incipient sociology of African-American knowledge that implies that personal meaning, spirituality, and moral order within the community are centered in women's wisdom. Harking back to Mary Church Terrell's insistence that the black community should be called "colored" because of its high degree of diversity, Walker described a "womanist" as "Traditionally universalist, as in: 'Mama, why are we brown, pink, and yellow, and our cousins are white, beige, and black?' Ans: 'Well, you know the colored race is just like a flower garden, with every color flower represented.'" For Walker, a womanist is also "[c]ommitted to survival and wholeness of entire people, male *and* female. Not a separatist. . . . "[14] This definition summarizes a diverse historical role played by black women. Historically, women have taken major responsibility for the integrity of the community and for its mobilization.[15]

From a sociological and theoretical perspective, Deborah King addressed the importance of black women's consciousness regarding the entire community. King offered an "interactive model" to account for the "evidence that the importance of the multiple discriminations of race, gender, and class is varied and complex" and to establish that "the relative significance of race, sex, or class in determining the conditions of black women's lives is neither fixed nor absolute but rather dependent on the socio-historical context and the social phenomenon under consideration."[16] Thus the interactions among gender, race-ethnicity, and class in black women's lives "produce what to some appears a seemingly confounding set of social roles and political attitudes among black women." King introduced the terms "multiple jeopardy" and "multiple consciousness" to depict black women's social reality and their ideological and practical responses. She wrote:

> A black feminist ideology . . . declares the visibility of black women. [It] . . . asserts self-determination as essential. . . . [A] black feminist ideology fundamentally challenges the interstructure of the oppressions of racism, sexism, and classism both in the dominant society and within movements for liberation. It is in confrontation with multiple jeopardy that black women define and sustain a multiple consciousness essential for our liberation.[17]

Anna Julia Cooper (1892) and W. E. B. Du Bois (1924), early analysts of the African-American experience, pointed out the importance of black people to the political and cultural life of the United States. One of the most important contributions was the persistent challenge to oppression that came from the black community. This challenge, considered a "gift of black folk" by Du Bois,[18] forced the extension of the Constitution beyond its originally intended population and "reconstructed democracy" in the South. For Cooper, the conflicts generated by black people were important to forging what she called a "progressive peace," or a more inclusive social order as the result of conflict.[19] It was W. E. B. Du Bois, who in his sociology of the United States, argued that America faced "three great revolutions." These were the freeing of labor, the freeing of black people, and the freeing of women, in other words, political and social change that simultaneously addressed class, race-ethnicity, and gender oppression. He saw in black women the intersections of these three great revolutions. Their value to the transformation of this society into the democracy he believed that the United States was in the process of becoming was therefore inestimable.

Additional observations led Du Bois to argue that black women should have the vote because they would use it more prudently and in proportionately greater numbers than black men. Calling them "unselfish intelligent voters," Du Bois stated flatly that "you cannot bribe Negro women."[20] In assessing the contributions of the black women's club movement, a movement through which black women emerged in the first decades of the twentieth century as "the intellectual leadership of the Race," Du Bois noted that "the women of America who are doing humble but on the whole the most effective work in the social uplift of the lowly, *not so much by money* as by personal contact, are the colored women."[21] Du Bois's emphasis on their lack of money indicates that the movement, fueled by the motto "Lifting as we climb," involved women of all of social classes.

Anna Julia Cooper also recognized the critical importance of black women to their race and to the society at large; her perspective is embodied in the now-famous quotation, "Only the BLACK WOMAN can say 'when and where I enter, in the quiet, undisputed dignity of my womanhood, without violence and without suing or special patronage, then and there the whole *Negro race enters with me.*'"[22] Both Du Bois and Cooper saw the full emancipation of black women as a key to America's greatness and as the nexus of a struggle involving the intersection of class and labor status, ethnic experience, and the special perspective of the femininity that had transcended the harem-like demands of the dominant culture. According to Cooper, "the colored woman of today occupies, one may say, a unique position in this country. . . . She is confronted by both a woman question and a race problem and is as yet an unknown or an unacknowledged factor in both."[23] Black women, then, had to be comprehended as a unique social entity and as the key to democratic progress and moral order. Their situation combined issues and experiences that presented a distinctive challenge to the society and to all other social movements.

Black women's multiple consciousness about the intersection of work (and therefore class), race-ethnicity, and gender in their experience led to political activism that was self-consciously female. The black women's club movement consciously reached across social classes to forge networks between women "in professions" and "in industry." The movement was also avidly antiseparatist. One key leader, Josephine St. Pierre Ruffin, invited men to join the movement and, therefore, to follow women leaders. Womanist insurgence, then, insisted upon leading men in a patriarchal society by means of autonomous women's organizations that were open to men. Their leaders made it clear that they were "neither alienating nor withdrawing" but simply "coming to the front" seeking to offer leadership.

The current political sophistication of these women, across class lines, is the product of this "personal contact" that was part and parcel of the club movement. One woman I interviewed described the way in which one of the clubs she founded dealt solely with the problems of black women who were household domestics, teaching them to carry their carfare to their daywork jobs and to "leave the money on the table" when employers sought to cheat them out of promised wages. Although her husband was a white collar technician who manufactured appliances for doctors, she worked as a household domestic before and after her marriage and therefore felt moved to reach out to "other women like myself." She noted that the clubs were training stations for black women leaders who learned the language and the politics that enabled them to lead clubs and become public women. Black church women similarly sought to develop grassroots leadership by training southern urban and rural women to be public speakers at the turn of the century. A notable example is found in Nannie Helen Burroughs's rationale for instituting "Women's Day" in black Baptist churches in 1907, a practice that spread to every predominantly black church denomination and to "black congregations within predominantly white denominations such as the United Methodist Church, the United Church of Christ, the United Presbyterian Church, and the Disciples of Christ-Christian."[24] According to Burroughs it was a day "primarily for raising women" and "a glorious opportunity for women to learn to speak for themselves."[25] Womanist insurgence, activism rooted in the multiple consciousness Deborah King[26] attributed to black women, entailed an individual and collective autonomy "in thousands of churches and social clubs, in missionary societies and fraternal organizations, in unions like the National Association of Colored Women . . . ministering to all sorts of needs."[27]

## Historical Discovery: Strength in Community

Such efforts fostered and continued a collective ethic among black women that had its roots in slavery. Only in the past two decades have we learned much about the communal lives of enslaved black people with the emergence of a dynamic social history focused on the slave community.[28] The roots of the black religious experience with its invisible church and formally organized churches[29] and of the family with its emphasis on commitments to extended kin[30] were developed during this period. These two institutions, we now know, contributed mightily to the physical and psychic survival of black people during slavery. This revisionist history of slavery is important because it provides an opportunity to examine the human response to slavery both as an inhumane economic institution and as a crucible for a human community.

Several scholars have pointed to the importance and durability of the family.[31] Although the administration of family life by slave owners was intrusive and arbitrary, family commitments were deep and durable with voluntary family disruption minimal.[32] Slave mothers took seriously the role of their husbands and Gutman[33] points to the importance of naming systems which indicated the importance of fathers and husbands to black people even though slave owners did not think them important enough to record. The high rate of mother-headed families in the urban experience should not be read backwards into slavery[34]. The family was also an important agency of socialization to a clearly articulated set of norms and values that enabled black people to survive and to cope. Women were prominent as principals in this process. Women's roles in religious and cultural socialization led to their participation as leaders for the entire community.[35]

Black people not only built a family tradition, but also a religious tradition. The church was an important broker in enabling black people to resolve the pain and stress of death and disruption. The "invisible institution" was open to the participation of women as religious leaders. Toni Morrison, in her recent book *Beloved*,[36] builds on this tradition in her characterization of "Baby Suggs holy"—inspired by Margaret Garner's mother-in-law, an antebellum preacher or "professor of religion."[37] According to other historians, black women played prominent roles in the organizational establishment and cultural maintenance of churches.[38] Men who left their autobiographies in the slave narratives attributed their early spirituality to the religious practices, especially prayer traditions, of their mothers and aunts, the women of their slave communities.[39]

The participation of black women in establishing the family and the church during slavery does not explain fully the collective ethos that binds black women across social class. Although their contribution to these institutions was and is considerable, another dimension of the black female experience must be taken into account. Deborah Gray White, the only historian to focus exclusively on black women's experience during slavery, has not only pointed to the centrality of women to the family and the religious experience, but also described and analyzed the life that black women shared with each other.[40] It is my conclusion that the "female slave network" White described was a third institution that, together with the institutions of church and of family, fostered the physical and psychic survival of black people during slavery.

White argued that the image of black women as strong is an accurate one, but that that strength did not simply appear. "Strength had to be cultivated. It came no more naturally to [black women] than to anyone, slave or free, male or female, black or white. If they seemed exceptionally strong it was partly because they often functioned in groups and derived strength from numbers."[41] In addition to the work that they accomplished with men and sometimes like men, White showed that slave women spent most of their time with each other. They depended upon each other for medical care and child care. Within their network, these women created and maintained a pecking order based largely on age and occupation. Their leadership sometimes extended beyond the bounds of the women's network and could disrupt plantation operations. Some women emerged as spiritual leaders and enslaved women possessed a tradition of autonomous rituals and prayer meetings.

The female slave network was necessary for the survival of slave women and their families. By extension, then, it was a necessary feature of life within the entire slave community. According to White:

> The supportive atmosphere of the female community was buffer enough against the depersonalizing regime of plantation work and the general dehumanizing nature of slavery. When we consider how much more confined to the plantation women were than men, that many women had husbands who visited only once or twice a week, and that on average slave women outlived slave men by two years, we realize just how important the female community was to its members.[42]

Black women continued to assume important public roles within their community after emancipation. Their commitment to that community was intensified through the female network and that female community continues to exert an important historical force to this day. White observes: "[S]lave women had ample opportunity to develop a consciousness grounded in their identity as females. . . . [A]dult female cooperation and interdependence was a fact of female slave life. The self-reliance and self-sufficiency of slave women, therefore, must not only be viewed in the context of what the individual slave woman did for herself, but what slave women as a group were able to do for one another."[43] It is such a consciousness that survived and was sustained in facing the problems of reconstruction and its aftermath. According to White, evidence of this strength in collectivism was found in the Sea Islands and other areas of the South.[44] The complex and concentrated character of black women's oppression formed the practical basis for such cooperation and bonding. White concluded: "Few women who knew the pain of childbirth or who understood the agony and depression that flowed from sexual harassment and exploitation survived without friends, without female company. . . . Treated by Southern whites as if they were anything but self-respecting females, [they] could forge their own independent definition of womanhood through the female network."[45]

The continuing force of this third institution comes through in the political and community history of black women. Echoes of this network are found in Du Bois's observation that "personal contact" rather than money is the principal resource through which black women did their work for social uplift. The continuing force of this network can also be found in the women's organizations of churches and the widespread popularity of "Women's Day" in nearly all black churches—a day in which black women's own "independent definition of womanhood" is ritually enforced.[46] Over a period of forty years, 1895 to 1935, black women managed to bring together a massive network of women's organizations that were able to mobilize leadership at national and local levels. Giddings points to the emergence of national leaders such as Mary McLeod Bethune as examples of this mobilization.[47] The effectiveness of their organizations was such that Betty Friedan, speaking to the Eastern Sociological Society in 1974, pronounced black women "already organized."

This collectivism and community integration among women accounts for the very different orientation of black and white feminists. Gloria Watkins, describing her first encounter with women's studies at Stanford University, observed, "white women were reveling in the joy of being together—to them it was an important, momentous occasion."[48] Reflecting on her own life among "black Americans living in a small Kentucky town" she described a life style that contradicted that of her fellow students. She wrote, "I had not known a life where women had not been together, where women had not helped, protected, and loved one another deeply." Watkins is acknowledging what other analysts have observed, that there is a collective ethos among black women within black communities.[49] The term "sisterhood," for white women a goal of the feminist movement, is a reality as part of the larger "familyhood" actualized in settings such as churches, community organizations, and fraternal orders where "mother," "father," "brother," and "sister" are the terms of address and family is the metaphor for community.

## Community, Class, and the Integration of Female Leadership

The diverse problems faced by black communities generate leadership from all social levels. Though one would expect that class origins would be a barrier, there are specific contexts that historically have integrated black women, sometimes consciously, across the possible barriers of social class. Indeed, more than any other ethnic group, black people have wrestled with class as an ideology and a social problem. Not only have there been publications that have criticized the role, behavior, and values of elites, E. Franklin Frazier's *Black Bourgeoisie*[50] to name only one, but there also has been a strong public critique of class as a reality that divides the community, especially in churches and political organizations.

As we have seen, the two contexts that have integrated black women have been the church and autonomous women's organizations. Because most sociological and historical analyses of religion examine the role of male leaders or congregational culture, we have little understanding of the role of black women in national religious networks from a perspective of institutional history.[51] One study, still in progress, argues that the negative impact of recent social changes affecting opportunities for black men (negative in their potential for siphoning off talented male leadership from the religious communities) has been blunted by the emergence of black women in the ministry. However, the recent movement of women into the more visible clergy positions is part of a larger history in which the very integrity of religious organizations has been tied to the enterprise of women. As the chief economic investors in religious organizations, black women found ways, collective and powerful ways, to exercise influence in spite of discrimination.[52] It has been through the church that poor women have had access to affluent women and that affluent women have maintained their commitments to poor women, regardless of other socially exclusive activities in which they may have participated. An important part of religious history has been the insistence of a model of women's leadership that stands with the masses and not above.[53]

The other context for the integration of black women across class lines has been autonomous women's organizations—the organizations that reflect Walker's definition of the womanist approach to women's politics: "Not separatist, except periodically, for health."[54] The emergence of the black women's club movement coincided with the very sexist assault on female leadership within black churches and what Evelyn Brooks Barnett describes as black Baptist women's loss of the battle over the pulpit. Not only did church women use their women's clubs to carry on leadership roles outside the confines of their churches, but they also formed autonomous and highly elaborate women's organizations within their churches. For these women, the development of acculturated grassroots leadership was a principal task. The club movement sent organizers into the rural South, particularly in states that were not represented at the national meetings of the National Association of Colored Women. Nannie Helen Burroughs, as the principal proponent of a national women's day in National Baptist Convention churches, provided speeches for women from the national office in order to foster the development of public speakers in local congregations—so women could learn to speak up for themselves.[55] Evidence from both fieldwork and historical sources indicates that a real motive of educated women in movement and church clubs was grassroots socialization and leadership development. Their Christian ideology made them insist upon outreach to foster a genuine equality among black women.

In the late nineteenth and the first half of the twentieth centuries (1895-1965), the shared experiences of racism in the labor force provided an additional context of shared consciousness. Women interviewed in my own study and in the Black Women Oral History Project described their activities working with household domestics. Queen Mother Moore, a former Garveyite, described her own privileged upbringing in Louisiana and her early campaign to challenge the consciousness of other privileged black people. Born to a Louisiana Creole family, she described an incident where, at the age of five, she "ordered" her "nurse" to return home and get her a new handkerchief. She told me, "I was raised to be a real bourgeois 'stinker.'" Later she was instrumental in forming the movement that influenced New York City Mayor LaGuardia to remove the "slave markets"—places where black women waited on street corners for opportunities for day work. Another woman, director of an organization that lobbied for legislation protecting domestics, described her sense of commitment, reminding me that her mother along with most other black working women had performed household service in order to enable her family and the community organizations she supported to survive. A number of the clubs affiliated with the National Association of Colored Women sought to provide women "in industry" with alternative cultural experiences that would be emotionally uplifting and to counter the effects of demeaning work. One working class churchwoman described the "beautiful cultural events" she attended regularly at a local club house. Another elderly club woman described the practice of *not* asking "What do you do?" in order to emphasize the importance placed upon getting to know the person at social gatherings rather than getting to know their occupational status.

Both club and church reinforced the consciousness of a shared racial oppression. Historically, as class differentiation became more evident, women in both settings actively countered the growing divisions among themselves. Although class and color are significant forces in marriage markets and socializing, many black women, whose privileges could easily distance them from the grassroots, participate in the church and community organizations that focus directly and indirectly on the shared suffering of black women. In those community contexts that directly challenge the dominant culture or foster material and psychic survival, conscious integration of women across class continues to be a significant manifestation of black women's strength through collectivism.

### Racism and Womanist Consciousness

It is no accident that racism is named in the events giving rise to autonomous black women's movements while sexism, until very recently and still ambivalently, is not named in black women's responses to patriarchal black institutions such as the church. Historically, evidence of racism has been the galvanizing force. In the late nineteenth century, the insults heaped upon Ida B. Wells and other black women as they sought to end lynching helped to mobilize church and professional women nationally. Newspaper editors, seeking to discredit black women activists such as Ida B. Wells, levelled accusations at her and black women generally.[56] Later, the women's suffrage movement appealed to the racism in the South for votes for women, while barring the participation of black women in the white suffrage movement.[57] In contemporary times, responses to the Moynihan report and its attack on the work and family roles of black women sparked a contemporary activism around the problems of black women.[58] Stereotypes of black women, usually some variation of the "Mammy" and "Jezebel," then and now, revolve around their work and family roles. Racist assaults typically intersect race with labor status and sexual status and manage to pervade the meaning system of the wider culture.

In one of the most dramatic examples of the pervasive cultural image of black women, Audre Lorde described her experience in a supermarket: "I wheel my two-year old daughter in a shopping cart through a supermarket in Eastchester in 1967, and a little white girl riding past in her mother's cart calls out excitedly, 'Oh look, Mommy, a baby maid!'" Lorde then pointed out that such a stereotype is reinforced in the reaction of the white mother. She added, "And your mother shushes you, but she does not correct you." Because of that failure to correct, the barrier of racism within the feminist movement is firmly in place; Lorde observed, "And fifteen years later, at a [feminist] conference on racism, you can still find that story humorous. But I hear your laughter is full of terror and dis-ease."[59]

What Lorde describes, a microcosm of so many of the culturally pervasive stereotypes of black women, is a fusion of work and its meaning (labor status), color, and gender that sees black women, regardless of age and social class, as perpetual characters on the stage of demeaning and degrading work. The cultural configuration is so formalized that young children have internalized these images of a permanent servant class. Many black women recognize that middle class managerial roles do not negate this image.[60] One woman I interviewed, a former college dean, described her humiliation at a university convocation reception when a new white woman faculty member approached her to ask for help in securing a domestic servant. Such incidents reinforced her determination to continue to live in "the ghetto" in order to be the kind of role model that others had been when she had been a member of the underclass. This sense of shared humiliation and the determination to resist its consequences have undergirded the community experience of black women and helped to define the character of their relationships with one another.

The community activities of black women and the political and cultural histories tied to these activities are the observable consequences of a distinctive multiple consciousness that transcends the boundaries of class. The shared problems stemming from racism moved women to organize consciously across class lines and consequently to discover the diverse dimensions of the economic and political problems faced by black communities. While sociological analysis still puzzles over the question of race *or* class, more recent approaches, particularly King and Collins,[61] address their interactive and interstructured reality in the lives of African-American women. Understanding the community connection among women and between women and men provides an important perspective on the way womanist practices and insurgence have incorporated the many particularities of history through a conscious class integration in the context of community and church work.

# PART 2

# CHURCH WOMEN
# AND THEIR WORK

# 3

# "Together and in Harness"

## Women's Traditions in the Sanctified Church

A ll human communities contain enterprising and historically aware members who struggle to maintain their cherished values, statuses, roles, activities, and organizations of earlier generations that serve to structure the group's presentation of self and, therefore, constitute tradition. Within the black community in the United States, women have been some of the most enterprising agents of tradition. Since sociologists have seriously neglected study of tradition, women, and black people, black women's traditions in community institutions represent the most underdeveloped topic of social inquiry.

Black women and men have perceived racial oppression to be the most pervasive source of their individual and group suffering, but it has not been the sole catalyst for their collective action. In addition to mounting organized responses to problems of political subordination, economic exploitation, and social exclusion, black people have constructed a historical community that has provided a context for traditions, distinctive ethnic identity, and group consciousness. When pressure to abandon tradition has come from outside the black community, maintaining tradition has become a matter of political resistance, even though this struggle may take place in parts of the community that typically avoid confrontation with the dominant culture. For example, religion and religious activity have been the most important spheres for the creation and maintenance of tradition. Black women have invested considerable amounts of time, energy, and economic resources in the growth and development of religious organizations.

Recognition of the variety of strong traditions that black women have established in the religious and secular affairs of their community has been obscured by sociologists' exclusive focus on family roles and on black women's deviation from patriarchal expectations in a sexist and racist society. The tendency to view black churches only as agencies of sociopolitical change led by black male pastors also obscures the central and critical roles of black women.

Throughout all varieties of black religious activity, women represent from 75 to 90 percent of the participants; yet there is little documentation or analysis of their role in the development of this oldest and most autonomous aspect of black community life.[1] This chapter examines the place and importance of black women and their traditions within one segment of the black religious experience, the Sanctified Church.

The Sanctified Church, a significant but misunderstood segment of a very pluralistic black church, comprises those independent denominations and congregations formed by black people in the post-Reconstruction South and their direct organizational descendants. In contrast to those Baptist and Methodist denominations organized before the Civil War, the Sanctified Church represents the black religious institutions that arose in response to and largely in conflict with postbellum changes in worship traditions within the black community. Although these congregations and denominations were part of the Holiness and Pentecostal movements of the late nineteenth and early twentieth centuries, the label "Sanctified Church" emerged within the black community to distinguish congregations of "the Saints" from those of other black Christians. This label not only acknowledges the sense of ethnic kinship and consciousness underlying the black religious experience but also designates the part of the black religious experience to which a Saint belongs without having to go through the sometimes dizzying maze of organizational histories involving at least twenty-five denominations.

The importance of the Sanctified Church lies in its relationship to black history, its normative impact on the larger black religious experience, and its respect for and positive redefinition of black women's historical experience. When black people were first making choices about their cultural strategies as free women and men, the Sanctified Church rejected a cultural and organizational model that uncritically imitated Euro-American patriarchy. In the face of cultural assaults that used the economic and sexual exploitation of black women as a rationale for their denigration, the Sanctified Church elevated black women to the status of visible heroines—spiritual and professional role models for their churches. At a time when Baptist and Methodist denominations relegated Christian education to the structural margins of their organizations, the Sanctified Church professionalized this activity, and women were able to use their roles as educators and the "educated" as a source of power and career opportunity. At a time when employment opportunities for black women were the worst possible, the Sanctified Church presented "professional" role models for black working women to emulate. Higher education and work were identified as legitimate means of upward mobility for black women, and they were encouraged to achieve economic power through white-collar employment. As a consequence, the women's growing economic power helped to maintain their collective autonomy and reinforced their heroic role in the church. Finally, taking their cue from the feminist infrastructure of the black women's racial uplift movement, churchwomen created an institutional basis for women's self-consciousness. The result was an alternative model of power and leadership within the most authoritarian and least democratic of formal organizations—the episcopally governed church. These religious organizations transformed the negative and contradictory experiences of black women into an aspect of community life that maintained tradition and fostered social and individual change.

Within the Sanctified Church, black women have created for themselves a variety of roles, careers, and organizations with great influence but with variable access to structural authority. Their activities and their consciousness represent a part of the black religious experience that underscores both the dynamic and unsettled nature of gender relations in the wider black community and the historical centrality of gender as a public issue within it. Although the women in the Sanctified Church have worked within structures that range from egalitarian to purely patriarchal, they have neither ceased nor relaxed their efforts to improve their status and opportunities within these organizations. In a variety of ways, their efforts are related to those of women in other black religious and secular organizations.

Women's experience in the Sanctified Church has been part of the larger historical role of black women, a role that emphasizes independence, self-reliance, strength, and autonomy and that contradicts the dominant culture's expectations and demands of women.[2] Like many of the black community's activities of the late nineteenth and early twentieth centuries, the rise of the Sanctified Church contained a gender-conscious response to the problems of racial oppression. Concern about the status and role of women was reflected in one among a number of cultural debates within the post-Reconstruction black community. In a response to black women's suffering and role demands in the context of violent racial oppression, the Sanctified Church took account of at least four specific aspects of their history when developing churchwomen's roles: the devaluation of black women by dominant culture, the education of black women and their recruitment as educators of "the Race" during the late nineteenth and early twentieth centuries, the "relative" economic independence of black women through sustained participation in the labor force, and the autonomous political organization of black women between 1892 and 1940.[3]

The rise of the Sanctified Church also occurred when "liberation of the race was the immediate goal of blacks, [and] the men attached great importance to the females' roles in the effort."[4] In 1896, black women formed the National Association of Colored Women after several years of autonomous organizing. Their efforts earned them W. E. B. Du Bois's admiration and praise as the "intellectual leadership of the Race."[5] The ethic sustaining their efforts supported women's leadership as a necessary part of the overall effort to benefit the community and the world. Clubwoman Josephine St. Pierre Ruffin stated this clearly in 1892: "Our women's movement is a woman's movement in that it is led and directed by women for the good of women and men, for the benefit of all humanity. . . . We want, we ask the active interest of our men; . . . we are not alienating or withdrawing, we are only coming to the front, willing to join any others in the same work."[6] "The Saints" carried this ethic and a positive perception of the role of the "Race woman" into their new denominational structures as they separated or were ejected from the more established Baptist and Methodist churches. Specific women's tradition reflected the high value placed on women's political and educational leadership.

Leaders of the early Sanctified Church were also responsive to the fact that the majority of job opportunities for black women were in domestic service and agricultural work. As black people migrated and the church became more urban, this consciousness generated a concern for the problems of black women as household domestics. As household workers, black women were subject to sexual exploitation by white men who assumed that all black women were morally loose and appreciated male advances. Many black parents saw the education of their daughters as a strategy to avoid such risks. As a result, white observers often criticized black parents' failure to discriminate against their daughters. These educated women were expected to play a role in elevating their sisters, and black women's gatherings were the settings of just such "uplifting" socialization. Church and community activities were organized around household domestics' "time off" as alternatives to the entertainments available in the world of "sinners." Churches encouraged both the educated and the uneducated to be "ladies." While not entirely feminist, these strategies fostered a high degree of woman consciousness within the black religious community.

The black women who responded to Holiness and Pentecostal preachers and evangelists represented the broad spectrum of Afro-American women. These women were as militantly pro-black, pro-woman, and pro-uplift as their Baptist and Methodist sisters were, and their political consciousness was fueled by spiritual zeal. They were somewhat more successful than Baptist and Methodist women in gaining access to the pulpit or lectern; in those churches where they failed, the "double pulpit" emerged as a compromise between the women's spiritual militancy and biblical patriarchy. In some cases, Baptist and Methodist women defected to the Sanctified Church in order to exercise their gifts.

The militancy of organized women in the Sanctified Church led to the almost total divergence of women's leadership roles from that of the "pastor's wife." Such separation of marital role from leadership status came more slowly in black Baptist and Methodist churches than in the Sanctified Church, where women's opportunities for leadership became more and more diverse, offering a wide choice of religious careers. In those denominations in which women were unable to become elders, pastors, and bishops, they assumed the roles of church mothers, evangelists, missionaries, prayer band leaders, deaconesses, and, most important, "teachers"; these alternatives were also available in those denominations in which women were eligible for all leadership roles. Where churchwomen were officially "the second sex," they achieved quite powerful positions of influence and structural authority.

The various women's traditions existing within these churches are as much a response to the sociohistorical realities of black womanhood as to perceived biblical mandates and doctrines. One could almost argue that these traditions are more woman-centered than religious. Although all Protestants read the same King James Bible, the black interpretation of scripture had radically different organizational consequences than the white male reading of the same texts. Whatever the degree of patriarchal control, black churches have been influenced in some way by the militancy of the women of the Sanctified Church.

### "Women God Raised Up": The Elevation of Black Women

At the time when white Americans were calling black people a nation of "thieves, liars, and prostitutes,"[7] Sanctified Church members were calling each other "Saints." They perceived themselves to be set apart for sacred purposes; these men and women were confident that God "had raised them up" for a special calling. Regardless of the intensity of racial oppression, it was the responsibility of the "Saints" to do everything in their power to prevent whites from casting them down. Black women represented the over-whelming majority of "Saints" in need of elevation and protection from the physical and cultural assaults of white racism.

The church's resistance strategies have included the adoption of distinctive dress codes and the refusal to use first names in any public settings that could be interracial. Even cornerstones and signs listing church officers give only first initials and surnames. It is important to recognize that this tactic to achieve personhood applies to women as well as men: if male elders are listed with initials, church mothers are similarly listed. In church publications, elders, church mothers, and all others are also identified in this way. All this was (and still is) intended to prevent white racists from calling black Saints by their first names, a white practice used as a strategy to depersonalize and to devalue black people. Although largely overlooked as a tactic in cultural resistance, the Saints' use of initials rather than first names remains a very forceful answer to the daily irritations and abrasions of southern race relations. Accommodation to racism is, in the context of the preaching of the Sanctified Church, an accommodation to sin.

Although white people withheld ordinary titles of respect for black people, such as Mr., Mrs., and Miss, they relaxed such overt racism when using the religious titles of fellow southern Protestants. In the Baptist and Methodist churches, such courtesies were often extended only to the black preacher. The Sanctified Church, however, saw as ministry those roles reserved exclusively for women and therefore included women when contemplating this problem of interracial protocol. This failure to exclude women from protocol is clear testimony to the woman consciousness of the Sanctified Church, a consciousness evident in the glowing terms used to describe both women's and men's activities in denominational newspapers and reports. If images of the Sanctified Church were derived solely from such reading, one could almost believe that the roles of mothers, evangelists, and missionaries were structurally equivalent to those of the male elders, bishops, and pastors. Unlike men in other churches, men in the Sanctified Church have not ignored or trivialized women's roles. Thus these women with their expanded roles, important careers, and influence have been perceived as "the women God raised up."

The Church of God in Christ (COGIC), largest denomination of the Sanctified Church, ostensibly does not permit the ordination of women, and churchwomen have never let the matter rest. While there is a widespread agreement to disagree within the church, Bishop O.T. Jones represented the quintessence of the truce when he wrote, "The proper place of women in the church is an age old debate and from all appearances it seems that it perhaps will be an eternal one—for most mortals at least."[8] Despite its sexism, the church became the structural paradigm for other denominations. Despite or because of women's exclusion from pulpits, the most powerful Women's Department of any black denomination arose within the Church of God in Christ.

The Women's Department is a characteristic feature of the Sanctified Church denominations. James Shopshire argues that a defining characteristic of the power structures of these churches is their control by "a board of bishops" and the prevalence of an independently organized "women's work . . . where female leaders assume much authority, but with deference and loyalty to the bishops." Although these churches adopt the terminology associated with episcopally governed churches, they reflect the Baptist roots of their leadership in a tendency toward a Presbyterian style of more or less sharing power between the laity and the clergy. As a result, "a person may be upwardly mobile . . . to regional and national positions of relative independence from local congregations."[9] This is especially true for Women's Departments, which offer career mobility for a wide range of women.

Women leaders include those called to the ministry and denied access to pastoral positions, women who prefer the role of evangelist to that of pastor, women who actually have charge of churches in the absence of a pastor, and women who are Spirit-filled religious activists and congregational leaders. The political skill of the early Women's Department of the Church of God in Christ was such that nearly all women's roles, including that of "laywoman," were eventually included in that denomination's official definition of ministry. The term "layman" was not so included. Thus the avenues of social mobility for women in the church branched out and were officially recognized. The diversity of roles allowed women to exercise influence beyond their congregations, which laymen were not organized to do. Women's Departments today retain unparalleled power in matters of policy and practice for all laywomen and continue to provide ladders of career mobility. They communicate both to the women of the church and to the male leadership and, regardless of restrictions, determine the role models available to churchwomen. This means that the choice of heroines of the Women's Department, and thus of the church as a whole, reflects churchwomen's values and view of reality.

In order to contribute to the construction of those role models in the early days of the Sanctified church, women needed to attend the regional and national conventions and convocations. For the black women of the late nineteenth and early twentieth centuries, such travel was full of risks, and Jim Crow laws made these undertakings all the more difficult. Since women played a large part in developing individual congregations, the church recognized as issues of common concern the problems of their travel and need for respect in public places. In order to counter the stereotypes used as rationales for the abuse of black women, Sanctified Church women were encouraged to "dress as becometh holiness." One early bishop was convinced that the sight of women of the Church of God in Christ dressed according to the dictates of the Women's Department would restrain the most ardent racists.

There was a decided contrast between the ecstatic style of worship of these churches and the formal style of dress. Women wore black or white uniform-like dresses, and evangelists and church mothers devised a uniform or "habit" called "the Saint" to wear in services and on trains. At regional or national meetings, the highest ranking woman—the district missionary, the district supervisor, or the national supervisor—determined the dress of all other women present and decided whether they wore white on a particular day. While this may seem a rather trivial matter, the problem of discipline was not, and clergymen were required to adhere to equally stringent dress codes.

Thus the women of the early Church of God in Christ and other Sanctified Church denominations achieved such a position of respect and autonomy that they defined the content of their own roles. Furthermore, church members could not advance ideologies of patriarchy that contradicted standards of holiness since "holiness" was the most important achieved status in these churches—and a status not humanly conferred. Biblical debate concerning women was confined to structural norms, not the nature, quality, or character of women *per se*. Denominations that ordained women to be elders and pastors argued about women becoming bishops; in others in which all roles were open, there was no controversy. However, the egalitarian denominations would not recognize a woman's call at as early an age as they would a man's.[10] Within the Church of God in Christ, the church was forced to argue that women were completely capable but that the Church of God in Christ did not recognize the feminist biblical argument.[11]

Since women evangelists or revivalists founded or "dug out" many churches, they could not be excluded from church histories; they were too important to the tradition of holiness and to church growth. When male church leaders identified in their spiritual biographies those preachers who effected their conversions, the revivalists were often women. Thus the personal and congregational accounts passed down in written records and oral tradition placed a high value on the contribution of women and men to the most important goal of the church—salvation and holiness.[12]

The extension of women's spiritual contributions into autonomous leadership networks and careers fostered the development of heroines and myth, the most important pillars of tradition. In a social setting that placed a primary value on spirituality, "the women God raised up" as "Mothers in Zion" could not be excluded simply for the sake of male domination. The many tensions created by the intrusion of patriarchal norms were eased by the fact that both men and women placed a high value on holiness, and women played a heroic role in upholding that value. Women's allusion to Deborah who "arose a mother in Israel" in their self-descriptions provided a legitimate counterideology to the patriarchal desires of churchmen.[13] Finally, elevation to clearly articulated roles of spiritual leadership guaranteed that female heroines were part of the culture of the church shared by both men and women.

## "Women May Teach": Education as a Source of Power

Education has represented a supreme cultural value in the black church and community. The Sanctified Church arose during the height of the struggle for black education, which led to the expanded role of women as educators. The parents of church founders were slaves who had made their children's education a life's goal that was often not realized. Church officials' personal accounts of conversion echo laments over their own lack of education. Because the Sanctified Church became stereotyped as the sects and cults of illiterate black masses and disaffected urban migrants, both black and white observers failed to apprehend the high value these denominations placed on literacy and higher education. Thus it is important not to view their teaching ministries as a devalued area of female segregation. Male denominational leaders recruited educated women precisely because of their importance to the future.

The Sanctified Church's emphasis on biblical authority made learning "the Word" an important means for living a sanctified life. Educational goals therefore comprised general literacy, biblical literacy, advanced academic and professional achievement, and biblical expository skills, and these goals apparently ranked second in priority after salvation and holiness. The Saints were encouraged to acquire "the learning" without losing "the burning." Those able to teach biblical and general literacy skills and to provide appropriate spiritual role models were chosen as teachers.

The growth in women's roles as teachers resulted from a combination of male decisions and female enterprise. The male church organizers shared the larger cultural value of education, and their decisions to recruit female educators converged with the women's desires for important roles in their churches and with trends toward black women's education in the wider community. Recruitment occurred during that period in black history when the education of women was a conscious response to aspects of their oppression and when they were also being encouraged to act as educators of "the Race." Thus the deployment of women teachers in black education was carried out with almost total disregard for the dominant culture's norms; these women were not limited to teaching children or relegated to roles subordinate to men's. Black women capitalized on their leadership in church education. The early Women's Departments revolved around the Prayer and Bible Study Bands which expanded the literacy skills of women collectively; these groups paralleled the clubs and seminar groups that were part of the early National Association of Colored Women. This collective self-education was reflected in the expansion of women's leadership roles in denominations and in the growth of the Women's Departments.

Although engaged in conflict with the larger black community over the importance of ecstatic worship, the Sanctified Church admired the same heroines in racial uplift and black education. The examples of prominent churchwomen such as Mary McLeod Bethune, Nannie Helen Burroughs, Ida B. Wells, and Mary Church Terrell prompted the founder of the Church of God in Christ, Bishop C.H. [Charles Harrison] Mason, to recruit Mother Lizzie Woods Roberson, a Baptist teacher and academy matron, to be the first "overseer" of the women's work. Encouraged to travel in order to enlist and appoint women leaders, she also conducted revivals as an organizer. Another woman, Arenia C. Mallory, was hired as a teacher at Saints' Academy in Lexington, Mississippi. Church histories describe her as a protegee of Mary McLeod Bethune. After the death of the first principal of Saints' Academy, Mallory became head of the school, which then grew from a primary academy to an accredited junior college. For a while, she was the only black woman college president. As conflicts over theology, doctrine, biblical interpretation, and church polity fostered differentiation within the Sanctified Church, women's importance as educators and the high value placed on educated women were not diminished. When denominations argued about the ordination of women, those that chose to ordain preserved the teaching roles of evangelist and missionary.[14]

In addition to their role in developing attitudes about and organizations for formal education, Sanctified Church women were permitted to teach the Gospel. Teaching the Gospel involved setting forth biblical doctrine, church polity, and duties; conducting revivals; presenting teachings in the morning service in lieu of and in the style of a sermon; and "having charge of a church in the absence of the pastor."[15] The tasks of the teaching role differed very little from the task of the preaching role reserved for men. In some denominations, evangelists not only could have charge of churches but also, as in the case of Pentecostal Assemblies of the World, could serve communion and perform marriages. In some instances, the difference between women's and men's credentials was merely internal; for all practical and legal purposes, women evangelists were clergy. Often members of particular congregations have been hard pressed to distinguish between men's preaching and women's teaching. One young woman I interviewed observed, "I went to the service and the elder preached. Then he invited the women to speak. They preached, and they were much better than the man."

In the Church of God in Christ, women developed their own standards for examining and promoting evangelists. While it is conceivable that a Church of God in Christ churchman may be ordained as an elder with very little preaching and administrative experience, the Women's Department sets radically different requirements for women aspiring to become national evangelists. In order to receive such a license, a woman must preach revival successfully in seven states.[16] Church of God in Christ churchwomen are strongly motivated to develop their gifts and to develop a national reputation as revivalists in order to receive approval from the Women's Department.

The most widely shared value in the total black religious experience is the high premium placed on good preaching, which is as important in the black church as good music—another area in which women are not restricted. In the Church of God in Christ, the women's system guarantees that their "teaching" skills are superior. The dynamic and effective teaching of these women stands in stark contrast to the official stance of the Church of God in Christ that women are not called to preach. The availability of women evangelists who are in theory skilled "teachers" but in reality excellent preachers allows the elder with minimal skills in the pulpit to provide good preaching for his congregation. Since black Baptist and Methodist denominations tend to call all evangelists "Reverend" and to call male pastors conducting revival away from their own churches "Evangelist," the uninitiated may believe that these women are preachers. In the formative days of the Sanctified Church, the role of evangelist was an alternative for those women in Baptist and Methodist denominations who were unable to exercise their gifts either from the pulpit or from the floor. Such women went "over" into the Sanctified church. Contemporary changes among Baptists and Methodists have reversed this earlier trend.

Women's concentration in educational roles in the early Sanctified Church was not simply a form a female segregation; instead it was the basis for alternative structures of authority, career pathways, and spheres of influence. More important, those leaders and historical accounts that provide the church with normative legitimacy and modify the stereotype of its members as poor and illiterate credit the influence of women's educational work. Given the overall, sometimes exaggerated, respect and deference that the black community confers on educators, these women have legitimized the image of the "professional" woman throughout the church. As a result, women in the Sanctified church have established a more differentiated model of social mobility and occupational aspiration than have the men.

## "$10,000 in a Paper Bag": The Economic Limits of Subordination

In the black community, educated women work outside the home. Contrary to trends in the dominant culture, the higher the social class of black women, the greater their rate of labor force participation.[17] Organizers of the black Holiness and Pentecostal churches were children of freedwomen who worked for wages and thus were more sympathetic to the problems of stereotypes black women faced. These church leaders learned that it was working churchwomen who decided what proportion of their earnings would go to the church. However, black churchwomen did not wait for their pastors to discover their economic importance; they demonstrated their economic power collectively. After 1906, black congregations, conventions, and denominational convocations became acquainted with Women's Day, when women take charge of the program and turn over to the congregation, the convention, or the denomination the money they have raised. In one church I visited, this contribution was one-third of the church's budget for the year. While black congregations also hold Men's Days, men have rarely matched the contributions of the women. The fund-raising ability of women remains a traditional source of male-female rivalry in black churches.

The overwhelming female majorities in the early Sanctified Church meant that women's economic enterprise and labor force participation were essential for church growth and survival. Thus women's financial power was a major contradiction to the ethic of male domination and control. This contradiction was intensified by the dynamics of economic decision making in black families and black women's relatively greater economic independence.

Strong Women's Departments retained control over the disbursement and allocation of their funds. Women paid the expenses of their leaders and staff members, collected offerings for the evangelists and church mothers "teaching" in the churches and representing districts and congregations at national meetings, and provided benevolence for unemployed men, women, and their families. Sanctified Church women raised money for their pastors' and bishops' wives to travel to conventions and simply to have some funds of their own. These women believed in economic cooperation with men, not in economic dependence on them.

Black women have a history of handling financial matters efficiently. Early Women's Departments often assessed each member an equal amount of money to meet goals, one of several monetary practices that paralleled those of the clubs of the National Association of Colored Women. As their activities grew, Sanctified church women adopted the practice of contributing money throughout the year and then presenting this collection at the end of Women's Day or of a convention. Such practices had their roots in benevolent and mutual aid associations, with the sacred and secular practices becoming mutually influential. In a sense, churchwomen extended their domestic economic practices to their households of racial uplift and their households of faith.

By 1951, the Church of God in Christ Women's Department had grown to such an extent that the women began meeting in a separate convention under the leadership of Lillian Brooks Coffey. Using the structure of state and district supervisors, Mother Coffey collected money prior to and during the convention and then presented it to the church at the end of the convention. She inaugurated this practice at a convention where she surprised the church by presenting Bishop Crouch with "thousands of dollars" in a paper bag.[18] The women's importance to the survival of congregations led some to the false belief that black women were better off economically than black men. Since women tithed faithfully and prominently, it was easy to perceive them as the most powerful economic segment of the black community. Such perceptions made the image of the matriarch so believable to black men.

Whatever their beliefs and ideologies concerning female subordination, men in the Sanctified church ultimately have been confronted with the economic necessity of maintaining good relationships with their female members. At some point during the church year, it has been in the interest of the most sexist and domineering pastor to advocate financial support for the local, district, and national women's work. Like almost all black pastors, these men also have acknowledged the collective economic power of churchwomen on Women's Day—and they often have vacated their pulpits to do so. Finally, the collective economic power of women has been reinforced at the district, jurisdictional, and national levels when the superintendents and bishops receive the quarterly or annual "reports" from the Women's Department.

## "The Women Stuck Together": Collective Autonomy

Women's economic power has limited attempts by bishops and pastors to impose themselves directly on the activities of women. Churchwomen have thus been free to discuss issues and problems that churchmen may not have wanted to hear. While the dynamics and degree of male domination of local congregations varies, black women, because of their autonomous organizations, occasionally remind their brethren, "If it wasn't for the women, you wouldn't have a church."

Although many denominations were formed between 1895 and 1950, those that survived and flourished were those with strong Women's Departments. Structures of female influence enabled denominations with charismatic male founders to grow after those founders died; other denominational movements with high visibility but no structures of female influence almost disappeared. The Women's Department of the Church of God in Christ was formed at approximately the same time that the denomination was reconstituted as Pentecostal in 1907 and after women's auxiliaries, missions, societies, and clubs had grown and developed in black Baptist and Methodist churches. The founder of the Church of God in Christ, divorced from a woman who was still living, could not remarry. His position as an unmarried head of a church was almost unique in black church history, a marked departure from the traditional pattern of a preacher married to a professional woman leader (usually a teacher). This historical "accident" generated the model of a nearly autonomous women's organization. Mason not only recruited Mother Roberson to head the women's work but also on her advice appointed women's overseers along the same jurisdictional and district lines as the male overseers who later became bishops. The title "overseer," a literal translation of the Greek word usually translated as "bishop," was used in the early days of the church for both men and women leaders in the church. Such usage implied that the founders of the Church of God in Christ and other denominations initially envisioned a church organized in parallel structures of both male and female overseers. This vision was closer to the dual sex political systems characteristic of some West African societies than to the patriarchal episcopal polities of European origin.

The founding of the Sanctified Church coincided with the most extensive and energetic period of organizing by black women. In the 1890s, the Fire Baptized Holiness Church of God of the Americas was founded as an egalitarian denomination. The Church of God in Christ began as a Holiness church in 1895 toward the end of, but distinct from, the Church of God movement that established an interracial and egalitarian denomination. In the same year, black women began holding national conventions focused on the problems of "the Race" and of black women. Women were eligible for ordination in the African Methodist Episcopal Zion (A.M.E.Z.) Church, the church of Harriet Tubman. During this period, they organized major women's auxiliaries among black Baptists and Methodists, and they formed the National Association of Colored Women, which assembled women across the boundaries of religion, class, and intensity of skin color. By 1907 and the beginning of the Pentecostal Movement, the black woman had a prominent image as Race woman, clubwoman, churchwoman, and educator in the black community. Black clubwomen and schoolteachers in the Sanctified Church were prepared to assume roles of leadership and possessed the skills to do so.

The period between 1895 and World War II was the era of "racial uplift." In addition to race relations, female employment, and the multiple problems of group advancement, black women made the "status of the ministry" a central concern of their national programs, first in the Colored Women's League and the Federation of Afro-American Women and, after the merger of these organizations, in the National Association of Colored Women.[19] Women in the Sanctified Church were committed to the cause of racial uplift. They retained their commitment to ecstatic worship, which black Baptists and Methodists were rejecting. They also retained an emphasis on women's interests, education, professionalism, and the cultivation of a black female image that contradicted the dominant culture's stereotypes.

Some of the organizational features of the Sanctified Church Women's Departments have since disappeared in the black women's clubs where they may have originated. One such example is the Women's Purity Class, where women still learn their "proper place" in their churches and homes. A Baptist clergywoman I interviewed who visited such a class remarked, "Those classes are interesting. One woman told me, 'The Bible says that I should be in subjection to my husband, but that's the *only* man!'" In these classes—as well as the meetings of the evangelists, missionaries, and church mothers; the Prayer and Bible Bands; the Sewing Circles; and the organizations of Deacons' Wives, the Bishops' Wives, and the Pastors' Wives—women are able to develop a perspective on their position in their churches that includes important critiques of church politics and structure. In such settings, women learn the language of biblical feminism and maintain their collective autonomy, arguing that it is not "proper" for pastors "to teach . . . things that women should know."[20]

In structuring their activities, women in the Sanctified Church retained the features of organizations founded during the most intensive era of Afro-American feminism; the network of small groups they organized around churchwomen's specialized roles formed a feminist infrastructure within a patriarchal organization. Many women belonged to several of these groups, which provided multiple perspectives on women's roles in the form of direct statement and biblical allusions. When churchwomen showed their strength, it arose from these many networks and was described in biblical terms.

The role of the Women's Department in the Church of God in Christ during the crisis precipitated by the founder's death illustrates the importance of the women's infrastructure to the survival of the denomination. During that crisis, while the men were fighting constitutional battles in the courtrooms, the Women's Department continued to function under the leadership of Mother Anna Bailey. While sources are cryptic, the Women's Department seemed to exercise veto power over the direction of policy structure, and choice of leaders. The women also participated in the election of the bishops, who in turn elected the presiding bishop. Finally, the church's newspaper took special note of Mother Bailey's approval of the final choice of the board.[21]

Writing later in an official church history, Lucille Cornelius emphasized the contribution of the Women's Department to the survival and integrity of the Church of God in Christ. She emphasized that "the women stuck together and held the church in harness until the brethren could find their identity in the form of leadership that we must have in this time."[22] The phrase "in harness," a biblical term meaning "prepared or organized for war," referred to the children of Israel leaving Egypt. The statement reflects some of the disdain that the well organized feel for the relatively disorganized; the women knew that they could do better. Cornelius's tone also suggests the frustration of many black women who, regardless of conflicts and inequities, were reluctant to abandon institutions they played a major role in building.

Churchwomen have advanced a public strategy of cooperation with men. While their oral tradition is militant, their written tradition is indulgent, eschewing overt conflict. Recently, church mothers were admonished to "remember . . . [that the pastors] are the Lord's people."[23] It seems that the biblical ethic of love and of church unity has reduced the temptation toward open rebellion. Yet these women are aware that other denominations have been founded by women more militant in opposing subordination. Examples of female leaders within the denomination heighten women's sense that entire congregations and perhaps the entire church could continue in the absence of male leadership. However, racial oppression serves to remind black women of the importance of unity. The tension generated by a hostile dominant culture encourages women to adopt a cooperative model of gender relations and to support male leadership that, as Cornelius wrote, is necessary "in this time."

Men in the early Sanctified Church were aware of the tension between women's leadership skills and the structural realities within their institutions. Although bishops and elders married evangelists and missionaries, historically a woman's marital status did not determine her access to leadership; only one of the four national supervisors of women was married to a man nationally prominent in the church. In a very few but significant cases where pastors died and were therefore "absent" from their churches, bishops did not appoint any other male leaders to replace them but left the widows, licensed evangelists, in charge. The Church of God in Christ discovered that such congregations were more efficiently managed.[24] Finally, while churchwomen today admonish their sisters to cooperate with pastors, many pastors head congregations that were "dug out" and managed by women until those women sent for a pastor.

In other denominations that do not restrict women, female evangelists have become elders or pastors through the prompting and encouragement of women's organizations. In the Church of the Living God, Christian Workers for Fellowship, for example, women recognized that the sacred traditions of the wider black community did not encourage women in ministry in the way they encouraged men.[25] Both churchwomen and clubwomen depended on their autonomous organizations to achieve positions of leadership.

The women's methods of leadership have evolved in direct contrast to the authoritarian style demanded by the nature of episcopal polity: hierarchical, individualistic, and dominating.[26] In comparison, women's leadership tends to be consensus oriented, collective, and more inclusive, involving larger numbers of people in decision making. Visible women leaders have been able to represent large organizations of women in both sacred and secular settings. Black churchwomen have thus transformed their autonomy into the form of power best described as influence and created a pluralist political structure in an episcopally governed church where pluralism was never intended.

The collectivism and autonomy of organized women has been the most significant historical factor in the survival of denominations within the Sanctified Church. In churches with structures derived from male positions, women's organizations with parallel structures maintain the visibility of female leaders.

Finally, this collectivist orientation has also kept alive a cooperative model of gender relations and pluralist political practice in an elitist organization.

### Beyond "This Time": Tradition, Cooperation, and Prospects for Change

Women's standing in the Sanctified Church presently ranges from subordination in the Church of God in Christ to equality with men in the Fire Baptized Holiness Church of God of the Americas and the Mount Calvary Holy Church of America. While access to authority is a problem for these churchwomen, they do not experience structural marginality, a major difficulty for women in white churches. According to Rosemary Ruether, churchwomen were marginalized because they "seldom controlled the processes of the cultural interpretation of their actions," which led to their exclusion from the myths and heroic accounts central to church tradition. Women's exclusion from leadership followed, except "in those areas where roles based on gifts of the Spirit were recognized."[27] Both men and women in the Sanctified Church attain leadership through their expression of gifts of the Spirit, which perhaps explains in part why marginality and exclusion do not characterize the type of subordination women experience in black Pentecostal and Holiness denominations. Where the processes of cultural interpretation have been external to the church, the entire Sanctified Church has suffered. Where the interpretive process was internal to the church, black women influenced and, in some cases, controlled that process.

The politics of sexism in the Sanctified Church are the politics of incomplete male domination, and the politics of feminism are the politics of cooperative protest, collective enterprise, and assertive autonomy. Therefore, strong and visible women's traditions are part of the total church culture that is passed on in the socialization of new members. Recruits and young people learn beliefs, values, and ways of thinking that depart from the dominant culture's notion of women's place in churches and other formal organizations. Church members also learn to admire the distinctive aspects of black women's experience and their historical role without accepting the negative images and stereotypes imposed by the dominant culture.

By writing symbolic accounts of women's participation in the extraordinary events that made the growth and development of these denominations possible, churchwomen continue to reinforce these heroic images. In American society, women have been permitted more expression of gifts of the Spirit, the most important aspect of these denominations' identities. Clearly, women must be included in the symbolic accounts or myths strengthening the norms of holiness that define the unique position of the Sanctified Church on the continuum of black religious experience.

The presence of prominent female heroines in holiness has prevented churchwomen from becoming alienated by their structural subordination in the Sanctified Church. The collective and self-conscious politics of female influence modify the politics and pain of male domination. Over time, black women in the Sanctified Church have drawn on the strength of their skills and historical experiences to create structural conditions tending toward equality. Yet even in denominations where women have full access to authority, some of which were formed in protest against discrimination, black women and men have not pursued a course of antagonism or separatism. Instead, a model of dual-career religious leadership has emerged. Where women church members have a higher status than their husbands ("Mr. and Rev.," or "Deacon and Elder," or "Mr. and Elder"), men express pride in their wives' achievements. Through a combination of heroic accounts, symbolic leaders, and an alternative organizational setting, black women have maintained a tradition of protest and cooperation—a dialectical tradition—within the Sanctified Church.

The Sanctified Church and its women's traditions are an important resource for the entire range of the black religious experience. Churchmen cannot ignore the written tradition of women's achievement, and they ignore the oral tradition of cooperative protest with great difficulty. In denominations that do not ordain women, female members point to their tremendous records of service and continue the conflict of their role in the church. If and when these denominations change their stance—and there are reasons to be pessimistic about this prospect—ordained women will have a greater impact than they now do as unordained evangelists. As has been the case in the area of music, the Sanctified Church continues to have a normative impact on the larger black experience greater than would be expected from its actual number of members, and that number is growing.

A major problem exists concerning the values of churchmen, which range from a commitment to patriarchy, domination, and hierarchy to a belief in male-female cooperation and mutual influence. The history of the Sanctified Church demonstrates that both sets of values exist in the world of black men. In the Sanctified Church and beyond, many black men want to achieve the pure patriarchy they have never truly experienced. The functional necessity of women to the very survival of congregations, convocations, and denominations opposes such a tendency. James Tinney suggests that some black men absent themselves from churches precisely because of authoritarian male domination.[28] However, such male resistance to religious patriarchy is undermined by the dominant culture's persistent denigration of black women as matriarchs who are too assertive, powerful, and aggressive. Such labeling feeds a sexist backlash within the black community that encourages a rejection of the model of womanhood black women represent and deepens intragroup hostilities.[29]

Thus it has become fashionable since the civil rights movement to dismiss the achievements of black women in church, community, and society at large as a mere consequence of economic necessity. Unfortunately, many black men perceived the message of the 1960s to be, If you will be sexist, we white men won't be racist. Such ideological assaults led to attempts to enforce

European or dominant culture patriarchy where it had been effectively resisted.

The disestablishment of sexism in the dominant culture remains a threat to many black males who perceive the traditional model of gender relations as a component of the goal of assimilation. In order to persist in this thinking, such men must reject as unseemly and inappropriate any institutional record that suggests a tradition of heroism by black women. They must refuse to transform their observations of women's church and community roles and of the historical records of the churches into an internalized norm of egalitarian gender relationships. The saving grace for black women in the Sanctified Church is that, even in a context of structural subordination, they do control the record books and therefore the written record of their role. As long as women are involved in this process of cultural interpretation, there exists a strong egalitarian potential within the Sanctified Church. Additionally, black women do have allies among pastors who have never adopted or who have abolished the separate lectern or "double pulpit" and among sympathetic bishops who will ordain them to take a charge outside the church (e.g., military chaplaincies) or to begin new churches.

Racial oppression and its gender-specific racist ideologies still invade the black experience. Black women who do not conform to patriarchal traditions have been particularly victimized. Unless black women's image in the dominant culture changes radically, their struggles against racial oppression must proceed both inside and outside the black community. They will continue to be tied to internal struggles to maintain what power they now have in the face of embarrassed black male opposition, as well as to the external struggles with white racism. As long as racism and patriarchy operate as combined forces in the oppression of black women and men, black women will not abandon those institutions that are responsive to the shared aspects of the problems. The history of formal and informal organization within the black community suggests that the cooperative and egalitarian model of male-female leadership would be the preferred outcome. Black women's traditions in the Sanctified Church yield great hope for the transformation of structures that alienate and trivialize women's experiences. In the meantime, black women will maintain their solidarity and organizational strength—"stuck together [holding] the church in harness"—until deliverance comes.

# 4

# The Roles of Church
and Community Mothers

## *Ambivalent American Sexism
or Fragmented African Familyhood?*

The slave's lament, "Sometimes I feel like a motherless child," was more than a mere commentary on the individual desolation and disorganization which accompanies the shock of enslavement a "long way from home"—the African Motherland. This melodious grieving also conveyed the slaves' loss of their West African political, religious, and family systems which attached importance, sometimes great importance, to the role of the Mothers as well as the Fathers of Civilization. Slaves came from social systems where men and women shared power in various ways, but most often through economic interdependence. The slaves correctly perceived their new life in the United States as a "war on African familyhood . . . those expressions and manifestations of individual/community/national life and organization which emerge from the African world view of relationships between Man, Woman, and the Universe."[1] The slaves not only lost their homeland, they also lost a social system whose culture and social organization was guided by the obligations of kinship and whose policies grew out of these obligations.

Aspects of the black religious and political experience in the United States reflect elements of this ethic of "familyhood." In both sacred and secular community settings, there are powerful and respected older women addressed by the title, "Mother."[2] In secular settings, such mothers are often the heads of black women's organizations and hold positions of power and authority in more broadly based community and civil rights organizations. In sacred places, particularly the churches, they are occasionally pastors, sometimes evangelists, more often pastors' wives and widows, but most often leaders of organized church women (missionaries, deaconesses, mothers' boards, etc.). Regardless of their institutional offices, these women wield considerable authority in both sacred and secular settings. The members of the community call them

"Mother" and their "children" are often religious and political leaders who owe their power and authority to the sponsorship of such women. The roles of these mothers represent an important yet unresearched aspect of the black experience that must be examined if the position of black women within the black community is ever to be fully understood.

At present, a movement dominated by white feminists is forcing rapid reorganization of traditional expectations based on gender. Black women's absence from or reluctant or ambivalent participation in this movement is overwhelmingly evident.[3] Although black women evince a clear understanding of their multifaceted exploitation by white Americans, male and female, they are ambivalent about aiming the same criticism at black institutions and black men.[4] The complicated response of black women to the women's liberation movement represents an unconscious and implicit understanding that black women's roles and status *within* the black community are *qualitatively* distinct although not independent from their roles and status within the dominant society. Black women, at various levels of consciousness, know that the feminist theories and critiques of American society do not entirely fit the facts of their existence.

Although the institutional arrangements of the dominant society are the source of the political-economic victimization of black people, white customs, traditions, and ideas do not fully explain the responses of black people to their victimization. Furthermore, not every aspect of black social organization and culture in this society should be seen merely as a response to victimization.[5] The cultural segregation which has accompanied racial oppression in America is remarkably similar to the indirect rule that has characterized colonialism everywhere. The concept of "internal colonialism"[6] is invaluable for understanding aspects of the behavior of black people in community and religious organizations. Additionally, the colonial model suggests that the history of black people as *Africans* is as relevant as their history in the United States for interpreting the black experience. Some cultural artifacts and symbols (music, language patterns, kinesics, and worship styles) have been explained only with some degree of reference to the African background.[7] Why not incorporate such references into histories and analyses of black womanhood within *relatively* autonomous social worlds?

Black women figure prominently in the sacred and secular affairs of black communities. Black women's church and community work represents more than mere support for male organizations aimed at social change. Black women community workers participate in the affairs of local, regional, and national black organizations. These women manage and administer large community and human services agencies and programs as well as serve on boards of many kinds. While at local and regional levels, they are likely to hold the same leadership positions as men, national leadership is available mainly through women's organizations.[8] Since much of the work involved in social change, group survival, and community politics takes place at the local level, black women's leadership is important. Black women's church work generally encompasses active membership in local churches, clubs, and religious auxiliaries, as well as teaching Sunday school. Depending upon the denomination or congregation, church work also includes founding churches, administering their affairs, and founding and maintaining national, state, and local auxiliaries of church women.[9] In a few but significant cases, church work also involves pastoring or, at least, "hav[ing] charge of a church in the absence of its Pastor."[10] Addressing such women as "mother" signifies the community's recognition of the importance of their various roles and length of service in the public institutions of Afro-American community life.

## Church and Community Mothers

The roles of church and community mothers represent impositions of familistic and pseudo-familistic ties upon social organizations and the process of social influence. These mothers serve effectively for a very long time and accumulate great prestige and in many cases very real authority. Not only are they role models, power brokers, and venerable elders, but the actuarial realities of black life are such that elderly black women provide the continuity necessary to promote unity in the face of ever-changing historical conditions. Such women are the senior members of diverse networks of community workers and provide a counterforce to the potential for fragmentation. In some religious settings, particularly the late nineteenth- and early twentieth-century Sanctified churches, these women provided continuity through the crises wrought by the deaths of charismatic local and national leaders. Their particular organizational roles and degree of power varied from one organization to another. Still their roles are part of a larger tradition of female leadership at various levels of community life. Finally these women, bridges between the women's world and the world of men, exercise authority not only in an autonomously organized world of black women but also in areas dominated by black men.

Within northern black communities and independent black women's organizations, the power of these mothers is a reflection of black women's independence from male authority and economic support.[11] Within several black Pentecostal and Holiness denominations, regardless of the level of "formal" sexism, an ethic of female autonomy operates to enforce a reality of more or less shared power in a "dual-sex" political system, a system in which "the major interest groups are defined and represented by sex."[12] When viewed with reference to aspects of West African social organization and culture, these diverse settings provide important insights into black women's access to authority. The positions these women hold are similar to those held by women in pre-colonial West African societies, thus supporting the claim that Euro-American models of sexual oppression are *not* totally reproduced in the public affairs of Afro-American life. Any analysis of the position of black women within the black experience must take into account the admittedly unconscious persistence of African processes within social organizations based upon Euro-American organizational models.

The first part of this analysis reviews the relevant features of the West African background, revealing both a legacy of female leadership within the context of a dual-sex political system[13] and an ethic of "familyhood."[14] The several contemporary issues confronting community and church mothers are described with reference to their African parallels in order to highlight the contradictions and dilemmas which exist in the organization of gender-based roles in Afro-American life. Finally, these examples are critically examined in terms of their implications for the future role of black women in a changing society.

## The West African Legacy of Independent Womanhood

West Africa was the source of the world view with which the newly enslaved Africans mediated and negotiated a harsh, shock-filled, and absurd new world.[15] In spite of violent and radical discontinuities, slavery reinforced certain aspects of black women's West African social and economic roles. Because "the social and cultural forces that have shaped Black women in America differed in subtle and sometimes sharp ways from those which molded white women," both the African and American historical contexts are "keys in determining the character of Black women in America today" even though "it is difficult to assess how lasting the influence of African norms [has] been in the American setting."[16]

In Africa, the themes of female independence and self-reliance were reflected in the organization of economic, family, and political roles. "In numerous West African societies, women were persons in their own right with responsibilities and privileges not derived from husbands and fathers." Women controlled the marketplaces and this economic monopoly provided the women with "considerable mobility and leeway for autonomous action." As a result, African women achieved "considerable economic independence; in religious ceremonies, women were priests, even leaders of some cults. Women also maintained their own secret societies."[17]

From this independent economic base, women wielded considerable power in African societies which were patrilocal and patriarchal. According to Judith van Allen, women had their own political institutions through which they were able to "express their disapproval and secure their demands by collective public demonstrations, including ridicule, satirical singing and dancing, and group strikes."[18] This "dual-sex organization contrasts with the 'single-sex' system that obtains in most of the Western world, where political status-bearing roles are predominantly the preserve of men. In the single-sex system, women can achieve distinction and recognition only by taking on the roles of men in public life and performing them well."[19] In West African societies such as the Igbo of Eastern Nigeria, women's organizations like the *otu umuada* (organization of the daughters of a lineage) and the *otu inyemedi* (organization of the wives of a lineage) represented the women's collective interests in the problems of mutual aid, violations of domestic law, decisions concerning agricultural labor, and the social control of men.[20] Economic and political independence were acknowledged in women's title societies, membership in which was based on economic advantage. Such membership then led to even greater economic and political advantage, since leadership in women's political organizations was often based upon titles.[21] Such social organization is found throughout West Africa. The additional presence of age-grade organizations, such as the "*otu umu agbogho* ('groups of eligible girls'),"[22] meant that the African woman existed in a "society of women her own age. These women are called sisters, and the women her mother's age were called mothers." The role of mother was more important than the role of wife.[23] Developing against the background of this social context, Afro-American sex-role ideology sees women's work outside the home as important and legitimate.[24]

Within the context of the dual-sex political system, the African woman had recognized access to authority. The roles of *omu* (loosely translated "queen" but meaning "female king" or head of the women's world) and the *ilogo* (women's cabinet) represented roles of real power. The term "Queen Mother" comes down to us as the English translation of this role in various West African societies. However, these women were not wives of kings but rather, in the context of decision making, the important contact points between the men's and the women's world.[25] The stability of women's power was guaranteed through the autonomy of a well-organized women's world. African women thus developed their own legacy of political leadership which included military campaigns against European colonialism as late as the early twentieth century.[26] Heroines of this legacy include Queen Hatshepsut whose trading skills renewed the wealth of Egypt, Queen Nzinga who insisted on her royal prerogatives when negotiating with the Portuguese and later led military campaigns against them, and the Ashanti (Akan) Queen Mother Yaa Asantewaa who is remembered as "the woman who carried a gun and the sword of state into battle."[27] One African queen, Candace, led military campaigns of such ferocity that "all later queens have borne the same generic name," *Candaces*.[28] Geraldine Wilson was correct when she stated that "women of Africa had the care, love, protection, and institutional and societal support of men as they—the women—carried out major military, governmental, and family economic responsibilities."[29]

The independence of African women did not mean that their lives were cut off from the lives of men. Slave traders discovered that if they captured African men, "these black women are so loyal to their men that they would follow them even into hell. Yet many of these same women would seek death directly, by attacking [slave raiders] and [their] armed guards. These [women] of course were beaten and chained the same as the male slaves."[30] Throughout slavery, black women were expected to carry the same economic load as men and to continue to be the primary caretakers of children. They also had certain opportunities for ad hoc leadership in religious affairs and resistance activities within the slave community. The equality of political powerlessness and economic exploitation which characterized the slave experience set the stage for those aspects of contemporary black women's roles which contradict traditional European presumptions concerning patriarchy.[31] The public prestige and real power of certain elderly black women in community work diverged from dominant (white) cultural norms.

### Community Mothers: Power through Independence

Mothers in community work have carried on the roles of elders in traditional West African societies where accumulated wisdom is power. They have occupied positions of leadership in women's organizations (e.g., the National Association of Colored Women) and in local branches of national organizations (e.g., the National Association for the Advancement of Colored People and the Urban League). They participated in the strategies that produced real changes for "the Race." Their successes over the years generated broad networks of appreciative community members who, in turn, became an increasingly valuable resource for confronting new community problems. The elders, reflecting on their successes and failures, offered advice, warnings, and cautions. The backing and encouragement of these elders were necessary for the mobilization of new movements and organizations and for the legitimation of new community workers. The blessing of the elders carried weight. Community mothers were living links to the heroes and heroines of earlier eras. They had met and worked with such women as Mary McLeod Bethune, Mary Church Terrell, Ida Wells Barnett, and Margaret Murray (Mrs. Booker T.) Washington. At public events like meetings and banquets, these elders recounted the victories which contributed to social change. They provided an important sense of the community's history and potential effectiveness. The women performed the *griot* or African storyteller role for the community just as the grandmothers in black families had been the keepers of the family records.[32] Community mothers are the guardians of community political traditions. Their ability to function as power brokers stemmed from their leadership within historical black women's movements and organizations.

In response to Jim Crow, oppressive work situations, and negative images and stereotypes, black women formed local and national organizations. The Colored Women's League and the National Federation of Afro-American Women were merged in 1896 to form the National Association of Colored Women.[33] During the Depression, black women led by Mary McLeod Bethune, organized the National Council of Negro Women.[34] Both organizations stressed the problems of "the Race" and the special problems of black women in the home and labor force.[35] In the late nineteenth century, these women insisted that their movement was a "woman's movement" in that it was "a movement led by women." While many of their concerns were feminist, they insisted that their movement was designed not to exclude men but to develop women leaders. They focused on the economic, social, and political problems of the entire black community.[36] Club activities grew out of involvements in the suffrage movement, mothers' clubs concerned with education and mutual aid, and the growth of the National Association for the Advancement of Colored People (NAACP). The problem of household domestics represented a significant area of activity. In the early years of this century, some women cooperatively purchased clubhouses which currently house and administer a variety of grants and demonstration projects. Contemporary community mothers are direct descendants of the leaders of these women's organizations. Their movements grew out of their economic independence as professionals, businesswomen, and working wives. Community mothers' influence and power has reached beyond the black community and into the world of intergroup conflict. In one major city, when community members staging a sit-in in a public building were threatened with arrest, they sent a taxi to bring Mother Williams[37] to the sit-in. When she arrived and joined the sit-in, the police immediately called their superior and were ordered not to arrest the demonstrators. These elder community workers, "Mother" to most of the younger black politicians, agency heads, and activist ministers, were women who had very long careers working for social change. Mother Braxton, whose passing brought twelve hundred grateful community members, religious leaders, and state, local, and national politicians together for her funeral, stated:

> That [change] is what we look[ed] forward to in this generation I'm in, and I worked in. And of course now that the generation is moving out and a newer generation of younger women, like the age of my daughter and people like that, are coming in and taking up where we left off . . . and seeing that we did start a movement, it gives them an opportunity to work for real change—permanent change.[38]

These elders recognized that it was their movement, "led by women," that was the source of the skills and authority that made it possible for them not only to become symbolic leaders and role models, but also to exercise real power from a base of economic and political independence.

The dual-sex nature of community work networks is not immediately obvious to the outsider, but this characteristic becomes apparent when the worlds of church work and community work overlap. Many male community workers are ministers from the larger and more prominent denominations (Baptist, Congregational, African Methodist Episcopal, African Methodist Episcopal Zion, and United Methodist). While women community workers are also churchwomen, their community work networks are grounded in secular organizations and agencies. Although the community elders are also called mother within their churches, they do not have the same access to religious authority that they have to secular political power and influence, nor was their devotion to their churches always recognized in secular community folklore. Still there was a more liberal attitude towards women's preaching in those churches where community mothers' "children" were pastoring, and being the "first woman to deliver a sermon at" was an important part of their public biographies.[39]

## Church Mothers: Varieties of Shared Power

The situation of church mothers differs from that of community mothers. The paradoxes and ambivalence surrounding the appropriate roles of women in public life are more obvious within the churches. Within larger Baptist and Methodist denominations, women are organized under a system of relatively unyielding male authority. Baptist and Methodist Church Mothers tended to be influential and venerable elders. Within the Sanctified Churches, those Pentecostal and Holiness denominations which were founded and managed by black people and which have retained more of the traditional southern and African elements of black religious worship and liturgy, there is a broader range of attitudes and practices concerning the position of women. Church mothers are not only role models and venerable elders—according to some ministers, "women who are important for moral guidance within our congregations"—but also older, venerated, Spirit-filled women who hold considerable power within *nearly* autonomous and well-organized parallel women's worlds. Such women may be known as heroic co-workers of powerful elders, bishops, and church founders. Others may owe their prestige, and occasionally real power, to their roles as wives and widows of elders, bishops, pastors, and church founders. Some are community prayer band leaders or prayer warriors.[39] Most importantly, some church mothers are church founders, preachers, and congregational leaders with full authority within congregational and denominational structures. While women's roles range from symbolic role models to nearly-independent power brokers, all are called "Mother." Their various positions exhibit some vestige of the African concept of familyhood or the dual-sex organization of power in religious life.

One of the most powerful and well-organized groups of church mothers is the women's department of the Church of God in Christ. From the time of Mother Lizzie Roberson, the Church of God in Christ recognized a parallel, but subordinate, women's authority structure. The writings of the founder and other former bishops of the Church advanced the beliefs that women should be led by women and that "neither is the man without the woman, neither the woman without the man."[40] These beliefs led to the appointment of "overseers" or "organizers" of women's work, a system which evolved into a separate women's convention whose jurisdiction and officers parallel precisely the authority of the elders and bishops of the church.

The position of church mothers reflected an ideological and theological ambivalence on the part of the church. On the one hand, the Church of God in Christ recognized "that there [were] thousands of talented, Spirit-filled, dedicated and well-informed devout women capable of conducting the affairs of a church both administratively and spiritually."[41] Histories of the church placed Mother Roberson among the founders (in one case, "founding fathers") and mentioned numerous women missionaries, evangelists, national supervisors, and state supervisors. Historians paid particular attention to Mother Lillian Brooks Coffey, "As a woman of distinction [Mother Coffey] has a great influence in her chosen field as a religious worker, humanitarian, and dreamer. . . . Like Lucretia Mott, she has combined her effective speech for [women's] suffrage [with her work] in the Church of God in Christ."[42]

On the other hand, according to some of these same bishops, "nowhere can we find a mandate to ordain women to be an Elder, Bishop or Pastor. Women may teach the gospel to others . . . have charge of a church in the absence of its Pastor . . . without adopting the title of Elder, Bishop or Pastor." The entire tone of the official church manual's section, "Women in the Ministry,"[43] reflected the ambivalence of men who were aware that "the 'proper' place of women in the church is an age-old debate and from all appearances it seems that it perhaps will be an eternal one—for most mortals at least."[44]

The debate over women's proper place was confined largely to those areas where participation required that one be a pastor, elder, or bishop. In the area of higher education, the church imposed no restrictions; thus, half of the students at the Charles H. Mason Seminary are women. The evolution of Saints' University, the Church of God in Christ's undergraduate institution in Lexington, Mississippi, was credited to Dr. Arenia C. Mallory, a protege of Mary McLeod Bethune.[45] Mallory started as a teacher in 1925, and in 1930 Bishop C.H. Mason appointed her president.[46] In 1975, while she was still president, the presiding Bishop appointed her Commissioner of Education. The resolution of the church's General Assembly stated that "many of the noted leaders of the Church of God in Christ owe a debt of gratitude to Dr. Arenia C. Mallory King for the great role she has played in grooming their lives for top leadership in the church."[47] In 1975, she was the only black woman college president.[48]

As the women's work in the Church of God in Christ expanded, so did the level of education of the missionaries and evangelists within its ranks. The high degree of consciousness among these women is evident in a more recent history of the Church of God in Christ. The author implies that women are indispensable to the functioning of the church, that the history of the church is *their* history.[49] One of the women's conventions made such a dramatic impact that "tributes were sent to Mother Coffey from everywhere. *The National Evangelist Women were presented from the Pulpit and felt free to tell the Great Story of Jesus and His Love.* Certainly Mother Coffey made giant steps through this great women's Convention."[50] After the death of Mother

Coffey, Mother Bailey was appointed to head the women's work. During her tenure, the Church of God in Christ experienced an organizational crisis precipitated by the death of its charismatic founder, C. H. Mason. Commenting on the importance of the Women's Convention during this period and revealing the level of women's consciousness, Dr. Cornelius writes:

> The Women's Convention has grown larger under Mother Bailey and we have added the plane to the cavalcade as we go to a foreign country on each Convention. We are enjoying the Women that God has raised up for this hour, and with much wisdom Mother Bailey has braved out the greatest storm in the history of the Church of God in Christ: The Church in its transition from Bishop Mason's leadership. *The women stuck together and held the Church in harness until the brethren could find their identity in the form of leadership that we must have in this time.*[51]

It is significant that Mother Bailey was given the equivalent of a founding Bishop's funeral: there were two memorial services for her attended by ten thousand mourners.[52]

In other black Pentecostal churches with similar restrictions, women's organizations take a similar form.[53] Typically, women's work is structured so that "female leaders assume authority but with deference and loyalty to the bishops."[54] Women appear to accommodate themselves to male power and authority. However, the histories of some Sanctified churches demonstrate that certain schisms occurred precisely because of disagreements over the role of women. Both the Mount Sinai Holy Church of America and the House of God, Which Is the Church of the Loving God, the Pillar and Ground of the Truth, Inc., began in just such schisms.[55] Both churches had their origins in groups which ordained women to be elders—the United Holy Church of America and the Church of the Living God, Christian Workers for Fellowship (C.W.F.F.)—but kept them the second sex. In the United Holy Church, women elders could elect bishops but not *be* bishops. In the Church of the Living God, C.W.F.F., discrimination was more subtle and regionalized.

The Church of the Living God, C.W.F.F., is important for allowing women to pastor churches. Like the Church of God in Christ, it had a well organized "women's work." Church mothers were recognized as special venerable elders, usually charter members of the churches or "Temples." The roles organized under the women's department did not carry the title of mother; women were organized as evangelists and missionaries and there seemed to be a number of pastorates that were partnerships between male elders and their missionary or evangelist wives. An important feature of men's careers was their tenure as evangelist prior to becoming elders and bishops. The partnership of husbands and wives working to build churches was emphasized in many bishops' and elders' biographies. In other sketches, wives were mentioned separately where their work fostered the maintenance of the denomination.[56]

One deceased bishop and his evangelist wife were described as having "teamed together in the Evangelistic Field. Together they preached through the [cities] of Birmingham, Ensley, . . . [in Alabama]. They suffered many hardships and had to have police protection in many of the mining quarters of Pratt City." The description goes on to say that "[the wife] organized the first church in Birmingham, Alabama, and *through her*" one of the then currently presiding bishops joined the church.[57] At one time, this evangelist also headed the women's work and the evangelist board. Their ministerial partnership was an important model for younger ministers, particularly women, and, in 1967, their "adopted" evangelist daughter was pastoring one of the churches they had founded.

In spite of the independence of women officers and the ordination of women within this denomination, differences existed in women's and men's pathways to ordination. Women were ordained as missionaries and evangelists first. Men usually advanced to ordination from their call to the ministry without any missionary service and with shorter periods of evangelism. One women's biographer recognized that others were slow to affirm the potential of females who received the call to the ministry at an early age. "Because of the nature of the surroundings and environments they [her parents] did not believe in women preachers, they did not encourage her to continue." This woman conducted revivals and ministered to young people for over twenty years before she was ordained and received a church. Her career symbolizes the difficulties of women ministers in a denomination which recognized that "women have a distinctive and indispensable place in the work of the church. No history of a church would be complete without the ministry of the hands and hearts of women."[58]

In spite of its dual-sex organization, the subtleties of discrimination led to conflict in the Alabama district where the president of the Women's Work admonished the women "to know their place in the church, and be subject to and support the local pastor in his program."[59] According to James Shopshire:

In rural Alabama, part of the District, a woman by the name of M. L. Esters came to exert considerable charismatic influence in that state. Her leadership exacerbated the problem of recognition of women clergy persons, and although details are scant, she accordingly led a faction which eventually split from the Church of the Living God [Christian Workers for Fellowship] and proceeded to build another religious body along the same holiness-pentecostal fundamentals as the original body, with greater and explicitly stated stress on Pentecostal ideas. . . . With apparently well-tuned sensitivity to the movement of people from rural

Alabama and Georgia to the cities, Mother Esters, who was later known as Bishop M. L. Tate, was instrumental in dispatching organizers to the North.[60]

The result of this conflict was a denomination called The House of God, Which Is the Church of the Living God, the Pillar and Ground of the Truth, Inc. It became a Pentecostal denomination with a strong tradition of women preachers and pastors. Women pastor, preach, and sit on the board of bishops. Ironically, the First Born Church of the Living God split from The House of God, Which is the Church of the Living God, the Pillar and Ground of the Truth, Inc., because some members felt that the latter's position on women was *too* liberal.[61]

These varieties of women's power and position indicate clearly that the role of women in the ministry and in the hierarchy of black churches remained a central and critical debate that often fueled the reorganization of social worlds within the black religious experience. Long before the women's liberation movement began shaping headlines in the dominant society, women in the Sanctified churches founded congregations and denominations, preached, pastored, conducted revivals, and generally did all of the work associated with authority in the church. The many denominations exhibit a range of shared powers and a diversity of opinions on the scripturally prescribed offices for women. Consequently, in those churches where women were barred from pastoring and preaching, there is a well-developed and powerful women's world which, while under the authority of male bishops, has carved out its own space within the church while maintaining a militant consciousness concerning the areas of exclusion. Where women are granted the full authority of ordination and recognized as preachers and pastors, their careers are still dependent upon a strong women's world and, as in the case of the Church of the Living God, Christian Workers for Fellowship, ministerial partnerships with their husbands. Additionally, some women pastors are the "children" of such partnerships. In such "liberal" churches, the strong positions of women and these ministerial partnerships exist alongside organizations which continue to accommodate the dominant cultural style of women's participation in the church, particularly as pastors' wives. Where women do have access to full authority, the debate over the role of women does not cease but continues to be an axis of reorganization within the black religious experience. Finally, the situation of even the most liberal church demonstrates that the position of women is affected by a larger social context where the response of others defines women's pathway to the ministry.

These varieties of shared power or of access to authority reflect the range of positions church mothers occupy. The similarities in organization of church mothers to West African social organization range from clearly articulated and established dual-sex political systems to fragments of familyhood, which modify the otherwise rigid lines of authority within episcopal style church hierarchies. These African overtones in social organization exist alongside and in spite of a dominant cultural tradition of European sex-role organization and church politics.

## Black Women in Black Society:
## Ambivalent Sexism or Fragmented Familyhood?

Early in their history, black women learned that American society would not provide them the protection and privileges of the pedestal. Rather, racial oppression generated material conditions which reinforced economic independence and self-reliance. Political disenfranchisement nurtured an independent movement to uplift and to advance "the Race."[62] The movement was not only effective in making changes in the wider society but it also provided a training ground for leadership that facilitated black women's entrance into the world of community politics as an effective, visible, and formidable force. Black women consequently developed a proud legacy of independent and collective struggle with several generations of female role models. These role models enjoyed the respect and admiration of both men and women.

The position of black women in their churches reflects fragments of African themes and ambivalent imposition of American themes regarding gender. On the one hand, black women have been well-organized forces in their respective congregations. On the other hand, they have waged a long and protracted struggle, with varied success, over the appropriate role of women. In some cases, black women have shared some level of power. In those Pentecostal and Holiness denominations which still ban black women from the pulpit, women militantly and relentlessly reject the role of dependent subordinates. Where subordination and dependence are formally decreed, black women have carved out unofficial spaces of independence. The patterns of conflict which have erupted within liberal denominations indicate that both African and European patterns of sex-role organization persist with a certain amount of tension between them. Both community and church organizations reflect various degrees of independence, interdependence, and shared power or *fragments* of the dual-sex political system of African familyhood.

The energy and competence of church and community mothers have generated some ambivalence among black men. When, in the secular world, black males were embarrassed by the depiction of black women as matriarchs, they insisted that women's place in the home was a strategy for advancing "the Race" or, at least, improving its image. Any attempt to argue that biology was destiny was contravened by the historical tradition of competent black women in the labor force. This is not to say that sexist ideology stemming from white patriarchal historical traditions is never invoked to oppose black women's militance and competence. Traditional Euro-American ideologies can figure significantly in conflicts with black men. In the secular world of community politics, black men confronted with well-trained women leaders bring up problems of sex, "unfemininity," and the reproductive needs of "the revolution." In the sacred world of the black Baptist and Methodist denominations, women are confronted with the ideologies of the Pauline epistles, women's physical inability to preach in a dramatic, energetic, and celebrative style, or the problems posed by pregnancy. In a world where "the call" is seen as something reserved strictly for men, black women preachers are sharply and persistently questioned. Sometimes it is implied that a sincere "call" has, by definition, a detrimental effect on the black woman preacher's sexuality. It is in such settings that black women, particularly those called to the ministry, confront a complex of attitudes and ideologies through which black men define their prerogatives. Such situations reflect European forms of sexism. Often these confrontations take place in the relative absence of a semi-autonomous world of organized women to provide support and counter ideologies.

Since the churches remain the most important social settings that black people control, the role of black women is critical for changing, developing, or reinforcing levels of consciousness regarding sex roles in the black community. The black church represents an important path to moral and political leadership within and beyond the black community. While black women community workers achieve their positions of leadership through the support of their autonomous women's world, they are easily excluded when local community politics involve any mobilization based on the ethic, "get to the ministers."[63] When ministers call meetings of ministers, the absence of black women from pulpits means an absence of female leadership in certain confrontations with white society. Since the dominant culture recognizes the role of the black preacher in the politics of the black community, white-initiated contacts with the black community overlook female leaders and inadvertently (or perhaps not) reinforce those aspects of sex-role organization most like that of the dominant culture. Since the legacy of militant black female leadership is not always visible to white society or is *not perceived as important by white society*, progressive "race relations" may mean regression in the relative position of black women.

The relationship of community and church mothers to institutions controlled and guided by black people indicates a qualitative difference between the position of women and the organization of sex roles within the black community and in the wider society. While there exists restricted access to the pulpits and executive suites of black churches and national change-oriented organizations, the nature, histories, and consequences of these restrictions vary. Black women have never passively accepted their exclusion from any level of black life and those black men who attempt to exclude them formally have been rather defensive about their behavior. A history of militance among black women within black institutions exists alongside a history of ambivalence among black men when they are tempted to exclude black women. Furthermore, the history and variety of church and community mothers demonstrate an imposition of familial organization over secular and religious bureaucratic forms. When one views the black community's collection of formal organizations, one sees a distinctly different organization of women's roles. The roles of church and community mothers are important indicators of the status and potential of black women within the black community. They exist separately from considerations of adaptation to poverty and the negative moral evaluations attached to black women's historical role in the impoverished black family.[64] These are not social roles created by default.

An evaluation of the West African background hints at some of the sources of the black community's ambivalence about adopting the sex-role organization of the dominant society. While patriarchy may have been present in West Africa, the world view of African slaves did *not* exclude women from religious and political authority. The realities of slavery guaranteed, furthermore, that black women were *never* treated as white women were. Black women were overworked, flogged, and otherwise exploited, just like black men. Moreover, they shouldered the burden of slave masters' exploitation of them as mothers and concubines. Slave socialization, morality, and religious organization affirmed the role of black women religious leaders and teachers in the slave quarters community.[65] In spite of pressures from the dominant culture to assimilate and the strong voices within the black community that advocate accommodation, there exist pockets of resistance to the total and uncritical reproduction of the dominant culture's sex-role patterns within the black community. Along with more widely recognized Africanisms, these pockets of resistance retain elements of West African familyhood within major aspects of social organizations controlled and guided by black people.

It is quite possible that the ambivalent nature of black male sexism and these fragments of African social organization represent the distinctive areas from which black women should seek to change the attitudes and ideologies of black men and develop positive alternatives for contemporary women. Indeed it may be healthy to devise strategies to retain those positive elements that have sustained and creatively advanced the sacred and secular organizations which are centers for moral development, political mobilization, and economic advancement. In the context of late twentieth-century racism and inequality, it is essential that there be a critical analysis of those internal community dynamics which will facilitate the development of women's leadership roles with the proud ideological and spiritual support of black men.

# 5

# The Role of Women
# in the Sanctified Church

*But all the same I said thank God, I got another chance. I wanted to
preach a great sermon about colored women sitting on high, but there
wasn't no pulpit for me.*

—ZORA NEALE HURSTON
*Their Eyes Were Watching God*

In a recent book of essays, Alice Walker fashioned a new concept from the
materials of African-American culture and tradition when she introduced
the term *womanist*.[1] A "womanist," according to Walker, was many things.
She was a serious person, a loving person, and one who had a strong motivation to achieve and to contribute to the "survival and wholeness of entire
people." Most of all, for our purposes, a womanist is one who has a very
healthy personal cosmology. Besides being nurturant, celebrative, combat-
ive, communal, and self-loving, she "*loves* the Spirit." Much of Walker's definition converges with the idea of "holy boldness" possessed by certain women
in our society. They are the women who occasionally remind us, quite asser-
tively, that "if it wasn't for the women, you wouldn't have a church." They
are Bible-believing women whose response to the admonition to be subject
to male authority will remind you that the Bible *only* indicates subjection to
their husbands and "that's the only man."[2]

Church women throughout the African-American experience have established important legacies in their respective denominations. Regardless of
the level of office or specific activity, these women have brought to bear their
historical role model that contradicts and criticizes the expectations for behavior and attitudes that culture defines as appropriate.[3] Indeed, the works
of Paula Giddings[4] and Dorothy Sterling[5] indicate that the special history of
black women in American society delivers important historical antecedents
that are instructive and prophetic for all women. The quintessential victims
have also become, at some times and under some conditions, a revolutionary
vanguard.

In the late nineteenth and early twentieth centuries, beginning at the end of Reconstruction and continuing through World War II and the civil rights movement, there arose a new set of religious organizations, denominations, and independent congregations to which black people referred collectively as "the Sanctified Church." Largely associated with the Holiness movement of the late nineteenth and early twentieth centuries and with the Pentecostal movement of the early twentieth century, these churches as they emerged attracted significant numbers of black women. Drawn by the preaching of charismatic black women and men, black women and men abandoned Baptist and Methodist churches which, in their zeal to regularize their worship and to assimilate culturally, had begun to trample upon the well-defended traditions of slave religion with its oral music tradition and its ecstatic praise traditions. Some of the grandchildren of those slaves whose spiritual independence (e.g., "every time *I* feel the Spirit moving in *my* heart, I *will* pray) had fostered the survival of individuals and communities under the regime of slavery felt deeply enough about the tradition to defend it on biblical and theological grounds. The revivals and revisions among the Wesleyans coincided with the emergence of this assertive black cultural revolution which fueled the sacred and secular popular culture of the American South and eventually the entire culture (e.g., "Oh when the Saints go marching in").

Women were the most numerous adherents to what Zora Neale Hurston called an old religion in the form of cultural revolution, the "Sanctified Church."[6] This essay attempts to develop an understanding of the role of women in the Sanctified Church. It uses the phrase "role of women in the Sanctified Church" somewhat loosely. The essay examines three aspects of women's experience. First, there is an exploration of the importance of the Sanctified church to women. The overwhelming response of women to this phenomenon requires interpretation. The black religious experience is heavily female,[7] but the Sanctified Church is overwhelmingly female.[8] Why? What women's issues are addressed by these organizations? Secondly, there is an exploration of the importance of women to the Sanctified Church—its denominations and congregations. While the denominations' positions on the proper roles for women vary, women are central to these churches' survival and growth. Additionally, women play a vital role in church order and organizational structure. Thirdly, there is a discussion of the importance of Sanctified churchwomen to the larger African-American community. How have the ethics of "the saints" affected the larger cultural experience? As community evolved and history was made, how did these women contribute?

This essay does not claim to be exhaustive. It is based upon research in progress. However, it is my aim to point out areas that may force us to revise some of the stereotypical views with which we approach the study of black churches, and may encourage us to rethink the manner in which we study and assess the cultural importance of churches, and may motivate us to be more holistic in our approach to the study of African-American culture and social organization. At the very least, I hope that this exploration will inspire others to read carefully the evidences of the diverse religious constituencies that contribute to the identity of the cultural whole.

The term "Sanctified Church" provides a cultural and experiential land-mark for most black Christians. It identifies an area of experience that is familiar yet not so familiar that its intricacies are instantly described. It is a significant but misunderstood segment of a very pluralistic Afro-Christian religious tradition, what we often refer to as "the black church." The Sancti-fied Church encompasses those independent denominations and congrega-tions formed by black people in the post Reconstruction South and their direct organizational descendants. These churches arose largely in conflict with the older denominations (Baptist and Methodist). As I have stated else-where, "although these congregations and denominations were part of the Holiness and Pentecostal movements of the late nineteenth and early twenti-eth centuries, the label 'Sanctified Church' emerged within the black com-munity to distinguish congregations of 'the saints' from those of other black Christians. This label not only acknowledges the sense of ethnic kinship and consciousness underlying the black religious experience but also designates the part of the black religious experience to which a saint belongs without having to go through the sometimes dizzying maze of organizational histo-ries involving at least twenty-five denominations."[9]

The Sanctified Church is important because its small size carried with it a large cultural impact. This relatively small phenomenon had a special rela-tionship to black history in that it operated as a vehicle for the reorganization of the post-Reconstruction black community into constituencies organized around answers to important cultural questions. While it is not possible to describe the complexities of the cultural conflicts that swept southern black communities and the crises faced in community organization in different regions of the South, it is important to note that the Sanctified Church had an important normative impact on the larger black religious experience, and a respect for and positive redefinition of black women's special historical back-ground. In addition to all of its other contributions to traditions of church history in the United States, "when black people were first making choices about their cultural strategies as free women and men, the Sanctified church rejected a cultural and organizational model that uncritically imitated Euro-American patriarchy."[10]

The Sanctified Church has been an important cultural repository and aesthetic resource. A 1985 article in *People Magazine* featuring De Leon Richards represents only one item in the uncounted contributions mem-bers of these churches have made to popular culture. The freedom of con-science that is most notable about the Sanctified style came through when this little eight-year-old member of the Church of God in Christ (COGIC) told the awed reporter, "God gave me the voice and told me to use it."[11] For a segment of the black religious experience that has been maligned for its seeming pie-in-the-sky orientation, the spiritual authority that this child's statement represents is an important resource in a society that seeks to destroy the individual spirit as well as the body and community.

## The Importance of the Sanctified Church to Women

The Sanctified Church came to prominence at a time when the role of black women in their community and the larger society was under tremendous negative pressure. Furthermore, the end of slavery had brought about a struggle in the renegotiation of social roles. Within the community, there were members who wished to see the community strive for social and cultural practices that mirrored totally those of the dominant culture. Within that context, the role of black women in their families and their communities and the practice of religion came under attack. Thomas Webber's analysis of the slave community reminds us that the last thirty-five years of slavery could be characterized by the "remarkable lack of sexism" that obtained in quarters communities.[12] Black women were the carriers of culture and tradition both within their families and the hush harbors of slave worship. When slavery ended, northern missionaries, white and black, rushed to the South and intended to make good Christians out of the former slaves.[13] These missionaries discovered Christians engaged in distinctive religious practices that they were reluctant to relinquish. One missionary recorded the fact that a woman testifying in one such service informed them that her Bible told her that if she were to hold her peace the very rocks would cry out and that she did not want the rocks to speak for her.[14] Not only was there a tradition to defend and to protect, but black women were not afraid to stand up to well-meaning white people in the defense of that tradition. After freedom, black women discovered some of their husbands had been anticipating the kind of authority over their wives that they had observed their masters enjoying over theirs. Dorothy Sterling's documentary history demonstrates that black women appealed to every kind of authority to enable them to resist that kind of domination.[15] Some women were so rebellious they were expelled from their churches and others walked long distances to offices of the Freedmen's Bureau to seek aid in renegotiating their relationships with their husbands. Along with the problems of interpersonal reorganization, the black community of the late nineteenth-century South was extremely sensitive about the denigrating characterizations of black women based on their history of sexual exploitation and their departure from the dominant culture's expectation of delicacy and idleness within womanhood. Black women's work history, identified by W. E. B. Du Bois as one of the cultural fights of black folk in the form of the "freedom of womanhood," was a source of shame to many black people.[16] There was a move to keep black women from doing the kinds of work that exposed them to the sexual exploitation by white men and separated them from their families. Black women disappeared from the cottonfields and only re-emerged as farmworkers when the work was reorganized into family groups.[17] When in 1896 a letter circulated that libeled "the Race" in general and black women in particular—calling black people a nation of thieves, liars, and prostitutes—black women organized their first national convention and began what developed into a full-scale social movement.[18]

At the turn of the century in the United States, black women faced several historical dilemmas stemming from their historical experiences. The rise of the Sanctified Church helped to resolve some of these dilemmas in a way that was considered positive. In the light of twentieth-century feminism, some aspects of this response may seem archaic. But in the light of the Victorianism and repression of the nineteenth century, the Sanctified Church affirmed "the freedom of womanhood" in a number of ways.

First of all, the assaults of the dominant culture in the form of ideologies and physical attacks made it clear that the world was an unsafe and unpleasant place for black women. The Sanctified Church dignified the role of black working women, providing the positive moral support for their role within their families and their communities. The churches took seriously the problems associated with the lack of respect regarding terms of address. Some churches, such as the Fire Baptized Holiness Church of God of the Americas, along with older Church of God denominations, actually ordained women to the ministry. In the context of the South, their ecclesiastical titles were respected in spite of their race. In other regards, churches such as the Church of God in Christ proffered social roles that carried titles of respect, dress codes, and institutional authority to travel throughout the South. These denominations accommodated the desire of women for leadership and autonomy, encouraging and permitting them to form strong women's departments. Shopshire in his dissertation on the Black Pentecostal Movement has identified the "Women's Department" as a characteristic feature of these churches.[19] Within the women's departments an important infrastructure developed that provided avenues for leadership training and "uplift." Like their counterparts in the women's club movement, Sanctified Churchwomen encouraged each other to be "ladies." The Social Purity class developed as a feature of both Sanctified Church Women's Departments and National Association of Colored Women's groups; these remain a feature of some denominations, notably the Church of God in Christ. In spite of their subordination within these denominations, black women carved out prominent and important roles for themselves. In spite of the biblical debate over women in the ministry, these women were able to preach revivals and found ("dig out") churches. Because of their importance, they could not be excluded from the political processes of these churches nor from the historical record of these churches. In the process of elevating black women in the face of a particularly pernicious historical period of sexualized racism, the Sanctified Church encouraged:

> [t]he extension of women's spiritual contributions into autonomous leadership networks and careers [and] fostered the development of heroines

and myth, the most important pillars of tradition. In a social setting that placed a primary value on spirituality, "the women God raised up" as "Mothers in Zion" could not be excluded simply for the sake of male domination. . . . [F]emale heroines were part of the culture of the church shared by both men and women.[20]

Another historical dilemma facing black women was their role in the struggle for black education. Black women during this period and their fathers and mothers felt the urgency surrounding the crisis of education. Fannie Jackson Coppin, for instance, opted to take the "gentlemen's course" at Oberlin College. She remembered her sense of collective representation every time she rose to recite in those courses. She stated, "I never rose to recite in my classes at Oberlin but I felt that I had the honor of the whole African race upon my shoulders. I felt that, should I fail, it would be ascribed to the fact that I was colored."[21] As a response to their degraded status and to the educational crisis facing "the Race" black women were encouraged to become educated and then educators of "the Race."

In spite of the stereotype of the Sanctified Church as churches of the uneducated masses, and in spite of the cultural controversy that swirled between the saints and their Baptist and Methodist cousins, the Sanctified Church encouraged black women to acquire educations and to use those educations in the service of the church. Regardless of the level of sexism in a particular denomination, women were permitted to "teach."

Women were quite enterprising in expanding the definition of teaching. Within the Church of God in Christ, "teaching" came to include "having charge of a church in the absence of the pastor."[22] Both women and men in these churches claimed the same role models from the surrounding culture. Women such as Mary McLeod Bethune, Nannie Helen Burroughs, Ida B. Wells, and Mary Church Terrell, were admired by "the Saints." The Church of God in Christ was proud of the fact that they had recruited Arenia C. Mallory to head Saints Industrial Academy since she was "a protege of Mary McLeod Bethune." Mrs. Lizzie Woods Roberson, the first organizer and leader, originally called "overseer," of the women's department of the Church of God in Christ was recruited because of her educational position at a Baptist academy.[23] Women's roles in the educational enterprise of the Sanctified Church provided for them alternative structures of authority, career pathways, and spheres of influence. Many of the men in the church were grateful for the "teaching" of the women that provided for them either literacy or salvation.

Finally, the Sanctified Church provided an opportunity for women to have a voice. The Sanctified Church, particularly the largest denomination—the Church of God in Christ, gained its most intense growth at the same time that the Baptists and the Methodists were restricting the activities of women. Women convinced that God had called them to have a voice in preaching or teaching the gospel "went over" into the Sanctified Church in order to exercise their gifts. Because there were so many women in these churches, and because the masses of black women were working women, these women made substantial contributions to the church, thereby increasing their functional importance to the church. In some denominations, this placed economic limits on their subordination. The women's collective economic power reinforced their ability to sustain large autonomous women's works which provided additional platforms for developing their skills as public speakers, as managers, as administrators, and as teachers.

## The Importance of Women to the Sanctified Church

The importance of the Sanctified Church to women has a direct, intimate, and dialectical relationship to the importance of women to the denominations that comprise the church. The question of what did the Sanctified Church do for women is inseparable from the question concerning what the women did for the Sanctified Church. Simply, black women built and maintained the churches. The economic and structural importance of women to most of the denominations of the Sanctified church cannot be overstated. Where women's relationship to the church is not cemented with a well-organized women's work with access to real authority, the death of the charismatic founder reverses the momentum of church growth. Where women have asserted their economic and structural importance, as in the Church of God in Christ, churches survive and even thrive after the deaths of their founders. In the words of Dr. Lucille Cornelius, describing the role of women in the Church of God in Christ after the death of Bishop Mason and by extension the role of women in other denominations, "the women stuck together and held the church in harness until the brethren could find their identity in the form of leadership that we must have in this time."[24]

The importance of the women to the growth and development of churches was not ignored by the men. Bishop O. T. Jones, writing in the fiftieth anniversary church history, argued, "Women in grateful acknowledgement of what Christ has done for their social as well as spiritual emancipation, have ever since been attendant to their Lord and to his cause. Indeed, who would dare deny that largely by their hands and feet and service has the Kingdom of our Lord moved forward?"[25] Women became such an eager part of the Holiness and Pentecostal movements that churches had to establish rules concerning the behavior of evangelists and missionaries. One evangelist, remembering her training at Saints Industrial Academy, said that, "Dr. Mallory used to sit us down and tell us how we should behave when we were traveling and preaching revival." She went on to describe the kinds of pitfalls that could face single evangelists. The women were encouraged to travel in pairs and to avoid meeting church pastors alone. Apparently the saints had a healthy respect for the frailty of fallen humanity.

In addition to their roles as evangelists, revivalists, educators, and economic supporters, women were also agents of church order. The Sanctified Church expanded the role of the home missionary into an important teaching mission under the direction of the bishops. It became the role of the district missionaries to travel around and teach churches their duties toward the bishops. This was a particularly important job, since the bulk of the saints, especially in the Church of God in Christ, were former Baptists. Most of the Holiness and Pentecostal denominations adopted some form of Episcopal polity where the individual congregations were now subject to the authority of a bishop. Some churches resisted, and even today, according to one observer, the conformity of individual congregations to national or regional policy remains a problem.[26] Conflicts between bishops and local congregations or between jurisdictions and national headquarters could lead to splits and the rise of new denominations within these movements. Thus the role of the district missionary was of vital importance to church order.

Because of the special role played by these women, they often carried more authority than the local pastors they were charged to teach. If these missionaries were married to ministers, such authority could present problems. Such dilemmas and contradictions in status became the focus of the 1941 convocation.

> Questions were asked Mother [Roberson, the first National Supervisor] concerning the power invested in District Missionaries and those excluded from serving. Those not serving are Minister's wives in the same district with the husband. They are privileged to work in any other district. All district missionaries are subject to the State Mother. No district Missionaries are to be called "Supervisors." Her appointments are under the supervision of her State Mother: both working in cooperation.[27]

Although it is not clear from the minutes, the discussion of the district missionary carried over into the next day's meeting. Obviously, the husband restriction did not set well with everyone. They wrote:

> Mother gave her daughters more instructions. Speaking, she said, that it was the part of the State Mother to defend the Overseer [later Bishop], and should the wife be serving with him in the capacity of District Missionary (in case of misunderstanding) it would become a husband and wife issue; for wife or husband will defend one another. People do not want all the church to be consolidated in one house. Go from this meeting and make the changes, then come back to a new appointment.[28]

Finally, the most important contribution these women made to the growth and development of the Sanctified Church was the urbanization of traditional

African-American Christianity. Although the majority of these denominations are patriarchal in that they do not ordain women to the full range of ministries in the church, the congregations are very, very female. Church memberships can be over ninety percent female. If one looks beyond the pulpit, it is possible to view the Sanctified Church as a women's movement. The success of Sanctified Church evangelists was often due in large part to the response of other women to their preaching. It was the habit of these women to preach a revival in order to organize a church, dig out the church (build the physical plant), and then send back to the headquarters for a pastor. Although we tend to view the Sanctified Church through the prism of the urban storefront, it is important to note that most of these churches have headquarters in the South. Furthermore, several of these denominations have their headquarters in cities that were not well developed in the early twentieth century.

One of the most important social facts in the history of black women is the movement of women's work to the city at an earlier point than the urbanization of men's work. Southern cities, and then later northern cities, were characterized by their excess populations of Negro women. Sociologists, especially Kelly Miller, complained about "surplus Negro women."[29] The number of women living and working in the cities, when compared to men, was overwhelming. Partly attributable to the encouragement of daughters to get away from the oppressive rural environment and to attempt to gain an education, black women moved to the city. They carried the Sanctified Church with them to the city. As they preached and dug out new churches, they sent for the pastors. They were enterprising in following the movement of black people from the areas in which particular churches started. Thus different churches have concentrations in different places. Furthermore, the growth of districts and jurisdictions reacted to and was informed by the movement of the church membership. Some jurisdictions in the Church of God in Christ make no geographical sense; however, they make perfect sense when the history of that jurisdiction is told with reference to the movements of a particular bishop and the migration patterns of members of his district churches. It is the enterprise of black women that provides the urban settings in which traditional black religion is able to thrive and to provide a haven for cultural developments. Not only was the tradition of ecstatic worship maintained, but the little urban versions of the Sanctified churches provided a home for the early gospel singers who were barred from singing in Baptist churches.[30] If it were not for the urban Sanctified Church, gospel music might not have survived as a *sacred* tradition. The urban storefront, the conscious extension of southern old time religion—not in reaction to the coldness of northern churches but as positive action on the part of proud and partisan saints— provided an important crucible for the process of urban ethnogenesis. It was black women who largely carried this tradition to the city.

It is in the cities that women emerge as pastors and the role of black clergywomen began to be developed and defined. Sociologists who have studied organizations and structures within urban ghetto communities have confessed to me the fact that they ignored the small churches pastored by women precisely *because* they were pastored by women. It never occurred to them to take note of the names of the churches and to ask the origins of the churches. Both black and white sociologists are guilty of such behavior. By not noting the historical origins of these small urban churches and examining the networks of which they were a part, chroniclers of the black cultural experience simply overlooked large segments. One sociologist, when discussing the revisions of his manuscript on black pentecostalism, confessed that he had never once traveled with the congregations he studied on their numerous trips to fellowship with other churches. He had no idea what other churches and what other networks were important to the identity and connectedness of the church. The fact that these were often other urban congregations in different denominations was important, because it is such interchurch interaction that gives the cultural referent, the "Sanctified Church," its social organizational reality. The urbanization of traditional black religious practices was important for the process of ethnogenesis. This process enabled black people who had made cultural choices in favor of tradition to maintain their choice within the context of a like-minded constituency. It is interesting to observe the current role played by the descendants of these church traditions in the more "mainline" congregations who are attempting to regain their spiritual and cultural identities.

### The Cultural and Social Importance of Sanctified Churchwomen

While it is easy to discuss the role of the Sanctified Church in the history of black spirituality, it has become fashionable to evaluate the cultural importance of black institutions on the basis of their observable role in social transformation. Regrettably, that becomes the sole question some students of the black religious tradition ask. In the case of the Sanctified Church, the question is misplaced. Unfortunately, the failure to appreciate the roles of women within the churches and the roles of the churches in the lives of women has led to a lack of appreciation of the ways in which black women shaped this religious tradition with reference to the political milieu.

The Sanctified church rose in importance at precisely the same time that black women were organizing their racial uplift movement. In a sense, black women carried their Christian missionary zeal beyond the walls of their churches and into the streets and houses and schools of the community. For many women who wished to be missionaries "in Africa"—Mary McLeod Bethune to name one example—they discovered their very own Africas right next door.[31] The uplift movement with its federations of women's clubs was the specialized political arm of black church women. During the period between 1896 and 1948, for black women at least, the church became a specialized religious institution while at the same time they organized a dizzying array of organizations that addressed every problem from scholarships and household domestics to the problems of international relations and the end of colonialism. The women organized homes for youth, homes for unwed mothers, purchased club houses, and provided housing for women college students, established organizations of cultural refinement for household domestics, organized political clubs, campaigned for woman suffrage, and participated in a wide variety of activities designed to promote social change and advance the interests of "the Race."[32]

Sanctified Churchwomen were very much a part of this movement. They were quite proud of the facts of their acquaintance with other progressive women. One of the most militant heads of the Church of God in Christ's Women's Department was Mother Lillian Brooks Coffey. She was extremely proud of her activism and her relationship with other women leaders. The men in the church also recognized and admired her activism, at least in 1957. Bishop Pleas wrote:

> As a woman of distinction she has a great influence in her chosen field as a religious worker, humanitarian and dreamer. . . . The ingathering of women from every nook and corner of these United States and Foreign Fields speaks for itself of the great influence of this woman as a leader for God. Mother Coffey's influence has been far, reaching the hearts of men and women of every walk of life. . . . Like Lucretia Mott, she has combined her effective speech to women suffrage in the Church of God in Christ.[33]

When Mother Coffey was installed as the supervisor of the Chicago jurisdiction, Mary McLeod Bethune attended as her special invited guest. Alternatively, Mother Coffey represented the women of the Church of God in Christ at various national functions organized by Mrs. Bethune. The minutes of the 1941 Convocation provided important insights into this relationship. Mother Coffey gave her report to the body saying:

> "I am a servant of the most high God. God gave me this appointment and no man can take it from me." Mother Coffey was blessed to have a consideration opened for her through Pres. [of Saints Academy] Arenia Mallory, to attend the National Federation of Negro Women's Clubs, as a representative of the Church of God in Christ; not as an invited guest but as a leader and a guest of the President's honored wife, Mrs. E. Roosevelt; together with Mrs. Bethune, as president of this organization and the many other women of national repute. We know of no one more eligible for such a position, and to embrace such an occasion, to express herself on "Religious Morale." Also among the noble women present we were happy to hear of the presence in this meeting of Miss Arenia Mallory, Pres., Saints Industrial School, Lexington, Mississippi

and Mrs. Alice Mason Amos, daughter of Bishop Mason. Each had a voice in this meeting. God has given them wisdom to come before rulers and magistrates.[34]

Mother Coffey's attitude toward public service went far toward paving the way for Sanctified Churchwomen to play a role in the shaping of political culture in the black community. Because women are often overlooked and the Sanctified Church has been virtually ignored, it is easy to miss the various contributions that have been made by women possessing the spiritual vision of the saints. One of the things that this research has made me do is to notice the denominational affiliations of black Christians in newspapers and magazines. [In 1984], *Jet* carried a where-are-they-now-type piece on Mrs. Mamie Mobley. Mrs. Mobley is a member of the Church of God in Christ and one of her favorite activities is working with the young people in the church, preparing them to compete in an oratorical contest concerned with black history. That activity in and of itself is interesting since it is continuous with the kinds of activities of women such as Nannie Helen Burroughs, the founder of the National Training School for Girls, and of the Women's Auxiliary Convention of the National Baptist Convention. However, I was struck by the fact that Mrs. Mobley is Mrs. Mamie *Till* Mobley, the mother of Emmett Till.

[In June of 1985], *Jet* ran another article concerning Mrs. Mobley. This time the article stressed the importance of Emmett Till's lynching for the heightened consciousness of the black community. According to Simeon Booker:

> Four months before Rosa Parks took the personal stand against segregation, a Black Chicago mother, Mrs. Mamie Till Mobley unknowingly but decisively jolted "the sleeping giant of Black people." Hurt and angered by the lynching of her only child, 14 year-old Emmett Till during a summer trip to Mississippi, Mrs. Mobley defied pressure from local authorities to immediately bury Till by demanding that his battered, mutilated body be brought back to [Chicago].
>
> Screamed the distraught mother, "Open it [the casket] up. Let the people see what they did to my boy." Her face wet with tears, she leaned over the body, just removed from a rubber bag in a Chicago funeral home, and cried out, "Darling, you have not died in vain. Your life has been sacrificed for something."[35]

Apparently, the implications of Mrs. Mobley's insistence that Emmett Till's body be displayed and the attendance of "almost a quarter of a million people" at the [church] for a viewing were similar to the consequences of public funerals in [apartheid] South Africa. According to Booker, her actions prevented Mississippi officials from hastily burying the body in Mississippi rather than shipping it to Chicago. Although the Booker article did not refer to her specific denominational affiliation, it did make mention of the importance of her faith for coping with the occasional reminders of her pain. Booker writes:

> Deeply religious, she believes that "the Lord knows best." When the Till case was revived on Chicago television, she pictured herself as en- cased in a "block of ice" because of the sudden onslaught of past memo- ries. "But then I had a dream," she told *Jet.* "I was standing on a bridge as high as any building in Chicago. I looked down at the raging waters far below me. Then I heard the Lord say, 'I have kept you far above the troubled waters.'"[36]

Mrs. Mobley is not the only "saint" to have an effect on the ethical and political culture of the black experience. Another famous member of the Church of God in Christ was the late Mrs. Lillian P. Benbow, a former presi- dent of the sorority Delta Sigma Theta. In 1976, she provided an important criticism of the behavior of black fraternal organizations. In an article titled, "It's Time to Stop 'the Dance,'" appearing in *Ebony* in October, 1976, Mrs. Benbow analyzed the financial cost of the "annual ritual" that is often "the single most successful and highly supported event of any program year." Segments of her critique were highly incisive and remain instructive. She wrote:

> When the figures are tallied, it is not difficult to see where this annual collective budget would place "The Dance" among the yearly income ratings of black businesses. Even in those instances where dances are sponsored as benefits, the funds realized from the event simply reflect and are limited to the financial input of the membership. . . . Since expenses usually exceed profits from such events, the major beneficia- ries turn out to be the white owners and concessionaires who rent and service the facilities.[37]

After citing the fact that such social occasions do not even provide the same kinds of informal economic benefits as similar occasions do for white people, Mrs. Benbow urged that a national vow of abstinence might be in the best interests of black people. She argued:

> The eight black sororities and fraternities alone represent more than 500,000 professionally trained men and women endowed with tremen- dous skills and resources. Each organization has a history of laudatory achievements in public service. It is time—high time—these groups take a collective *vow of abstinence* from the giving of the annual dance and use the money and the energy in the interests of the more serious needs of black people. And it is even more timely that responsible black leadership demand that black professionals cease this annual pampering

of themselves—stop this dutiful use of money as a sacrificial offering on the altar of white profits, which affords *no* returns.[38]

Mrs. Benbow's ending was consistent with the message of self-help and self-reliance that has been an unheralded tradition among women and men in the Sanctified Church, long before it became popular among members of the larger black community. She concluded:

> Black fraternal organizations can no longer validate the routine dissipa-tion of huge sums of money by citing their numerous public service contributions. There are no contributions significant enough to justify such colossal waste so long as there exist such great needs within the black community. Paramount is the need to support black businesses and black causes, and to build black institutions. We can maximize our ability to do so by throwing off the yoke of "The Dance."[39]

Within the same October 1976 issue of *Ebony*, the achievement and self-reliance that saints attempted to cultivate was underscored in an article titled "A World without Sight or Sound." The article featured the story of a Cleve-land woman who had been elected the first and only black officer (president) of the National Association of the Deaf-Blind of America. Not only is Mrs. Callahan a nationally noted advocate for the deaf-blind, but she is also a national evangelist in the Church of God in Christ. Her husband is an elder. Not only does she preach and give Bible readings, but she is also an excellent pianist. Her message to others when helping them to cope with their handi-cap highlights the importance of this spiritual tradition for coping and asser-tively moving beyond the confrontation with suffering. She says:

> "Look at the splendor of His art work," she said sweeping her arms over the camp grounds. "The same God that did all of this, created you and me too. Don't worry about not being able to see and don't worry about not being able to hear. God gave you a spiritual sight and a spiritual hearing. One day, you shall have it again, and when you do finally see, you'll see all goodness and righteousness. There will be no sickness and no affliction."[40]

These isolated cases point to the need for closer examination of the im-portance of women in the Sanctified Church for the larger community. If we look at them as isolated women in their churches or if we view the churches without reference to roles of the members in the world, we are not able to have a better understanding of the complex dynamics that obtain in the rela-tionship between religion and social change or between women and reli-gious institutions. When we consider the role of women in the Sanctified Church—their importance to the church, the importance of the church to them, and the importance of these churchwomen to society—we should carry away the importance of a complex and dynamic analysis in the area of black church studies. The roles of Mrs. Benbow, Mrs. Mobley, and Mrs. Callahan, point to a contribution to the politics and ethics of the black community that has been overlooked simply because students of black religion and community organization chose to overlook certain churches. Furthermore, in light of social and historical research on the role of black women in American society,[41] women in the Sanctified Church are part of the larger tradition of black women who are able to transform their victimizations into a prophetic vanguard.

### Conclusion: A Foundation of Strength and Commitment

The varieties of situations black women confront in the many denominations of the Sanctified Church point to the importance of black women to any endeavor of significance in the black community. Black women are central and vital members of the community. The growth and development and survival of small organizations is dependent upon not only their membership, but their access to leadership, leadership training, autonomy, and community. The observation of Anna Julia Cooper, that the levels of access and respect accorded black women reflect the status of the entire group, is underscored in the case of women in the Sanctified Church. Only where black women are able to enter with some modicum of respect, does viable organization for the entire community thrive.[42]

It has been argued that black people have no culture to defend or protect. The role of women in the Sanctified Church should call into question such an assertion. The Sanctified Church has been a vehicle of traditional black culture—those aspects of culture that contribute to the ethnic distinctiveness of black communities. Elsewhere I have written about the importance of women's roles in the preservation of fragments of African tradition. Even from a partial and exploratory analysis, it can be argued that these small denominations and congregations have been essential aspects of the social organization that fosters what Ronald Taylor has analyzed as black ethnogenesis—the social production of black ethnicity.[43]

Additionally the women are responsible for the care and cultivation of tradition. Edward Shils has argued that tradition is one of the most neglected concepts in sociological analysis. He argues that in a society that prides itself on being innovative and nontraditional, the agents of tradition tend to be ignored and sometimes stigmatized.[44] Sanctified Church women have been enterprising agents of black religious tradition. They have in a number of circumstances provided the discerning voice that distinguishes between spirituality and "show." They have opted to preserve the sacral nature of an ecstatic worship tradition that has been popularized and prostituted in any number of ways. One woman commented to me, "It seems that the gospel music of the Sanctified Church is so much more sacred." While I am sure there are church members who can argue that the Sanctified Church has maintained the sacred character of gospel music, I am also sure that there are Sanctified Churches that have wandered just as far away from orthodoxy as is possible. However, it is important to note that at the cultural level, the role of the Sanctified Church in the maintenance of cherished traditions and true spirituality is recognized by others outside the experience.

Walter Brueggemann in his study of the prophet Hosea has reminded us that one of the tasks of the prophet is to call to our remembrance traditions that are important for coping with crisis and to remind us of the spiritual foundations of our communities.[45] If we can only say one thing about women in the Sanctified Church, we should be able to say that they are prophets in this tradition. They have maintained the faith as delivered to "the saints" and it stands available to anyone at a point of personal or collective crisis. In their persistent refashioning of tradition in the context of the continuing crisis of the black experience, the Sanctified Church and its churchwomen have contributed to the internal strengthening of the community and its ability to effect the kinds of external transformations that are necessary to create a just society.

# 6

# The Politics of "Silence"

## Dual-Sex Political Systems
## and Women's Traditions of Conflict

*Let your women keep silence in the churches: for it is not permitted unto
them to speak.*

—PAUL
1 Corinthians 14:34 (KJV)

*The "proper" place of women in the church is an age-old debate and from
all appearances it seems that it perhaps will be an eternal one—for most
mortals at least.*

—BISHOP O. T. JONES
Church of God in Christ, ca. 1950

*As the Bible is an iconoclastic weapon—it is bound to break down images
of error that have been raised. As no one studies it so closely as the Baptists,
their women shall take the lead.*

—MARY COOK
American National Baptist Convention, 1887

Religion and politics, we are told, do not mix. Yet any superficial observation of religion in contemporary society will demonstrate that religious
organizations contain within them structures and mechanisms which allocate
power and authority. Religious systems are political systems, and very religious people can be quite political. Indeed, Alexis de Tocqueville in his travels
through the United States commented on the political enterprise of the nation's
preachers and the religious fervor of its politicians. The most dramatic contemporary religious politics revolve around issues of gender—specifically the power,
authority, and prominence of women in churches and in public religious life.
Because many Christian churches have recited Paul's admonition to the women

in Corinth to "be silent," the proper activities of women in leadership roles have been a problem to be resolved in dramatic, public contests of power. In addition to these gender contests, the African-European confrontation persists in our national life. It is not only a political-economic conflict; it is also a cultural confrontation, and at the core of culture is religion.

The responses of Africans and their descendants to Christianity, we are now discovering, highlights the contrasts and contradictions between European and African worldviews. In one area alone—that of church polity and women's roles—we can recognize many of the tensions that existed between Western logic, which selected Paul's admonitions as privileged parts of the canon, and African logic, which tolerated a high degree of religious diversity, emphasized community and experience over doctrine and dogma, recognized women's religious authority, and gave a prominent place to the feminine in its cosmology. One result of these tensions is that a part of the religious experience of African-Americans involves coming to workable terms with European organizational forms that presume the subordination and marginalization—that is, the silence—of women.

This analysis attempts to confront and interpret the experience of African-American women in their churches. Women have emerged in every African-American religious tradition as persons with significant power in spite of the overwhelming resistance of the largest church bodies to women's ordination. On the issue of ordination there is pluralism. Even in episcopal polities where the practice is ostensibly "illegal," some bishops will ordain women. Women's roles in the African-American tradition have been constructed largely through the assertiveness and enterprise of women within a system of contested gender relations. That system was shaped in a societal context of competing cultural forces. I call this confrontation between the women and the larger system "the politics of silence."

Within this tradition one must examine the women, their religious roles, practices, and ideas, and then the entrenched conflicts that exist in the churches. First, I describe briefly some of the distinctive aspects of African-American women's experience. Then I look at the distinctive religious emphases fostered in slavery and nurtured thereafter in a wide variety of settings. I focus on those aspects specially related to the shaping of women's roles and to gender relations. Finally, I examine some of the conflicts that persist in the complex institutional arrangements of religious life.

### African-American Women's Experience

Although students of race relations and social change have acknowledged the primary importance of religion in the social and political life of the black community, there exists a critical lack of understanding of the historical process of institutionalization of black religious traditions and their cultural importance. At the same time, the role of women has become an important question in the formal study of religion and in the contemporary expressions of Jewish, Christian, and Islamic traditions. While material concerned with the historical importance of African-American religion and with the role of women in society is expanding at an unprecedented rate, far less has been written about the role of women in African-American religious traditions.

The legal, economic, and social status of African women, Paula Giddings argues, was perhaps the foundation upon which the unique experience of Africans and their descendants in the United States was constructed.[1] Sexuality, cultural roles, and gender relations early became central problems in the organizational and cultural responses of African-Americans to their enslavement and to their subsequent experiences. Those responses, of which religion and church were integral parts, fashioned a complex community whose diversity has lived in historical tension with its need for unity.[2] Women, through their networks of ideologically and practically diverse organizations and constituencies, have been keys to that unity in the face of diversity. Deborah King employs the terms "multiple jeopardy" and "multiple consciousness" to develop an integrated theoretical approach to the experiences of African-American women.[3] Instead of an image of abject victimization and paralysis, she points to race-ethnicity, class, and gender as interactive terms that both locate and constrain experience at the same time as they interact to provide a unique perspective on culture and society. This "multiple consciousness" enables African-American women to shape a multifaceted critique of oppression and its diverse expressions as well as to develop strategies aimed at social change. Thus, in the face of crushing victimization and brutalization one finds a complex basis for resistance and self-actualization.

This resistance has manifested itself in the observations and writings of African-American women throughout their history in the United States. Frances Ellen Watkins Harper and Nannie Helen Burroughs, to select just two, insisted that the role of African-American women involved an assertive and persistent solidarity with their communities. They also pointed to a strength and pride that emerged from African-American women's resistance to the slave experience. Harper in particular asserted that in the process of adjusting to the social change associated with the new experience of freedom, African-American women drew upon their experiences in slavery as the source of a militant solidarity evinced by African-American women of all backgrounds, and particularly privileged ones. Often that solidarity was expressed in the language of religious covenant and Christian mission.

Literary, historical, and social scientific perspectives point to the emergence of a "role model" in which African-American women were perceived as autonomous, independent, strong, and self-reliant. This model was identified by Dill as a contradiction to the expectations of the dominant culture (white).[4] It has been stereotyped and trivialized in popular culture, creating powerful conflicts and tensions within African-American women themselves and within their communities. Nevertheless, it embodies features of the individual lives and organizational careers that are distinctive within the African-American religious tradition.

Alongside the experience of oppression in the United States, another cultural tension stems from the religious imaginations that Africans brought with them to the New World. In West Africa, women were recognized as competent religious leaders. They were priestesses and cult leaders, and they were responsible, as wives and mothers, for the socialization of their children into the diverse and sometimes competing demands of household and family cults. Furthermore, African religions contained within them female deities and feminine imagery of the creator deity. Mbiti and others have argued persuasively that these African understandings of God the Creator stand squarely within the canons of monotheism and Judeo-Christian understandings.[5] Cultic service in West African cultures was never restricted to men. Moreover, women also maintained their own independent cults which reinforced their autonomous economic roles. The importance of West African women to production and markets was reflected in the religious life, and the religious life exalted the roles of women in a way that Europeans, particularly the English, would find unthinkable. This prominence (not dominance) of women in a context of patriarchy has led some, particularly Cheikh Anta Diop, to argue that African societies should not be viewed through the same lenses with which we examine European traditions and societies.[6]

The emergence, then, of an independent network of slave women was a function, according to Deborah Gray White, of African cultural foundations and American oppression.[7] Within this world, which enabled women to support one another in sickness, childrearing, childbearing, and work, enslaved women also conducted a religious life with one another. This autonomous world, relatively impenetrable, provided a basis for women's leadership and authority in the larger slave community. According to Webber, there is considerable evidence for women's leadership within the slave quarters community, and that leadership extended occasionally to the role of preacher.[8] Observations in missionaries' accounts and biographies document the fact the women were accomplished leaders of worship and teachers of religious tradition coming out of slavery.[9] Women's commitment to their religious life and the larger community continued in the aftermath of slavery and remained a source of tension between black women and their employers.[10] Their prominence in the slave community and their commitment to the religious life guaranteed that women would emerge as part of the leadership class—particularly as educators who were so essential to the development of a stable post-emancipation black community.

The tensions surrounding the historical role of black women in the United States—their work roles and their political roles—have contributed to the contemporary organizational shape of historically black denominations and congregations. At the same time, the churches that black women made together with black men became effective normative, social, and psychological resources for black women in their economic and political roles. Like other areas of African-American life, the black religious experience exhibits apparently contradictory characteristics. These characteristics stem from the historical, social, and cultural dilemmas related to the intersection of race oppression and gender oppression. One aspect of the intersection of gender and race in the shaping of black religion is the existence of diverse expressions of a dual-sex political system in historically black churches, stemming from black women's traditions of autonomy, independence, and self-reliance. A second aspect is the existence of a tradition of conflict stemming from black women's consciousness concerning their special history, their political activism and community work, and their resistance to the imposition of Euro-American patriarchy. These two aspects of African-American women's religious experience are not the only distinctive ones, but they point to the depth of the historical and cultural roots that have shaped the black religious experience in America and the centrality of "the woman question" to the dynamics of that experience.

Although African-American life in contemporary society is diverse and complex, religion has been a diffuse phenomenon that has helped to shape and to organize orientations to family, work, politics, economic behavior, and education. The problems of race and gender have been and continue to be salient in all of these, to be part of larger religious questions, and also to be part of an understanding that black women and men have both suffered.[11] While black religion is patriarchal, it sometimes exhibits an ambivalent patriarchy. In the history of sociological analysis and American racist ideologies, the failures of black people to conform precisely to the norms of Euro-American patriarchy in their family lives and labor histories have been the cause of much victim blaming and innumerable cultural assaults. As Giddings points out, gender, particularly the status of African-American women, is a foundation for the status of the entire community.[12] An understanding of the dynamics of gender relations in the black community is essential, but remains incomplete because of the failure to analyze those relations in the religious experience.

The contested gender relations of black religion are obscured because of the exaggerated focus on the preacher and the edifices. While important, the role of the preacher has unfortunately overshadowed other forms of religious leadership. By reading the dynamics of the Civil Rights Movement back into black religious and political history, the complexities, multiple traditions, and alternative models of power, authority, and leadership have been ignored. In addition, the elevation of the edifice of a church to a sociological concept (with the storefront imaged only as an isolated sect and cult) has obscured the linkages between institutionalized religion and women's experience. (One sociologist told me that he noticed the little storefronts pastored by women but it never occurred to anyone to ask whence they came.) Equating the preacher with the black church and the edifice with the sociological reality has also diminished our capacity to appreciate the historical and evolutionary processes contributing to the emergence of national church networks.

The additional failure to account for tradition has limited our view of religion as a cultural force. All these failures of perspective have combined to intensify the practice of ignoring and minimizing the importance of women. To correct these failures, it is important to focus on those aspects of gender relations which give the religious experience a distinctive character. Analysis of the role of women highlights the ways in which black women and men manipulated elements of two cultures and their respective social organizations to fashion a distinctive pillar of American Protestantism. The duality and conflict associated with women's roles point to the dynamic complexity and "multiple consciousness" underlying issues of gender, race, and their intersection.

### The Roots of Contradiction and Paradox: African Culture and American Slavery

The organization of gender in the black community has been influenced by the manner in which black people extracted meaning from their experience as slaves in the antebellum South. This extracted meaning was brought to bear on such questions as the proper role of women in black social life. Answers to the questions that arose during and after slavery took into account black women's capabilities, the needs of the race, and the ways black people were expected to adopt in order to become acceptable members of the dominant culture. It is easy to ignore the conflict and tension over the woman question because the conflict transpired in the privacy of black churches and of community organizations that often met in black churches. Such an intersection of settings in sacred space meant that questions pertaining to the spiritual were deeply political and, among women and men who were both political and religious leaders (preachers and teachers), the political issues were also spiritual.

Whatever the Euro-American religious forms appropriated by the slaves, the content of these forms was not appropriated without extensive critical reflection on the source—their oppressors. Black Christians share every denomination label of white Christians, as well as many of their own. In spite of shared labels and affiliations, black denominations and congregations embody unique aspects of the African-American experience. As slaves, Africans arrived with a religious perspective that did not exclude women from cult service. Indeed, African religious systems, regardless of how patriarchal they were, exalted both the male and female in their various collective expressions of the holy (the cult). There was a tradition of religious independence as well as leadership among African women. According to Letitia Woods Brown, "in religious ceremonies, women were priests, even leaders of some cults. Women also maintained their own secret societies."[13] Furthermore, religions centering upon goddesses and female ancestors thrived in the African context. The survival of these religions, such as Cuban Santeria and Haitian

Vodun, in the Catholic societies of the New World attests to the fact that women's cult service and the veneration of both the male and female ancestors were not forgotten during Middle Passage. In the United States, the African-American expression of Christianity during slavery was largely Afro-Baptist and African-Methodist.[14] In the slave and Reconstruction South, the Baptist/Methodist division was not always meaningful, although in terms of cultural influence and numbers, Baptists dominated.

Another influential element in the African perspective was the relationship of the cult servant to the larger community. The cult servant (priest or priestess) embodied culturally constructed differences between the sacred and the profane. However, the role was not necessarily an elite one. It did not carry with it the aura of professionalism that implied social distance, deference, and autonomy. Although there was the understanding that the role required specialized knowledge, the structure of social relationships between priest/priestess and community was more akin to the relationship of the Israelites to their prophets than to their relationship to their priests. Later on, with the coming of European missionaries to West Africa, this tension between the African and European notions of the cult servant contributed to the religious rebellions that gave rise to the African prophet movements and the independent churches. African communities believed that the cult servant was a specialized religious role subject to the authority of the community. European priests and preachers believed that their cult service was a specialized religious role with authority to which the community was subject (cf. John Calvin). The polity (and not necessarily the theology and doctrine) that matched the African model most closely was the Baptist polity. Furthermore, Baptist churches provided a certain degree of autonomy to slave communities under the most oppressive—and, after 1820, repressive—circumstances. Raboteau and Sobel both suggest that the slave response to missionary preaching was a reasoned choice among diverse Christian polities.[15]

Africans confronted Europeans at a point when religion was becoming increasingly specialized, compartmentalized, and segregated from everyday public life. Religion was increasingly the product of evangelical enterprise. The lack of an established religion was one of the features of antebellum life that prompted Stanley Elkins to introduce the concept of unopposed capitalism into his analysis of American slavery.[16] In contrast, every aspect of African social organization involved religious ceremony. The segregation of the cult from everyday life that characterized Euro-American society was alien to African religious practice. Since women's societies and other collective enterprises were important components of African culture and social organization, women's experience carried with it a set of independent religious traditions. In addition to their performance as cult servants for entire African communities, women possessed their own ceremonies and cults. Their work and political roles varied from culture to culture, but all of these roles carried with them some type of religious ceremony. Furthermore, women's roles were not remanded to a sphere of social life that could be labeled "private" as they are in the public-private dichotomy of contemporary social life.

In the context of African patriarchy, the African woman's role as an individual political person could be severely limited. However, particularly in those cultures that contributed heavily to the British and American slave trades, African women effectively imposed themselves on the political process as a collective body. African women's response to New World slavery was influenced not only by the distinctive nature of cult service and the religious foundations of their everyday life, but also by their traditions of collective politics. African women's effective collective politics stemmed from their economic roles. The economic impact of women on their cultures was (and still is) considerable. According to LaFrances Rodgers-Rose:

> The African woman was more than a mother. . . . She was instrumental in the economic marketplace. She controlled certain industries—the making and selling of cloth, pottery, spinning, and the sale of goods of various kinds. The economic position of the African woman was high. The women were traders, and what they earned [often] belonged to them. Some women became independently wealthy. The West African woman was also responsible for raising the food for her family—she planted the crops and maintained them.[17]

It was this independent economic base that paved the way for the collective political participation that was institutionalized in West African societies.

West African women developed their own political institutions, according to Judith van Allen, through which they were able to "express their disapproval and secure their demands by collective public demonstrations, including ridicule, satirical singing and dancing, and group strikes."[18] Okonjo highlighted the importance of dual-sex political systems "in which the major interest groups are defined and represented by sex [or gender]." She suggests:

> Dual-sex organization contrasts with the 'single-sex' system that obtains in most of the western world, where political status-bearing roles are predominantly the preserve of men. In the single-sex system, women can achieve distinction and recognition only by taking on the roles of men in public life and performing them well.[19]

Okonjo points out that African organizations of the daughters of a lineage and of the wives of a lineage represented women's collective interests in the problems of mutual aid, violations of domestic law, decisions concerning agricultural labor, and the social control of men. Such collective power was related to the salience of women's title societies in which membership was based upon economic advantage and which in turn led to even more economic as well as political advantage, since status in other groups was often influenced by titles. Women's organizations were based upon age as well as family relationships. African women existed in societies of women their own age and status; their peers were called "sisters" and their elders were called "mother."[20]

Occasionally these collective politics led to institutionalized authority as well. The roles of the *omu* (loosely translated queen but meaning female king or head of the women's world) and the *ilogo* (women's cabinet) held real power and represented important sources of authority for women. Eva Meyerowitz points out that in spite of the English translation of *omu* as "queen mother," these women were not wives of kings but rather were the important points of contact between the men's and women's worlds within the context of decision-making.[21] During the struggle against European colonialism, some of these women emerged as leaders of entire African communities.[22]

The West African women who came to the New World came with a highly developed sense of their importance to a polity and an economy. Slavery, then, was a loss of authority for women as well as men. Any struggle to gain autonomy and regain authority over their lives, from an African perspective, was a struggle for both female and male authority. The organizational and sexual politics of historically black denominations contain evidence of this struggle for autonomy and of dual-sex political systems. The exigencies of survival and the impact of sexualized racism reinforced the collective political consciousness of black women. The failure of these collective politics in the contexts of European colonialism, such as the Ibo Women's War, highlight the differences between European and African patriarchies.

The paradoxes introduced by the African perspective were intensified by the material conditions and gender relations of slavery. This process was aided by the visible and invisible slave churches. These congregations consisted of women and men who shared a world of work, a reality which shaped a conscious egalitarian ethos within the slave community. As Angela Davis reminds us:

> Black women were equal to their men in the oppression they suffered. They were their men's social equals within the slave community; and they resisted slavery with a passion equal to their men's. This was one of the greatest ironies of the slave system, for in subjecting women to the most ruthless exploitation conceivable, exploitation which knew no sex distinctions, the groundwork was created not only for Black women to assert their equality through their social relations, but also to express it through their acts of resistance.[23]

Davis (1981), Dill (1979), and White (1984) argue persuasively that what emerged from this political economy of slavery and the counterculture of the slave community was a distinctive (in the context of Euro-American patriarchy) model of womanhood.[24] Davis insists that it was slave women "who passed on to their nominally free female descendants a legacy of hard work, perseverance and self-reliance, a legacy of tenacity, resistance and insistence on sexual equality—in short, a legacy spelling out standards for a new womanhood."[25] Dill suggests that this model of womanhood, with its constituent elements of independence, autonomy, self-reliance, and strength, was a contradiction and a source of dialectical opposition to the female role model dictated by Euro-American patriarchy.[26] Emerging as it did from strength through community, this model of womanhood was derided in the Jezebel and Mammy stereotypes and in the racist imagery labeling black women dangerous and deviant mothers and "bad black women."[27]

Black men evaluated black women's experience in both positive and negative terms. Regardless of the degree to which they agreed or disagreed with the dominant culture's model of gender organization, black men have never been free (from the influence of women) to impose either equality or total male domination. Since northern and southern antebellum churches were political as well as spiritual centers of their communities, women were an integral part of emergent black political organizations. Black women argued persuasively that they should be included and a comparison (by both men and women) between racial oppression and white male behavior toward women was often raised in these arguments.[28] As a result, black male political discourse acquired some feminist content through such spokesmen as Frederick Douglass, W. E. B. Du Bois, and Martin Delany. Rosalyn Terborg-Penn demonstrates that as early as 1789, black men and women participated together in organizations devoted to abolition and racial uplift.[29] Although there was some resistance by black men to full participation of women, for the most part they accepted women's participation in their conventions, elected black women to office, invited them to speak publicly, defended their right to an education, and recognized their role in the workplace. In 1848 a resolution was proposed at the National Convention of Colored Freemen that, according to Terborg-Penn, invited "females hereafter to take part in our deliberations"; after some debate, the convention ruled that "all colored persons" could be delegates, "that the word 'person' be understood to include 'women'."[30] Women's inclusion in deliberative bodies carried over to religious bodies such as the American National Baptist Convention and the African Methodist Episcopal Church. Any refusals that arose surrounding the right of women to preach had to be addressed directly to them. It is this process that made possible the emergence of women such as Maria Stewart, Sojourner Truth, and Frances Ellen Watkins Harper as public lecturers and as role models, enabling other black women as well as white women to become activists and lecturers.

Vestiges of African tradition combined with the political economy and the gender relations of slavery to produce tensions within both slave and free churches. Yet according to Thomas Webber's analysis, the shared suffering and oppression of slavery produced a slave community characterized by a remarkable lack of sexism.[31] Although the black male *preacher* was the leader recognized by whites and their religious institutions, black women emerged as worship leaders, preachers, catechizers, exhorters, prayer warriors, singers, teachers, and storytellers—all authoritative agents of the black religious tradition. Many slave churches existed without a black pastor (male preacher) of its own choosing in the last decades of slavery. The tasks of worship were not dependent on "his" presence. Shared notions of "real" religion were not dependent upon a properly built edifice, special training in the arts of ministry, or the gender of the worship leader. The various tasks necessary for adequate worship—expounding upon a scripture, praying, raising a song, teaching religious doctrine and practice—were broken down and distributed among the members of a congregation according to their talents. The essence of black religious tradition was completely portable. Whereas the integrity of slave families was dependent upon having its members present in an enduring household, the "household of faith," or one's "church home," was dependent only upon the gathering of "two or three who touch and agree." In order for the free black church to conform to its counterpart in the dominant culture, it was necessary to suppress the freedom with which black church women had exercised their roles in the churches of the antebellum South and in the evangelical campaigns of both the North and the South. When the invisible institution of slave religion went public, the woman question was one of considerable debate. These debates and conflicts gave rise to practices and institutions that reflected a range of opinions on the roles of women, and to a complex set of women's organizations which exercised considerable power and influence and nurtured a tradition of feminist/womanist biblical exegesis and theological discourse. Although the dual-sex politics of black church women and their unyielding tradition of conflict concerning the proper place of women have not toppled patriarchy, these have profoundly influenced the institutional expressions of sexism and the content of male ideology. If the interpretation of these two aspects of black women's religious experience is correct, the strategies of black male preachers to maintain the traditional exclusion of black female clergy from the National Baptist Convention will differ in content from those used recently in the Southern Baptist Convention.

## The Dual-Sex Politics of Black Churches

The institutional expression of gender-based politics in black churches varies from congregation to congregation and from denomination to denomination. Recent observations and comparative analyses of contemporary African and black American church traditions have acknowledged a parallel between the prayer leadership of black women in all variations of black Protestantism and the African Queen Mother and between the distinctive role of black pastors' wives and African female leadership.[32] In addition, the roles to which the labels "teacher," "missionary," "evangelist," and "deaconess" are affixed are wide-ranging in their rights, duties, obligations, authority, and structural relationships within a congregation or a denomination. For those black denominations formed after the end of Reconstruction, conflict over the role of women contributed to the reorganization of churches and the founding of new ones. The end of Reconstruction was a time of violently imposed changes and community reorganization, and, of the many denominations that emerged from that period of community reorganization, those that continued to grow after the deaths of their founders seem to have been the ones that contained the strongest "women's departments" or that ordained women to pastoral roles.[33]

The most distinctive aspect of dual-sex church politics is the role of the Church Mother. While most black churches in the Baptist, Methodist, or "Sanctified" (Pentecostal, Holiness, Apostolic) denominations have a woman to whom members refer as the "Church Mother," her position varies. In almost all cases, she is an older woman, often elderly, who is considered an example of spiritual maturity and morality to the rest of her congregation. Her career as a Christian is usually exemplary and long, and most members know of her various activities in the missionary unit or on the deaconess board. Perhaps she is the widow of a pastor or a bishop or a deacon, but not necessarily. She is one of the few people whose seat in the congregation is formally or informally reserved. When she dies, her seat may be draped in black. Most important, she is publicly addressed by the pastor, the bishops, and the members of the congregation as "Mother."

As a spiritual and moral leader, she is expected to know her Bible. Since most black churches are "Bible believing" churches, she exemplifies the tradition of personal devotion through the reading and knowing of one's Bible. While she may not teach Sunday School, she may also be the leader of the adult class. She is the type of person that one pastor described as someone "who offers you spiritual advice that you learn to take." However, she can also be a source of exhortation for the congregation. When she speaks, she speaks in little sermons. On one occasion, the official "Church Mother" of a Baptist Church gave a rousing and spirit-filled exhortation at a special occasion. Later, the nationally known male preacher from another denomination rose to speak and mentioned that his decision to "preach" rather than simply to "speak" was based upon the divine "direction" that he had received through the Church Mother. One Church Mother, Mother Pollard, is famous for her participation in the Montgomery Bus Boycott and her remarking that, although her feet were tired, her soul was rested.

Occasionally, the Church Mother performs the role of a stage manager and director of public worship. Where tension exists concerning certain practices, her opinion may prevail. In one Baptist congregation, the insistence by the Church Mother that "this is not a Sanctified Church!" moved the deacon board to call an emergency meeting with the pastor in order to persuade him to withdraw his permission for drums to be used during the morning service: the Church Mother prevailed. Other members of the congregation may walk out when they disagree with the pastor, but their actions will be ignored. The Church Mother is never ignored.

In the Baptist and African Methodist traditions, her role is largely one of influence. Although she may be formally installed in her office, she does not have formal authority. Yet her influence may grant her considerable power, even an effective veto, in church politics and affairs. Her role as Church Mother may on occasion reach beyond the congregation if she is active in public politics. Her force as a role model may also affect the tradition of activism in her community. Not only her personal religious history, but also her labor force participation and her political career become informal models for others to follow. As a community activist, she may be the first woman to break some of the sexist barriers in black pulpits, or she may be given a permanent seat on the board of directors or the executive board of a community organization. Her stature in the overall politics of the community may occasionally modify the operation of oppressive political structures, such as the police department and the mayor's office. Sarah Evans and Paula Giddings observed fragments of this tradition in the southern rural wing of the civil rights movement. The southern "Mama," according to Evans's corrupted description of church and community mothers, served as a role model to white women whose experience in the civil rights movement motivated them to become the nucleus of the contemporary women's movement and to insist on the right to participate equally in the anti-war movement with radical men.[34] According to one activist, those white women observed that women such as Fannie Lou Hamer and Ella Baker had not internalized a sense of female inferiority.[35]

While space does not permit discussion of the importance of music to the black worship tradition, being able to "raise a song" is counted as an important spiritual skill in the black religious context. Howard Thurman remembered that the congregation of his childhood was highly concerned with such a skill. New members were adopted by older members and carefully taught the skills of public prayer and raising a song.[36] Thus the role of such women as Bernice Johnson Reagon and Fannie Lou Hamer in revitalizing the Civil Rights Movement using traditional sacred music was consistent with expectations placed upon church and community Mothers. "Singing was the tool that helped to forge that unity—and the strength to deal with the consequences of Black resistance," and women were crucial to that process.[37]

Although Church Mothers have no fixed structural power in Baptist and African Methodist traditions, they do have such power within churches organized in the late nineteenth-century South. Collectively referred to as the "Sanctified Church," black Holiness, Pentecostal, and Apostolic denominations institutionalized the role of the Church Mother and she became the basis for woman-centered church politics affecting entire denominations. The largest of these, the Church of God in Christ (COGIC), treated the role as that of an overseer or bishop of women during the early days of the denomination.

In every geographical jurisdiction, a man was appointed overseer along with a woman "overseer" of the "women's work."

These overseers or "state mothers" were charged with the task of "organizing" the women. As a result, mother's boards were formed in the various congregations which affiliated with similar state and regional structures. One woman overseer was appointed for every male overseer. In the Church of God in Christ, the founder, Charles Harrison Mason (who was a widower), believed that only women should instruct other women in proper religious and moral behavior. Mason and many of the other church founders of this period (male and female) were the children of slaves who had been raised in the independent slave Baptist churches of the rural South. In these churches, male deacons governed the behavior of church men and female deaconesses governed the behavior of the church women; these boards were also organized according to the status of slave or free.[38] The women's departments and their Sanctified Churches survived in part because of the earlier female slave network, which had prepared southern religious leaders to be comfortable with such expressions of collective autonomy. Dual-sex politics were part of their childhood experience.

The organizational politics of black women in the local and national black community also influenced the models of women's participation in churches. When conflicts erupted among black Baptists and Methodists during this late nineteenth-century period concerning traditions such as the "ring shout" or "holy dance," black women were beginning to make an impression on the community as activists and educators. By the end of the nineteenth century, women who were prominent activists in their denominations carried that activism into a movement for racial uplift, which culminated in the formation of the National Association of Colored Women. At the same time, the importance placed on education meant that educated men and women were recruited as teachers in the South, and within the community the emerging leadership class consisted largely of "preachers and teachers." The insistence by Baptists that women (who were as well-trained in theology and biblical studies as the men) could not "preach" but could only "teach" meant that these labels came less to define different activities and more to define male and female versions of the same activity.

As founders of Holiness and Pentecostal denominations sought to improve the status and the educational levels of these churches they recruited educated Baptist and African Methodist women to join in their work. The women who responded had been frustrated in their attempts to exercise their gifts in Baptist and Methodist congregations. In the new denominations they not only established schools and educated members of the clergy, but also preached revivals, founded churches, and maintained charge of those churches until a pastor was assigned by the bishops. These educated professional women, full of gospel zeal, were also the women chosen by founders, bishops, and pastors as wives. An interesting cultural contradiction emerged when the most prominent [female] role model married to the "best catch" in a church was an educated, professional woman. Usually she was a school teacher or community activist. Occasionally, she was a "superwoman" in the person of someone like Dr. Susan McKinney. A physician and pastor's wife who managed two medical practices in Brooklyn, New York in the late nineteenth century, Dr. McKinney was also a community activist, an organizer in the National Association of Colored Women, and organist in her husband's church. When she was widowed, Dr. McKinney married another preacher, Theophilus Steward.[39]

Within the Church of God in Christ, it is not unusual for male church leaders to testify to the fact that their salvation was preached by a woman revivalist. It was on the foundation of the role of the Church Mother's role, that the infrastructure of the women's department was built. Within these structures, the roles of missionary and evangelist evolved in response to the prohibition on women's ordination to the roles of pastor, elder, and bishop. In my research, I have not met a Church Mother who is not a licensed missionary or evangelist. However, missionaries and evangelists are not necessarily church mothers. In order for these missionaries and evangelists to "teach" (actually preach) they must have the signatures of both their pastor and church mother on their license. In order to teach within the jurisdiction, they must have the signatures of both the bishop (formerly overseer) and jurisdictional supervisor (state or jurisdictional mother, formerly overseer) of the women's work. These signatures and a letter of recommendation from the jurisdictional supervisor are necessary for a woman to move to another jurisdiction as a missionary or an evangelist. Finally it is the jurisdictional mothers or supervisors who determine whether a women can become national evangelist.

In some jurisdictions, the general category "missionary" includes all of the various women's roles and the term "minister" encompasses all pastors, elders, bishops, and male evangelists. These groups meet first separately and then together, on specified days of the month. After their separate meetings, the missionaries and ministers meet in the same room with women sitting on one side and men on the other. In those congregations within the Church of God in Christ that enforce the "double pulpit"—the lectern for women and the *real* pulpit for men—church mothers and evangelists sit on one side at the front of the church and the pastor and other elders sit on the other. Some evangelists informed me that older pastors in smaller and more traditional churches do not enforce the "double pulpit" and women speak from the same place that men *preach*. In these smaller churches, evangelists have the opportunity to become "pastors in truth" when an elderly pastor dies or ceases to preach regularly. A number of Church of God in Christ congregations are "pastored" by widows of elders and bishops who were well-known missionaries, evangelists, or church mothers and who administered the church and did the teaching each Sunday after their husbands became ill and incapacitated. One evangelist implied that there was a certain incentive for young evangelists and missionaries to marry elderly pastors and bishops since doing so might present the opportunity to inherit a pastorate.

Some dualism exists in black Baptist churches. In these congregations, the missionary shares the same role as the missionary in the Church of God in Christ. She may "teach" and lead worship from the floor but she may not "preach" from the pulpit. Many elderly Baptist women hear the term "missionary" as a euphemism for woman minister. The organization of a Women's Auxiliary within the National Baptist Convention antedated and paralleled the growth of women's departments in the "Sanctified Church." There was much borrowing and interaction among women across denominations and within women's community and political organizations. Nationally known leaders such as Mary McLeod Bethune, a Methodist, preached from the pulpits in Baptist and Sanctified churches.

Not only are these dual-sex politics reflected in the role of the church mother, thus providing a basis for autonomous woman-centered organizations, but such politics are also evident in the evolution of missionary role in home and foreign mission societies. Black women manipulated these positions in creative ways to generate autonomy and power for themselves in denominational affairs. Such a position also provided a base for addressing larger social issues and questions concerning women's roles in the larger society. While the women disagreed over the role of women in the pulpit, they were consistent in pressuring male church leaders to support women's rights to education and labor force protection. When men resisted such ideas, women could persist by turning to their organizations outside church structures for support and political leverage. Evelyn Brooks's analysis of the role of Nannie Helen Burroughs in the organization of Baptist women and the maintenance of the National Training School is instructive in this regard.[40]

Fragments of the dual-sex political system are evident in the role of the deaconess in black churches. In Baptist churches, this board is often the organization (along with the missionary board) from which women are elevated to the status of church mother. In some churches, the missionary board is for any woman with the appropriate calling and evangelistic zeal and the deaconess board is reserved for the wives of deacons. In other churches, the congregation elects women to the deaconess board on the basis of their perceived spirituality. Some churches actually ordain deaconesses along with deacons—usually those boards that elect deaconesses because they are deacons' wives or which elect deaconesses who feel "called" to the position. The diverse traditions among Baptist churches illustrate how different Baptist communities resolved contested questions of the role of women in church and society. While the context is clearly patriarchal, black women have constructed a wide variety of leadership roles that provide opportunities for both married and single women to perceive and to be role models for other black women. These positions of leadership and their histories are also the contexts in which the alternative models of womanhood that have their roots in slavery, black women's education, community activism, and labor force participation, are affirmed in spite of patriarchy. Although the male preacher is the clearly acknowledged authority in the public sphere, failure to examine the women's roles has obscured the varieties of shared power that the collective politics of black women have in fact produced. When one examines the "Sanctified Church" as a cultural phenomenon, it is clear that it has kept a great deal of the antebellum egalitarianism in the context of the patriarchal Euro-American polities which have become the organizational contexts of black church culture.

## Traditions of Conflict

Dual sex politics alone do not make black women's experience distinctive. The fragments of African gender organization contribute to a more persistent and prominent thread of tradition: conflict. Conflict did not always take the form of assertive, direct action; rather it was acted out through traditions enacted to resist marginalization and silencing. The dominant culture's pressure to regularize had a devastating effect on African-American Christian women. They fought back by establishing traditions which reflected the importance they attached to strength and self-reliance.

The patriarchy of the black church has never been peaceful. The content of that patriarchy—a patriarchy that can be labeled ambivalent in its various expressions—has been severely modified by the persistent tradition of conflict that black women have maintained within black religious structures. Although women remain subordinate persons in structures where males hold nearly all the highest positions, the ideologies advanced by these men in defense of their domination reflect the embattled nature of their position. Simply stated, there are certain arguments that black preachers dare not advance in public regardless of how much they believe them; for instance, those arguments assailing women's competence were lost in the debates of the nineteenth century. In interpreting any conflicts within African-American religious traditions, however, it is critically important to remember that they take place in organizational settings where the operating metaphor and ideology for human relations is family. They take place among "brothers" and "sisters," between "fathers" and "mothers" and "daughters."

To understand fully this tradition of conflict would require a comprehensive socio-historical analysis of women's roles in all of the historically black denominations. However, even a cursory examination highlights the importance of two examples: an aggressively articulated biblical feminism, and a persistent reminder of women's material importance through the annual "Women's Day." In addition, black women have been known to oppose the sexism of black preachers by ostentatiously changing churches and occasionally even by founding their own churches. Throughout the history of black church women, one can find significant expressions of their opposition to total patriarchy. Even among those women who sincerely believe that preaching is a man's province (and sometimes even more among such women) there is a tradition of a militant assertion of personhood and a sincere belief in their own competence and capabilities in the larger society.

The Church of God in Christ (COGIC) insists that women are not called to preach. However, the church's manual contains the biblical argument for women's ordination, clearly stated although militantly opposed. Rather than elaborate arguments for women's inferiority or sinful nature, or the reasons they should be silent, the manual simply states that it does not recognize certain scriptures as constituting a mandate to ordain women to the offices of elder, pastor, or bishop. Having been reminded innumerable times by the women of the church (both pro-preaching and anti-preaching) of the importance of women to the founding of congregations and to the salvation, education, and financial support of ministers and bishops, the Church of God in Christ then allows women to oversee congregations when there is no pastor. Since the women's "teaching" is indistinguishable from the men's "preaching" there are no tasks of ministry that are the monopoly of elders. There are, however, tasks that are the monopoly of bishops.

The Church of God in Christ is the largest and one of the oldest of the Pentecostal churches founded by the children of former slaves, and it is one of the continuous expressions of slave religious tradition. When one examines all of the debates in various black denominations and the positions taken by other early churches on the women question, it is clear that the position of the Church of God in Christ carries the scars of a protracted conflict. The effectiveness of the women's arguments is reflected in the arguments of men who are able to argue the positions of the biblical feminists.

The origins of black biblical feminism probably lie in the African Methodist Episcopal Church, whose founder, Richard Allen, was faced with the question of licensing Jarena Lee.[41] Black women did not argue in isolation from the biblical arguments that took place among white feminists. In order to continue participating in the variety of leadership roles they had held during slavery, they had to learn to justify these roles when, after emancipation, black and white missionaries attempted to "regularize" black churches and their practices.[42] Both black men and women argued in defense of their more ecstatic worship practices[43]; some ex-slaves, like Howard Thurman's grandmother, even insisted that the Pauline epistles were not inspired scripture meant to govern their lives.[44]

As early as the 1830s, black women orators refuted biblical arguments demanding their silence as public speakers. Giddings suggests that "the moral urgency of their being black and female . . . suffused black women with a tenacious feminism."[45] She argues that black women "bypassed the barrier of religious thought that circumscribed even radical white activists until the late 1830s."[46] She presents the arguments black women advanced for their right to public participation, especially as orators. One such woman, Maria Stewart, insisted:

What if I am a woman?. . . . Did [God] not raise up Deborah to be mother and a judge in Israel? Did not Queen Esther save the lives of the Jews? And Mary Magdalene first declare the resurrection of Christ from the dead?[47]

When it came to the arguments that stemmed from the Pauline scriptures, Giddings demonstrates that Stewart rejected their use to "justify slavery and sexism."[48] Stewart in her speeches did what biblical critics before her had done: give priority to the statements and actions of Jesus so that they became arguments for the limited nature of Pauline injunctions.[49] Her biblical feminism was also informed by an argument based on world religions, which took into account the roles of women as cult servants and deities in non-Christian religions. In addition, she appealed to the roles of women in early Catholicism, and to their histories of militance as a source of legitimacy. Finally, the biblical record that described God as deliverer led her to declare that in "light of the role of women in the past, 'God at this eventful period should raise up your females to strive . . . both in public and private, to assist those who are endeavoring to stop the strong current of prejudice that flows so profusely against us at present!'"[50] Concerning the public role of black women, Stewart admonished, "No longer ridicule their efforts, . . . [i]t will be counted as sin."[51]

Although Sojourner Truth is the most famous of black women orators, her role as a biblically-grounded preacher is often ignored. The change of her name from Isabella Baumfree came through her divine calling. On a road on Long Island, God called her to *sojourn* over the land and (because she asked for a last name) to preach the *truth* concerning slavery. Her famous speech at the Seneca Falls women's rights convention was not only a very personal feminist argument but also solid biblical theology: she appealed to women's role in the redemption of humankind from the consequences of the Fall. In discussing an abolitionist heroine, it is important to note that the denomination of Harriet Tubman never waged an effective biblical argument against the ordination of women; in fact the African Methodist Episcopal Zion (AMEZ) Church was one of the earliest black denominations to ordain women.

It was in the Afro-Baptist tradition that arguments surrounding women's roles proved most troublesome. Between 1880 and 1900—the end of Reconstruction and a time or reorganization among constituencies in the black community—an intensive struggle surrounding women's roles occurred. The issues were leadership and conformity to dominant group patriarchy. It was then that the institutional basis for black feminism and organizational autonomy was established. Evelyn Brooks has examined the feminist theology of the black Baptist Church within the American National Baptist Convention [ANBC]—the forerunner of the now predominant National Baptist Convention (Inc.) and the smaller conventions with which it co-exists, the

National Baptist Convention ("unincorporated") and the Progressive National Baptist Convention.[52] After one hundred years, these conventions differ in their official policy toward women clergy, yet all of them contain member churches pastored by women. In spite of the overwhelming sexism among black Baptist men, even the content of their arguments against women's ordination has been shaped by the tradition of biblical debate established by the women theologians of the ANBC.

Since black women educators were often educated in the same settings as black men, they were quite competent to argue theology and biblical interpretation in public. Like African Americans during the time of slavery, they saw the Bible as an instrument of liberation. Evelyn Brooks points out that unlike Frances Willard and Susan B. Anthony, women such as Virginia Broughton, Olive Clanton, Mary Cook, and Lucy Wilmot Smith accepted the Bible as a whole and perceived it as a valid basis for religious life.[53] Thus, their arguments revolved around questions of interpretation. Brooks's analysis sees the emergence of a Women's Auxiliary in the N.B.C., Inc., as a direct result of the feminist biblical tradition. It was probably the loyal opposition of these black women that deposited a fund of arguments supporting black female leadership roles into the oral tradition of the black Baptist community and the black women's club movement.

Although Brooks's analysis focuses on the women's speeches at meetings of the ANBC, she reminds us that such women also engaged in public lectures, house-to-house visitations, and prolific amounts of correspondence. Virginia Broughton capped this twenty-year period with the publication of a 1904 work called *Women's Work as Gleaned from the Women of the Bible*. In addition both Mary Cook and Lucy Smith, like Mary McLeod Bethune, Ida Wells Barnett, and Nannie Helen Burroughs, wrote extensively in the black press. Along with others in the ANBC, these:

> Baptist interpreters of the Bible perceived themselves as part of the vanguard of the movement to present the theological discussion of woman's place. They used the Bible to sanction both domestic and public roles for women. While each of the feminist theologians had her own unique style and emphasis, the basic arguments resembled each other closely on four essential roles for women: in the home, in the church, in social reform, and in the labor force. In every case, the Baptist women emphasized biblical passages that portrayed women positively.[54]

Sometimes these women expressed the opinion that women had a revolutionary role to play in the reformation of the Church; at other times they lifted up the importance of the home as having primacy over the institutional church. Even in the context of biblical feminism, these Baptist women never agreed upon the role of women in "establishing new churches, baptizing, or administering the eucharist" since there were no recorded precedents for such activities in the Bible.

The women did find biblical sanction for some independence from their husbands and for the pursuit of professional careers. Brooks states:

> Depicting Deborah as a woman with a spirit independent of her husband, Cook asserted: Her work was distinct from her husband's who, it seems, took no part whatever in the work of God while Deborah was inspired by the Eternal expressly to do his will and to testify to her countrymen that He recognizes in His followers neither male nor female, heeding neither the "weakness" of one, nor the strength of the other, but strictly calling those who are perfect at heart and willing to do His bidding.[55]

According to Brooks, "Biblical examples had revealed that God used women in every capacity and thus proved to Cook that there could be no issue of propriety despite the reluctance of men." It was biblical feminism that insisted that women had a right to engage in "all honest labor." Thus, what began as women's insistence concerning their right to participate fully in their churches emerged as a full-blown support for the alternative model of womanhood based on black women's historical experience and for black women's full participation in society. All of the elements of the role model that Dill describes as being in dialectical opposition to the role prescribed by the dominant culture for women were more than adequately defended by these women.[56]

One of the outcomes for this stream of argument was the emergence of the uplift movement at the end of the nineteenth century.[57] The same missionary energy that prompted Baptist women in the A.N.B.C. to write their articles and deliver their speeches was applied to the problem of racial oppression and social uplift. The development of an autonomous black women's movement was a logical outcome of their feminism, and this movement provided an alternative to fighting with black preachers over their monopoly on congregational leadership. The club movement was also an alterative avenue to public leadership. Whereas the dominant culture ignored the black women leaders, members of the black community did not. The women's commitment to the advancement of "the Race" was placed alongside their interest in developing their role as leaders. In 1892, Josephine St. Pierre Ruffin stated the goals of the black women's movement:

> Our women's movement is a woman's movement in that it is led and directed by women for the good of women and men, for the benefit of all humanity. . . . We want, we ask the active interest of our men; . . . we are not alienating or withdrawing, we are only coming to the front, willing to join any others in the same work.[58]

The creation of this independent avenue to community leadership coincided with the formation of Holiness and Pentecostal denominations. The Baptist and Methodist women who joined these new black denominations brought with them the biblical justification for their leadership roles. Both the Holiness and Pentecostal Movements provided black Baptist and AME women the opportunities to expound on the gospel (and in many cases to preach, pastor, conduct revival, and found churches) that they were denied in the older denominations.

With a fully developed women's agenda, other black women continued their organizing within their denominations. The reorganization of church constituencies that came with the growth of the Sanctified Church often addressed directly the conflicts over the roles of women. As was previously stated, the largest group, the Church of God in Christ, did not ordain women to be elders, pastors, or bishops. Women who could not compromise on this issue found or created other alternatives. Several other smaller denominations ordained women to be elders. Some of these, however, would not ordain women to be bishops. The Presiding Bishop of the Fire Baptized Holiness Church of God of the Americas, a black denomination with interracial origins, incurred the ire of other Presiding Bishops when he consecrated a woman to be Bishop in a denomination that she herself had founded. (The FBH Church is an egalitarian church that has always ordained women to full ministry; in theory women may be Bishops but none has ever stood for election.) In the Church of the Living God, Christian Workers for Fellowship, women had difficulties even though they were ordained and assigned to pastorates. Their careers took longer to develop than those of men, although men used the same career ladder—tours of duty as missionaries. A conflict that challenged the authority of pastors erupted in the Alabama District and women left the Church to form a new denomination. Conflicts among Baptists and their Sanctified relatives were so numerous and intense, that W. E. B. Du Bois complained about the fractiousness of the Baptists (meaning the men) and lauded black women as "the intellectual leadership of the race."[59] The conflicts over women's roles in church leadership and their proper place in society continued to fuel the politics of congregational and denominational reorganization throughout the first half of the twentieth century.

Black women never ceased to maintain an organized resistance to patriarchy within the black religious experience. The tradition of biblical feminism was maintained in two ways. Women in the Sanctified Church expanded upon the foundations laid by the Baptist women. They expanded their analysis of women's roles to the point that women's issues are articulated in the sermons of the men and the arguments surrounding scriptural prohibitions have become more finely tuned and elaborated. Using their woman-centered imaginations to expand upon the biblical texts, Church of God in Christ evangelists have established traditions that even name the unnamed women of the Bible. In one Church of God in Christ congregation I observed, a

National Evangelist was preaching on the biblical woman with "the issue of blood." As she developed her sermon (or "teaching"), when she came to the point of calling the woman's name, the entire congregation chimed in with her, "Safronia." I turned to my informant, and asked, "Where did she get that name?" My informant replied, "We have a book that names all the women!" It was their own book in which they had expanded upon the perspectives of women in the Bible in ways similar to earlier perspectives advanced by Virginia Broughton and Nannie Helen Burroughs.[60] Thus, the first way in which the tradition of biblical feminism was maintained was by extending women's arguments begun in the nineteenth century and refining these arguments to answer new questions and repel new assaults on women's leadership.

The second and more universal way in which the tradition of biblical feminism was maintained was through the establishment of Women's Day. According to Evelyn Brooks Barnett, Nannie Helen Burroughs was a pivotal leader in the maintenance of black women's feminism in the National Baptist Convention, Inc. (NBC) as well as in the larger community.[61] She continued the tradition of prolific journalism and lecturing begun by her foremothers. In the convention of 1906 she presented the idea of Women's Day, a Sunday when women would lead and speak in worship service, as a national event. According to Evelyn Brooks, in Burroughs's travels to other Baptist women in their state conventions, she had observed the celebration of the day in their communities. She urged black women Baptists to observe it nationally. Although Women's Day would advance the goal of raising money for foreign missions, Burroughs's feminist imagination saw the day as a way "the Convention could discover and develop public speakers for church programs. . . . This day was not thought up as a scheme for raising money, but primarily for raising women."[62] In an undated pamphlet that criticized the appropriation of the day by local churches for fund-raising, she described the breadth of her vision:

> A million women praying? A million women singing? A million women desiring? A million women laboring for the coming of the kingdom in the hearts of all men, would be a power that would move God on his throne to immediately answer the petitions. It would mean spiritual dynamite that would blast Satan's greatest stronghold and drive sin to its native health.[63]

Burroughs went on to describe the practical considerations that her spiritual vision entailed. She wrote:

> [W]e are in desperate need of women learning to become public speakers, and dedicated to a definite cause for which to speak. . . . Women's Day was intended to raise the women themselves—training them for public speaking and informed leadership through authentic, prepared,

challenging speeches. . . . The day offers a glorious opportunity for women to learn to speak for themselves.[64]

In spite of her lamentations about its misuse, Burroughs lived to see Women's Day spread to every segment of the black religious experience. Even black congregations in predominantly white denominations celebrate it. Regardless of the sexism a pastor may harbor, once each year he is obliged to sit in the congregation and listen to a sermon or "teaching" delivered by a woman community leader, missionary, evangelist, denominational executive, educator, minister, or professional. Occasionally these speakers are women who have left for college and are returning home as successful professionals. It is rare that a black woman with a graduate or professional degree escapes such an invitation and responsibility. Although the day may represent a form of tokenism, it is important to remember that tokenism is an attempt to resist more revolutionary change and an indirect acknowledgement of pressure to effect meaningful change. Moreover, over the years of Women's Day, a Sunday which often involves morning and afternoon services and a meal served by the men of the church, black women have been exposed to a wide variety of female professional role models who are accorded honor and prestige. Finally, Women's Day is the link between the dual-sex politics of the black church and the tradition of conflict that has maintained black women's loyal opposition to the patriarchy that characterizes their religious experience. The positive presentation of diverse female images who are also successful in the dominant culture represents the kind of hope that the black religious experience has provided black women over the years. At the same time, the practice sidesteps the issue of permanent pastoral and denominational leadership within the institutions where black women have invested so much time and money. Nevertheless, the final result is to insure the presence of a woman-centered perspective in the life of the church; that perspective has occasionally converted a pastor to the position of feminist advocacy.

### The Dilemmas of Commitment

Recent research on the historical and contemporary experience of the black woman demonstrates that her experience diverges from that of the white woman. The intersection of both gender and race oppression has generated a number of paradoxes that are evident in political and economic roles within the community. As we begin to examine her religious experience, the black woman of radical tradition seems to disappear. However, when one ceases to equate the black church with its pastor and its edifice, the black woman's religious experience emerges as both complex and connected to her other experiences.

In spite of its male domination, the black church functions for women as a women's institution. Dual-sex politics mean that women have the autonomy necessary to provide their own leadership training. While their access to authority within the church is limited, women occupy roles which are authoritative within the scope of the entire tradition. Although they are rarely pastors, black women have negotiated a wide variety of expressions in the roles reserved for them and have managed to impose themselves on the political process of their churches through collective strategies. As a result, they have established veto power in the context of black worship and congregational management, and they have restricted the content of black male sexist ideology.

The dual-sex framework has enabled black women to maintain a persistent tradition of conflict in the post-emancipation churches. The maintenance of a loyal opposition has created important alternatives for women aspiring to religious leadership. In spite of their opposing views, most black women who participate in the dynamics of conflict are proud of their commitment to the structures they are trying to change. This apparent paradox becomes intelligible in the context of the overall cultural role of black women. Black women's feminism is an anti-racist feminism. Furthermore, throughout their entire history they have experienced two kinds of patriarchy. The patriarchal racism they have experienced in the United States has been the most destructive, in terms of their own experience and the experiences they observe among their men. The high levels of commitment exhibited by black women to the black church can be understood when one recognizes the historical evolution of their role in maintaining the organizational integrity of the black community. In spite of the problems their pastors may present, black women clearly see the survival of their churches as their responsibility.

The consciousness of black women is informed by their historical role as agents of black community survival. Both dual-sex politics and the tradition of conflict permit black women to communicate this aspect of their historical role to black men. Occasionally, such as on Women's Day, black women's feminism becomes a statement of their primary functional importance to the church and, by extension, to the community. Black women have been assigned their places in the social structure because they are black *and* female. Furthermore, the structures of exploitation and oppression have involved a politics of death, physical destruction, and social disruption. As Angela Davis has pointed out, the preservation of life and the maintenance of a domestic reality in the lives of black people have been revolutionary acts in the context of slavery—and often I would add, in the contexts of later historical periods.[65]

What is simply an assignment to preserve life in other social contexts has been a more complex task for black women. Their role has become focused upon the maintenance of community integrity in the face of pressures which would divide and atomize. The failure to examine the ways in which black women have fulfilled this role in their churches has created a vast gap in our understanding of the foundations from which black women construct an anti-racist feminism. Furthermore, we have missed the ways in which black women have asserted their personhood while maintaining the integrity and continuity of a diverse and pluralistic religious experience. While the organizational shape of the black religious experience, with its wide range of denominations and orientations toward women's leadership roles, exhibits a complexity that is difficult to grasp, the continuities that exist across the various segments of that experience are largely the results of the work of the women. Women's Day is just one example; many others still need to be explored.

James Harvey Robinson (1927) has reminded us that "history books are a poor place to look for history."[66] They are an even poorer place to search for African-American history and African-American women's history. The religious experience of black women, in spite of their strong commitment to their churches, has offered a persistent challenge to the European model of church order and to the technologies and biblical interpretations which defend oppression and exploitation. In the process of maintaining that challenge, black church women have asserted their spiritual independence and have explored alternative models of power and authority. Their various experiences represent an important contribution to the current discourse surrounding women, religion, and social change.

In her survey of black women's experience, Paula Giddings suggests that the role of the black woman is of "utmost importance" because of the pivotal link between race and sex that she represents. Giddings is quite correct in her insistence that the transformation of a sexist and a racist society will not be effected without the guidance of black women's experience in social change and intellectual revision. When one examines the course of the black church in both its slave and free histories, it becomes apparent that beyond the prevailing images of preacher and edifice exists a complex set of politicized networks of women whose resistance to the masculinization of the churches they themselves helped to build has institutionalized a feminist perspective and a progressive female role model. Perhaps their persistent commitment to the institution is the most revolutionary stance of all. One nationally known preacher and civil rights veteran is reputed to have stated that if women ever leave the movement, "I am going where the women go, because nothing will ever happen without the women." The need for many things to happen still tends to pull members of the black community together, in spite of their disagreements. This is true in their religious communities as well. The dual-sex politics and tradition of conflict maintained by black women have enabled them to resolve their dilemmas of commitment while building a rich religious experience that remains one of the most important social, psychological and spiritual resources they possess.

# PART 3

# WOMANIST CULTURE

# 7

# "Some Mother's Son and Some Father's Daughter"

## Issues of Gender, Biblical Language, and Worship

Feminism has illuminated the role of the Christian church in the construction of social knowledge about gender, but its light has illuminated very different kinds of shadows and social problems. Both black and white Christian women identify problems in their churches and in society, but they define those problems differently, and they allocate their time, energies, and passions in distinctive, sometimes divergent, directions. These differing understandings of the treatment of gender in religious institutions reflect profound differences in social experience.

### Feminism and Social Knowledge: Locating a Social Problem

Contemporary sociological thinking about women has moved beyond the problem of social roles to comprise several interrelated problems focusing on institutions, culture, inequality, and the sociology of knowledge. Both sociological analysis and the feminist critique of culture recognize the importance of the production of social knowledge. Multitudes of cultural materials "carry explicit and implicit suggestions regarding the appropriate social roles for women and men," writes Margaret Andersen in her examination of "sexism and the social construction of knowledge." She argues:

The ideas about women and men that these cultural objects portray greatly influence our thinking about gender roles in society. As images, they convey an impression about the proper role of women, their sexual identity, and their self-consciousness. The ideas we hold about women and men, whether overtly sexist or more subtle in their expression, create social definitions that we use to understand ourselves and the society we live in.[1]

The images of women projected by the media distinguish between black and white women. While media reinforce a cultural vision of white women that is subordinating, they project for black women a profound cultural humiliation that includes black men. Since sexist images are always racially specific, and racist imagery almost always specifies gender, such images may be attributed to simple value reflection, to conscious role modeling, to organizational gender inequality, or to prevalent patriarchal interests within capitalism.[2] Andersen suggests that the exclusion of women from the pursuit and production of knowledge is the key to the problem of sexism and the social construction of knowledge.

Isolation and tokenism, as well as exclusion, are central features of women's experience in institutions of all kinds. Such social realities operate to keep women not only from contributing to the apprehension and interpretation of cultural experience, but also from a certain attachment to oppressive institutions. Their "stranger status" may produce a degree of indifference to the dominant perspective of the group. Andersen argues that while women's exclusion, isolation, and detachment hinder their effort to transform patriarchy, such detachment also "creates critical distance."[3] Thus what the powerful may take for granted, the excluded and the powerless may question and protest. Utilizing Hegel's analysis of master-slave relations, Andersen, like Angela Davis earlier, compares the world view of women to that of slaves. In relations of domination and subordination, the subordinate have a more complete or encompassing world view—their view includes themselves *and* the dominant party. The slaves' world view includes a perspective on their owners, while the owners fail to see the slaves. Women include men in their world view while men do not always "see" women. Similarly, black people may "see" white people to whom they are are physically and socially invisible. Like the labor of Hegel's slaves, the work and experience of white women tends to be invisible to white men. Andersen points out that:

> Women's labor shapes men's experience in the world (through house-
> work and the maintenance of social and bodily relations). Women's
> labor makes the male mode of operation . . . possible; yet, it remains
> invisible to men as the dominant class.[4]

For black women, however, the situation is more complicated. They share with black men the problem of rendering all black people visible to those who control a racist society. Historically, however, black women have been visible in the black world, and their attachment to that world can be seen in many places—including the slave narratives, where the accounts of slave women's abuse, rape, and physical punishment are often vividly documented by slave men. As early as the 1860s, some black men claimed to be conscious of the errors of white men in their view of women. According to Linda Perkins's analysis of racial uplift and black women's education in the nineteenth century, "cooperative efforts between black females and males" were prevalent in the nineteenth-century community, "since liberation of the race was the immediate goal of blacks, [and] the men attached great importance to the females' roles in this effort." Providing an example of this black male perspective, Perkins writes:

> While sexism was not completely absent from the black community, black men became some of the earliest advocates of women's rights. In 1869 when black men formed the Colored National Labor Union, they admitted black women and elected a female to the executive committee of the group. The body voted to uphold equal rights for women and further stated that they were "profiting by the mistakes heretofore made by our white fellow citizens in omitting women."[5]

The consciousness of slaves and freedpeople of the nineteenth century was informed by the heroic status of several black women. Sojourner Truth and Harriet Tubman were two particularly prominent women whose roles within the community raised questions about every assumption concerning the capabilities of women. Furthermore, the historical separation in legal tradition between "'incorrupt' women" who were white and imported to be wives, and slave women who were black and imported to be beasts of burden, created a historical centrality of women to the fate and future of black people as a self-conscious community.[6] In addition to heroic black women, what Angela Davis has called the "deformed equality"[7] between black women and men generated by racial oppression held distinct implications for the organization of gender roles and relations and consciousness about gender in the black cultural experience. Particularly in the black experience, the social problems that surround gender in the black community have not been problems of invisibility for women. The roots of the black community's sexism are not grounded in a perspective that renders women invisible or excludes them from the social world.

### "Largely by Their Hands and Feet": Religious Ideas about Gender

In a church history commemorating the fiftieth anniversary of the Church of God in Christ, Bishop Ozro T. Jones wrote in 1957:

> The "proper" place of women in the church is an age-old debate and from all appearances, it seems that it perhaps will be an eternal one— for most mortals at least. This is because too often humanity has looked to the misty heights of theory rather than the lowly foothills of practice and necessary human service.[8]

Bishop Jones then argued that Christianity addressed the problems of the status of women more dramatically and positively than any other religion by insisting that they are "persons for whom Christ died." Reflecting on Galatians 3:28, Jones wrote:

> But lest we forget, this has been possible only because Christianity has defined women to be persons. In so doing, Christianity has insisted that women are not commodities or an inferior breed, or something like "factory rejects" of the human race, conceptions which held (and hold) sway wherever humanity has lived in the era of B.C. (before Christ). FOR PERSONS FOR WHOM CHRIST DIED any incidental physical condition is no longer a barrier to freedom, or dignity, or value as a person whether that physical condition be social distinction, be race ("Jew or Gentile"), class ("bond or free"), or sex ("male or female"). They all share one spiritual destiny and nature and value in Christ. They all are "fellow heirs" of the promise in Christ.[9]

This statement is important because it was written by a black male bishop in the mid 1950s—the time period so clearly identified with women's exclusion and oppression in the United States. Although the statement contains problematic assumptions about the history of religions and cultural universals, it prefigures by nearly two decades some of the major (and no less problematic) arguments of contemporary Christian feminists. Jones observed that the overwhelming response of women to Christianity was "grateful acknowledgement of what Christ has done." He then advanced a rhetorical but important question: "Indeed, who would dare deny that largely by their hands and feet and service has the Kingdom of our Lord moved forward?"[10] The purpose of his essay was a tribute to the Women's Department of the Church of God in Christ. It was also to express support for the women's autonomous convention under the leadership of Mother Lillian Brooks Coffey, whom Jones called "the guiding spirit and leader of this momentous army of the church."[11] Oral tradition within the Church of God in Christ indicates that Mother Coffey was a militant leader of legendary proportions who was a feminist and an energetic supporter of the black women's club movement.[12] Not only was she central to the history of the denomination—she organized the complex structure of organizations within the Women's Convention— but also she engineered the Women's Convention's participation in larger black women's movements through her close relationship to Mary McLeod Bethune.[13] As a first-generation member of the Church of God in Christ and a former Baptist, Jones recognized the continuities of his church with the larger Afro-Christian tradition. His statement represents a central confession concerning the importance of gender to black Christians and their churches, and the centrality of women to the growth, spread, and development of the structures and traditions. Tacitly and tactfully, Bishop Jones suggests that if it were not for women, Jesus Christ would have no church.

While there are many sources of ideas and images concerning the proper roles of women and men in society, religion is the most powerful, elaborate, and historically persistent source. The dominant perspectives of contemporary feminism have criticized the role of religion and identified religious institutions as an ideological source of oppression. Indeed:

the symbolism of religion [is] so very powerful [because] it expresses the essential facts of our human existence. That is why religious symbolism has incorporated ideas of human identity as well as of social obligation, why there is the idea of soul as well as some kind of god or spiritual force that rules the universe. And since religion symbolizes the major facts of society, it has always had to make room for social conflict in its system of symbols.[14]

Contemporary feminism's cultural critique advocates the transformation or abolition of those ideas about identity, human obligation, and social conflict that consign women to diminished human status, dependent servitude, and victimization. Many feminists recognize that patriarchal Christianity, especially in Europe and the United States, supports institutional arrangements and ideologies that control other forms of oppression and inequity. Black women, however, directly and by their absence from and ambivalence toward white feminist activities and ideologies, question whether the religious and cultural critique of contemporary feminism is adequate for assessing traditions within black congregations and denominations. Indeed, black feminist theory has explicitly affirmed that "our situation as black people necessitates that we have solidarity around the fact of race."[15] Black feminist churchwomen have not approached black religious institutions with the same level of indictment that white women have carried to theirs, in spite of the struggle over women in the pulpit. Harriet Pipes McAdoo's research suggests that contemporary black single mothers rely quite heavily on the oral tradition of the black religious experience, and that these women utilize aspects of the tradition as practical ideologies in their every day lives in order to cope with the stresses of single parenting and of economic deprivation.[16] Churched and unchurched black women persistently attest to the sustaining power of their religious tradition, irrespective of any formal relationship to it.

This chapter explores the importance of women and their experiences to the construction of the African-American tradition and traditional religious knowledge. Four pillars of the Afro-Christian religious tradition are discussed—preaching, praying, singing, and testifying. The analysis aims to suggest and invite, highlighting the need for systematic investigation of gender within the context of religious roles and symbols. Several questions arise in relation to black women and their religion. Do the oral and written traditions of black churches speak about women's experience? Are women and women's experience visible within the traditions and rituals? Has the subordination of women within most, *but not all*, congregations and denominations been reflected in their role in the fashioning and maintaining of the pillars of the worship tradition? Have black women been silenced or silent about their positions in the church? If black women have been persistent and even enterprising agents of religious tradition, and if issues of gender are apprehended by the tradition (and this chapter suggests that such is the case), then precisely what roles *do* women perform? What is the sociological importance of women to the entire black religious enterprise? Has black women's historical role been marginal and trivial, or central and vital? What is the relationship between the importance of black women to the social construction of black religious knowledge and the ambivalent response of black women to white feminist movements, and to those issues, for instance inclusive language, that are central to the white feminist critique of religion?

Such sociological investigation presents a methodological problem. Oral tradition tells us something about the purpose, meaning, and importance of socio-cultural events, but not much about their sequence and frequency. However, oral tradition operates as a connective tissue among aspects of the black religious experience and is therefore relevant to the problem of gender in the Afro-Christian tradition. Let me note here that I use the phrase "Afro-Christian tradition" in place of the usual "black church" because of the plurality of experiences touched upon in this discussion. We are speaking of many congregations, denominations, and settings, and when we address the issues of preaching, praying, singing, and testifying, we are focusing on phenomena that extend far beyond the walls of black churches and are passed along through the intergenerational and interactional processes that constitute tradition. What is handed down, defended, protected, popularized, and occasionally prostituted is something that was essentially forged during slavery in a variety of settings, and it is greater than the institutional boundaries implied by the term "church." "Afro-Christian" recognizes that our African ancestors constructed a complex and dynamic tradition not only from the materials provided by the missionaries and other Europeans confronted in the nighttime of slavery, but also from the cultural imaginations of their African backgrounds, in which women were essential to cultural and religious practice. Slaves did not forget about the women priests and queen mothers in their ancestral societies.[17]

This chapter is not a complete and systematic study of the problem of gender and the pillars of Afro-Christian religious tradition, nor can it answer all of the questions raised above, or all the questions such an investigation generates. My aim is to suggest new directions for sociological research on the black religious experience. Recognizing the importance of gender in the structuring of society and the content of the racist "cultural humiliation"[18] contained in social oppression, we must explore the importance of gender and the realities surrounding it in the black religious experience. I assume that such a reality cannot be properly analyzed by appropriating the white feminist critique of culture, and that scholars must first explore the black experience whose organization of gender we wish to examine.

## The Pillars of Afro-Christian Tradition

Any interpretation of the Afro-Christian tradition must take into account the centrality within it of the English Bible. The African imagination, in its criticism of white oppression, valued the vivid depictions of liberation within the Hebrew Scriptures and their New Testament connections. The Afro-American religious imagination is a biblical imagination. Generations of black Christians who endured slavery, Reconstruction, Jim (and Jane) Crow, urban migration, and the civil rights era constructed and fashioned their songs, prayers, testimonies, and sermons with the English (King James Version) Bible as a resource for the interpretation of past and present sequences of events, and for the envisioning of futures and of strategies to achieve those futures. The suggestion that black people and their preachers do religion with the Bible in one hand and the newspaper in the other reflects this tradition. The title of Zora Neale Hurston's great work, *Their Eyes Were Watching God*, also captures the interpretive principle governing the everyday life and wisdom of black people in the segregated South. In the context of racial oppression, Hurston's observation, "They seemed to be staring at the dark, but their eyes were watching God,"[19] underscores the fact that the Afro-American cultural and political imagination is at its foundations a theological imagination. After reflection on their own experience, the most important critical tool used by black people has been the Bible.

Sermons, prayers, songs, and testimonies utilize the English Bible as a mediator between individual experience and the community. Since slave owners attempted to appropriate the Bible for ideological purposes, black people made it their business to de-ideologize their "blessed book." Anyone who could read it was valuable to the community, and the learning ethic "each one teach one" became a reality in some slave communities.[20] The early recruitment of women as teachers helped to establish their inclusion among the ranks of "educators," a status claimed by male preachers. Later those educators comprised the preachers and teachers who constituted the earliest free leadership class.[21] Their role as educators provided black women with access to leadership in other fields, especially in the area of business. Maggie Lena Walker, Ida Wells Barnett, Myrtle Foster Cook, Lucy Campbell, and Mary McLeod Bethune are famous examples.[22] Carter Woodson argued that the faith of black washerwomen, evidenced in their willingness to invest in black-owned business ventures, fostered substantial social and economic development.[23] All of this activity took place in the context of religious tradition. Reading meant reading the Bible, and most black leaders of the time left some record indicating that a biblical imagination shaped their admonitions and ideas. According to Paula Giddings, Maria Stewart was the first woman of any race to give a public lecture [and leave a manuscript record]. As early as the 1830s, Stewart defended herself against critics by appealing to the role of women in the Bible, especially as carriers of the Gospel message.[24] Recent investigations of slavery and its aftermath suggest that black women were central to the development of individual spirituality as well as institutions and ideologies.[25] Black women were important actors in the historical process from which the black religious experience grew.

Although black churches, with the exception of the African Methodist Episcopal Zion Church, did not support women's ordination, during the eighteenth and nineteenth centuries women did participate in the deliberative assemblies (religious and secular) that took place in church buildings.[26] Black women were rarely forced to justify their presence in any setting involving the welfare or future of black people. Since issues of social change were framed in religious terms, and religious perspectives focused on social change, black women participated in religious discourse even in settings where their right to preach was not affirmed. Often, they could only be "teachers." The opening lines of Lucy Campbell's famous hymn, "Something Within," indicate the extent of these teachers' participation. She wrote:

> Preachers and teachers would make their appeal,
> Fighting as soldiers on great battlefields,
> When to their pleadings my poor heart did yield,
> All I could say, there is something within.[27]

Black women were also "troublers" or prophetic critics in their community and the larger society. Sojourner Truth, a powerful preacher with a feminist hermeneutic and liberating ethic, once confronted Frederick Douglass in one of his more cynical moments, asking the question, "Is God dead?" In a similar manner, many black women worked to maintain the link between questions of faith and questions of social change.[28]

By World War I, black women were performing the central roles that fostered the growth and development of black churches. As missionaries they led devotions and preached Women's Days. As evangelists within the Sanctified Church (black-founded Holiness and Pentecostal denominations and congregations), they preached revivals and "dug out" churches. In those denominations that still do not fully ordain women as pastors, their historical role as organizers and builders of churches fuels the persistent conflicts surrounding the discrimination they experience. Sometimes black women left churches and organized new congregations and denominations where they could participate in every aspect of church leadership. Small denominations such as the Mt. Sinai Holy Church of America, and the House of God, Which Is the Church of the Living God, the Pillar and Ground of the Truth, Inc., were organized in this way. In other denominations such as the Fire Baptized Holiness Church of God of the Americas and the Church of the Living God, Christian Workers for Fellowship, women pastored churches and shared more equitably in the work. Usually they were forced simply to develop strong

Women's Departments which were essential infrastructures to the life and expansion of congregations and denominations.

Subordination and subservience were evident problems, but not silence, isolation, and exclusion. Not only did black church women fashion important and necessary roles for themselves, they also had a powerful effect on religious discourse. When we examine preaching, prayer, testimony, and song, it is clear that women's experiences and church activities are reflected in the stories presented, the images of God, and the pattern of biblical usage. Phyllis Trible has identified the stories of Hagar, Tamar, Jepthah's daughter, and the Levite's concubine as neglected aspects of the church's concern and she calls these biblical stories "texts of terror."[29] Within the Afro-Christian tradition, these women's stories are familiar, and they are preached. They illustrate the way in which both biblical imagination and women's experience are important sources for the interpretation of the black experience. Traditionally male and female preachers (and "speakers" and "teachers") have presented Hagar as the archetype of the slave woman (and by extension of all suffering black women with children), raped and abandoned by her owner and "'buked, scorned, tossed, and driven" by his jealous and selfish wife. Ishmael is often described with the black cultural term "outside child."[30] Langston Hughes's "Aunt Hagar" and E. Franklin Frazier's essay on "Hagar and Her Children" reflect secular appropriations of the Afro-Christian tradition's use of the experience of Hagar.[31] Not only do women in the Order of Eastern Star utilize Jepthah's daughter as a central character in their rituals and a role model for faithful behavior, but black women's organizations and benevolent societies have appropriated women in the Bible for their autonomous rituals.[32] Even the rape of Tamar and the tragedy of the Levite's concubine are familiar sermon topics. Vashti, the queen whom Esther replaced, receives a highly favorable response in the naming of baby girls, in black women's preaching, and in the poetry of Frances Ellen Watkins Harper.[33] Biblical material pertinent to women's experience, while neglected in the European and white American churches, has been woven into the biblical imagination that undergirds the Afro-Christian tradition. Women are active in the process of producing religious knowledge, and the effect of their activities can be found in the kind of attention that the biblical material has received within the context of preaching and the other aspects of worship tradition.

### The Eagle Stirreth Her Nest: Black Preaching

The tradition for which the Sunday service is noted is its preaching. In spite of racism, white people have often recognized the special talent evident in the preaching of black churches. Within black congregations, bad preaching is the unforgivable sin. Preaching is the most masculine aspect of black religious ritual. In spite of the progress of women in ministry, preaching remains overwhelmingly a form of male discourse. Within this male discourse, however, one finds evidence of the centrality of women to the evolution of religious tradition.[34] Black preaching, even in its most androcentric, masculinist, and sexist expressions, is forced to make some reasonable connection with the community at which it is aimed—primarily a community of women.

Black preaching depends upon its connections with the congregations' experiences and their visible assent, their response to the call. Interdependence is an essential condition for effective preaching. The question "will it preach?" is not simply one of form and exegesis; it is also the question, "will the congregation respond in a visible, audible, and meaningful way?" Those preachers who utilize the community's perspectives and biblical imagination as presented in prayer, testimony, and song are probably most successful in making the connections with their congregations that are perceived as successful preaching. When preachers use these other pillars of tradition in their sermons, they enhance the inclusive potential of the preaching tradition, in spite of its masculinist character.

Prayer often frames the preaching event and provides a general charge for the preacher. James Weldon Johnson noted that the black preachers who inspired his work *God's Trombones* were often preceded by a special prayer, and that prayer was often delivered by a woman. Preachers usually acknowledge their dependence upon the prayers of the people for God's arrival in the form of "my Help." They actively and sometimes repeatedly call upon "my Help" and welcome its arrival during the sermon.[35] Historically, new members of churches were trained in the art of public prayer and of raising a song on the assumption that it was a skill that every church member should have.[36] Women are visible participants in the prayer tradition and therefore in framing and shaping the preaching event. Often their "words of prayer" can be found in the words of the preacher. The missionary who begins her prayer by thanking God for waking her "clothed in my right mind" may hear those words come back as a declaration about the God who "wakes me up clothed in my right mind."[37]

The music tradition is another vital resource for preaching. Music functions in several ways within the context of preaching. In some churches the traditional pre-sermon prayer has been replaced by the pre-sermon solo, and like prayer, it often frames the preaching event. Like the prayer, it functions to provide a pathway for the Spirit, thus actualizing the oft-stated belief that "the Spirit comes on the wings of a song." Since the restriction of women in the music tradition is unheard of, the church soloist is often "she."

The music tradition is also a resource for the actual sermon. Familiar songs illustrate and reinforce aspects of the sermon. It is not unusual for a sermon to build toward a dramatic conclusion based on a hymn, spiritual, or gospel song. Some preachers use the song lyrics as a form of meditation at the beginning of their sermons. Black congregations underscore the importance of the music tradition through their preference for the preacher who sings, and some of these preachers have been known to use a talent for song to compensate for homiletical weakness.[38] Songs often fix important theological and biblical images in the congregation's and in the larger community's consciousness. Ideas about God and Jesus are often carried in very familiar terms by song lyrics. Furthermore, images of heaven, models for prayer, and responses to suffering are carried along in the songs. Music tradition is an important tool for the preacher in making a sermon memorable and connected to the community's experience.

Testimonies are priceless resources for sermons. Not only do examples of church members' testimonies provide cogent sermon illustrations, but also such testimonies provide connections between the situations of biblical characters and contemporary problems and experiences. Testimonies provide believable examples of faith that may motivate others to try a particular strategy for confronting and coping with problems. For black congregations whose troubles are disproportionately numerous, effective coping is an important aspect of spiritual well-being. Overwhelmingly, it is women who provide the testimony from which preachers are able to draw illustrations. Women lead many testimony services, especially in Pentecostal congregations, and are particularly effective at encouraging their sisters to speak out. It is this value of testimony for preaching that increases the significance and visibility of women in the shaping of Afro-Christian tradition. The appropriation of their testimonies for sermon illustrations is quite common and extensive.

The late Rev. Clarence LaVaughn Franklin may serve as an illustration for the appropriation of women's testimony for biblical preaching. Not only is he important because of his classic style, but his influence was wide-ranging within and beyond his denomination. To illustrate the importance of steadfast hope (a theme that characterized most of his preaching), Rev. Franklin used the testimony of two women who sent their sons off to war. One of the mothers had five sons, all of whom she accompanied to the train station. In her testimony, the first mother claimed to have asked the Lord, "if it be His will, to bring all of my sons safely home." Franklin claimed that she testified, "the Lord heard my cry" and brought her sons safely back home. The second woman, who had three sons, prayed the same prayer and lost all of her sons and yet she got up to "thank the Lord also . . . because He gave me the strength to get through my situation," and because "the Lord is still watching over, . . . opening doors, . . . and making a way for me" and, therefore, consistent with the central theme of Franklin's sermon, "nothing can separate me from the love of God."[39]

The manner in which Franklin and many other preachers use such testimony is instructive for our understanding of the consciousness of gender in black churches. First of all, Franklin had just been talking about Job. He used the testimony of the women to connect the problem of Job with the problem of contemporary experience. Beyond that, he transferred a biblical story centered on male experience to the experience of contemporary black women.[40] Secondly, Franklin and others often locate the problems of black suffering, through the direct or the indirect use of women's discourse and testimony, to the actual experience of suffering shared by black women. In other words, by reflecting women's testimony back to the community in the sermon, the black preacher affirms for black women that they have suffered, and unreasonably so. Finally, the black preacher not only contextualizes black women's suffering with reference to a document and canon that focuses largely on males, but also conveys the entire text to women as an appropriate possession for black women as they negotiate their purpose and meaning in a racist and sexist society. Women are encouraged to use the Bible as a resource for their own spiritual well-being. Unless one understands the active role of black women as the community to which the preacher is connected, and the centrality of a shared understanding of the biblical text, one cannot begin to understand the tenacity with which black women cling to the King James Version of the English Bible. Women who defend its use in church settings often argue their affection for this text on the basis of its literary style and its importance to tradition, not on the basis of its providing infallible revelation. A vivid example of this view is found in the Bible Study manual of the Church of God in Christ. The manual is taught largely by missionaries throughout the denomination. It emphasizes the details of the translation process for the King James Version, so that the laity are admonished to recognize that they possess a translation of the Bible.[41]

Male preachers manage to include women in their sermons in other ways. One strategy is to draw illustrations from female biblical characters and to place in the mouths of these biblical women an ordinary discourse that is recognizable as that of contemporary black women. To highlight the necessity of suffering for the maturation of the Christian, C.L. Franklin used the example of the mother of James and John. Portraying this woman in a sympathetic light, he attributed to her all of the concerns and care about the future of her children associated with an heroic perception of the role of black women in their families.[42] Another strategy involves calling women's names when the sermon rhetoric includes a roll call of characters of a specific type. In one sermon where "the grave" attested to its role as "landlord of the universe," the preacher included in his list of inhabitants great women church officers and community leaders in a roll call of the deceased.[43]

Finally, black male preachers occasionally provide androgynous or feminine imagery in the context of a sermon. Some of them are masters of the androgynous sermon. Such a sermon is grounded in imagery of God that transcends specifically male or female attributes and occasionally manages to dispense with human reference altogether. One sermon, called "Who?" was preached by an elderly Boston preacher notorious for his refusal to approve or affirm women preachers. At a regional [Baptist] convention, however, he preached his sermon as an answer to the question, which he happened to ponder in his study one day, "Who did all this?" The entire sermon was a long epic poem about "Who" and focused entirely on God's biblical activity without referring to God with a personal pronoun. God remained "Who" for the entire sermon. It is not unusual for preachers to transcend human attributes in the inspired endings or sermon conclusions characteristic of the black preaching style. Such endings, if they do not transcend specifically human attributes, draw upon the images of God as nurturer and combine these with other metaphors to disengage gender from divinity.

One of the most vivid examples of the tendency to emphasize God as mother in black preaching is Franklin's sermon, "The Eagle Stirreth Her Nest." It is his most popular and, perhaps, most often-borrowed sermon. Within that sermon, Franklin goes to great lengths to stress that the Bible speaks of God through a variety of images. He then proceeds to describe in deep and lively detail the ways in which God operates in our lives as a mother eagle. It is a masterful sermon that stresses the ways in which God's eagle nature is representative of *his* majesty, and then, continuing in masculine language, insists that people must not confuse the "puny" kings of the earth with God. Although the masculine language surrounding the pronouns attached to God remains through the sermon, the admonition against patriarchal idolatry is very clearly present. Franklin then discusses the problem of suffering with reference to God's role as a mother eagle. Franklin points out that the mother eagle makes a nest in high places where she feeds and cares for the baby eagles. However, as they begin to outgrow the nest, she begins to pull the soft feathers out of the nest so that they are less comfortable and want to go out on their own. Such imagery is consistent with his view of human suffering as a way of creating a mature Christian. Finally, Franklin develops indirectly the themes of godly benevolence and providence in his description of the mother eagle's flying lessons for the baby eagles. She takes them out of the nest and drops them, and continues to catch them up on her wings until they finally learn to fly on their own.[44] The sermon is a masterpiece of feminine imagery set in the framework of male discourse. When one hears that sermon, one is able to hear Franklin's glancing references elsewhere to the motherly nature of God. In other sermons such as "The Lord Is Good," one can experience God as the heavenly keeper of the human nursery.[45]

Preaching, as one of the pillars of Afro-Christian worship, is most prominent in the central ritual event—the church service. It is also the most masculine of the pillars. While systematic study of sermons, through such strategies as content analysis and in-depth studies of influential preachers, is needed, it is important to note that this male tradition is connected in recognizable and important ways to black women's experience. The other three pillars of tradition are even more directly tied to women's experience and more directly responsible for black women's sense of ownership of their churches and their traditions.

## Women Warriors: The Prayer Tradition

The song, "If I Could Hear My Mother Pray Again," highlights the centrality of women to the prayer tradition. Most black Christians have been taught to pray by their mothers. The poet Joanne Braxton has stated that her goal in life is to write poetry the way her grandmother prayed. Another writer and literary critic remembers the impact of her grandmother's morning prayer on her entire household. Harold Carter in his reflection on the "prayer tradition of black people" cites the importance of women to the vitality and sustenance of the tradition.[46] It is an area of the black experience within which women have never been silent. In his study of socialization in the slave quarters community, Webber attributes the deep spirituality of the slaves to their early exposure to prayers for freedom among mothers and aunts in the cabins.[47]

The label "prayer warrior" runs deep in black tradition. Mamie Garvin Fields relates the story of the events surrounding the purchase of a church from whites by freedmen and freedwomen in Charleston, South Carolina a year after the Civil War ended. She tells the story she heard growing up in the parsonage of that church. She said:

> The money had to be to the bank by twelve noon, sharp. So a small boat was hired to row out to the ship and unload the gold, while the warriors of the church prayed and prayed for the money to get to the appointed place at the appointed time. The staunchest in the congregation were praying very hard, because they had given up the monies that they had buried in cans, savings for their funerals. Anyway, this little boat went out and back, the men "rowing for life," as the story goes. When they got back to the wharf, the drayman was waiting with the best horses he could find, and the drayman whipped those horses through the streets of Charleston. All this time the prayer warriors kept on.[48]

When describing the outcome, Mrs. Fields stated simply, "The Lord brought us the rest of the way." In the black tradition, church mothers who have a mighty gift of prayer are called "warriors." Men with such gifts are usually deacons.

Thus when preachers say "some old warrior," the referent is usually "she." In a sermon that laments the waning of certain worship traditions, Jasper Williams demonstrates the manner and the style of these "old warriors":

> They had those old time covenant meetings; they had those red hot covenant testifying services. People would get up and talk about how good God had been to them. . . . You'd see some old warrior, when time came for her to testify, she'd get up and come down the aisle and

lock her arms back behind her back. And she'd cry a while; and then walk a while. And just stand before the altar and say, "Rev., I'm sorry but it's all over me, it's all in me, it's all under me." And she'd stand there and shout a while. And finally when she would regain her composure, she'd tell the church: "You all remember last month I stood here and asked you to pray for my son. . . . I'm happy to report to you this month that God has heard our prayer."[49]

The importance of these women to the church tradition is attested in black literature as well. James Baldwin's character, Praying Mother Washington, is such an example.[50] Langston Hughes incorporates the prayer warrior tradition into his novel *Not Without Laughter* in the character of Aunt Hagar.[51] The link between black women and the prayer tradition is firm and well recognized in letters and folklore.

Rosemary Ruether argues that one of the principal means by which women are subordinated within the religious tradition is through enforced silence.[52] The prayer tradition is a blatant contradiction to this tendency. Whatever the various interpretations of Paul's admonition to women to be silent in dominant culture churches, black denominations have interpreted this to mean "from the floor." Thus it is not unusual to see, in churches that do not permit women to preach or otherwise use the pulpit, women (missionaries and evangelists) leading worship services and praying from lecterns placed below or near the pulpit. Thus while black women may not pray from the pulpit, their "silence" speaks loudly in the literary, oral, and preaching traditions of the black experience.

### A Mother to the Motherless: The Musical Tradition

Women are most prominent and visible in the area of music. While this is true in any Christian communion, black women are largely responsible for shaping what is distinctive and defining in the black sacred music tradition. The crystallization of the image of God as "a Mother to the motherless and a Father to the fatherless" is but one important indication of their importance. Music has been the most powerful vehicle for this dramatic and well-articulated litany of deity that reflects both genders. This description of God is so entrenched within Afro-Christian tradition that the average church member is able to recite it and use it. The song, "Surely Our God Is Able," written by a man in collaboration with a woman and popularized by women requires consideration.[53]

Popularized by Clara Ward and the Ward singers, the song was written by the Rev. Herbert Brewster. Brewster believed that "a gospel song was a sermon set to music. It must have sentiment and doctrine, rhetorical beauty and splendor."[54] The singers for whom Brewster wrote were primarily women. As a result, this gospel composer often used inclusive language in his songs.

Popularized by Mahalia Jackson, Brewster's hit song, "Move on Up a Little Higher," states, "All God's sons and daughters,/ Will be drinking that healing water. . . . "[55] In Brewster's song "Surely," the characteristics of God combine masculine and feminine attributes. As part of an extended chorus to the song, singers sang:

> Don't you know God is able, He's able;
> God is able, Yes, he's able.
> Clouds may gather all around you
> So dark and sable.
> He'll be your mother when you're motherless;
> He's your father, when you're fatherless;
> He's your sister, when you're sisterless;
> He's your brother when you're brotherless.
> He's a doctor in the sick room;
> He's your lawyer, in the courtroom;
> When you go down to the Jordan,
> He will be there to bear your burden.
> He will step out before you;
> And my God will know you.
> Surely, surely, God is able to carry you through.[56]

The words of the chorus, with their theological affirmations, are probably older than "Surely." However, "Surely" fixed the images of God as a mother to the motherless in popular language and culture. The words of the chorus are heard, consequently, throughout the prayer and the preaching traditions, and they appear in the testimonies of prayer meetings. The words are also heard beyond the walls of the church.

Although such examples do not resolve the very real crisis of exclusive and inclusive language, they remind us of the importance of the gospel music tradition to the imagery black people share concerning God and other theological subjects. Visions of heaven, understandings of the role of Jesus, and a host of other concerns have been conveyed by gospel music. Popular religious music assigned a role flexibility to God and Jesus that went beyond dominant social conventions concerning gender. The gospel songs have also fixed in the oral tradition the importance of such [biblical] characters as the woman at the well, or Mary and Martha.[57]

Within the music tradition women are often the principal insiders in the production of religious knowledge. They not only sang men's compositions, they wrote their own. Mahalia Jackson, Roberta Martin, Beatrice Brown, B. Alma Androzzo ("If I Can Help Somebody"), and Mattie Moss Clark are a few names in a very large pantheon of women who both sang and composed gospel music. Clark not only composed [music] but headed the music department of the Church of God in Christ, participating in the relationship between canon and black community. Women are also prominent and powerful members—and occasionally, chairs—of hymnal committees. For some women, gospel singing became an alternative to preaching; some women achieved fame as "evangelists" within this musical movement. Mother Willie Mae Ford Smith and Shirley Caesar are the most prominent examples. Because of these and many other singers, music is the most widespread and popular aspect of the Afro-Christian tradition. It has crossed racial boundaries and represents a central characterization of black religion—to some minds, too central. Women are its most prominent and responsible agents, fashioning and communicating this critical category of religious knowledge. Two major publishing houses of Gospel music were founded and owned by women, Sallie Martin and Roberta Martin, and within the annals of gospel musicology, women are cited as agents of style. The centrality of music to the black religious tradition is well known, and women are central to that tradition; the tradition explicitly includes them and their consciousness in both the production and the product.

### This Joy I Have: The Testimony Tradition

The importance of testimony to the process of preaching has already been stated. However, it is important to examine testimony with reference to the black community itself. The shared nature of the experiences to which black religion speaks depends upon testimony. Testimony transforms the collection of worshippers into a community. Oppression and suffering make testimony important for psychological survival. Testimony does not resolve black problems but does transform them from the private troubles of distressed individuals into the public issues of a covenant community. Testimony is one of the important antecedents to movements for social change. Black women are the best testifiers in the community. They carry forward the slaves' determination to survive. It is not unreasonable to attribute black women's relatively low suicide rate to the survival value of testimony. It is not surprising that testimony figures prominently in the success of secular self-help groups such as Alcoholics Anonymous, and in the consciousness-raising groups of contemporary feminists.

For women, testimony can be a form of protest against some of the constraints of being female and a means of lament over the brokenness in their relationships with men. Occasionally one can hear testimony that includes these lines:

> This joy I have, man didn't give it to me;
> This peace I have, man didn't give it to me;
> This love I have, man didn't give it to me;
> Man didn't give it and man can't take it away.

Not only do such manipulations of the androcentric dimensions of the King James text occur, but the generic "man" is subverted into a usable women's perspective—a protest perspective. Women will rise up and testify about their struggles as women alone. In any pre-revival devotional session, one can hear a litany of the social problems affecting black women: abandonment, assaults, aging, poverty, violent crime, single-parenthood, and their children's futures. Testimony may also be responsible for the ideology of sisterhood among black women. It sometimes serves as an instrument of reconciliation. For his reflection on church tradition, Williams's sermon is again helpful:

> When he (the old preacher) got through, some old mother would get up and say, "Brother pastor! I'm sorry to cut across you but I've got to say this! I can't go another [step] further. I've got this grudge I've been carrying around in my heart against Mother Jones. And I can't sleep at night. I can't even pray. And I promised God I wasn't going to leave here until I got things settled. And here we are getting ready to take the Lord's supper. And I can't eat of my God's body, drink of His blood with what I've got in my heart against Mother Jones." And right there in front of everybody, she'd walk over to Mother Jones and give Mother Jones her hand and say, "Mother Jones, if I have hurt you or wronged you in any fashion, I want you to forgive me. Charge it to my head and not my heart."[58]

Because of the fragmented and fragmenting nature of life in black communities, this integrative dimension should not be overlooked. The potential for debilitating bitterness on the part of many black women is reduced while the potential for community and for collective action is enhanced. Since the feminist movement strives to develop sisterhood, black women's activity in this tradition represents an important resource.[59]

## Some Mother's Son and Some Father's Daughter: The Creative Tension

Historically, black preachers often substituted the phrase, "some mother's son and some father's daughter" for the terms "man," "somebody," or "someone." This traditional public rhetoric symbolizes the creative tension surrounding the imagery of gender that exists within the Afro-Christian tradition. Preaching, prayer, song, and testimony are historically derived pillars of the Afro-Christian tradition that transcend congregational and denominational boundaries. They are vehicles for women to construct meaning and imagery that become part of the religious experience women and men share. These pillars also reflect images of humans and of the Deity in ways that expand and relativize the androcentrism of the Bible, making it possible for women to appropriate and to own the Bible and the church tradition, and their experience is, therefore, explicitly included. While not inclusive by contemporary feminist standards, there exists an important foundation for change and inclusion. This inclusive potential influences roles and rhetoric. It can contribute to arguments for more egalitarian approaches to religious practice that may revise some of the existing strengths of the community while constructively criticizing some possible political excesses.

For instance, one problem that developed in the late 1960s was the impact of a more exclusive political rhetoric within a growing black power movement, when the problem of "the Negro" became the problem of "the black man." The transition from "Negro" to "black" was a necessary phase in the public politics of race relations and in both black and white cultural consciousness and awareness, but an element of gender inclusiveness was lost in the process. Black women had always felt included in the term "Negro." Since one of the important themes of black preaching in all denominations was the problem of racial oppression, the rhetorical switch from "Negro" to "black man" at precisely the moment that gender and women's rights became one of the most central issues of public politics may have been one of the most unfortunate contradictions of black liberation. Preaching and other forms of public male discourse that had been more or less inclusive of women and women's experience became more exclusive. I think it is reasonable to argue that this shift invited a problematic departure from tradition that must be assessed in our reflections of the intersection of gender and race-ethnicity, particularly in the area of consciousness.

Pauli Murray reminds us that the experience of racial oppression has incorporated both Jim Crow and Jane Crow. She criticized the social implications of this rhetoric, observing that the rhetoric of black power sounded as if it were merely a movement for black males to share power with white males. She links this new language to the ideological consequences of the Moynihan Report. Pointing to the failures of the black family by exaggerating the insubordination of black women, the report engendered a sense of shame concerning black women's putative achievements in the political, economic, and cultural life of the black community. Murray's criticisms suggest that the black power movement was a successful masculinist movement within the black community.[60] The particular expressions of racism against black men generated conditions for the movement's success. Such an irruption is intelligible in a patriarchy that sought explicitly and particularly to destroy all black male claims to manhood. Such specialized destruction existed to negate, violently if need be, all claims of black females to womanhood. The more important result of this dual process was the negation of the peoplehood and humanity of all black people. Thus it does become necessary to criticize a definition of humanity that rests solely upon "black manhood." The preaching tradition did indeed generate that criticism.

C. L. Franklin addressed this problem when he complained about the members of his church and his community walking around boasting "I'm a man!"[61] His complaint was then followed by the admonition that every Christian should boast about how much of a "child" in the kingdom of God he was. In other words, black "manhood" was not an important or positive concept in Christian community.[62] In his sermon, "The Meaning of Black Power," Franklin addressed this masculinist tendency. After castigating black power advocates for their violation of Christian ethics in their bid for separatism, he concluded:

> If there is any meaning at all to black power, . . . we must know that we are God's children. Proud black men and women—creative, resourceful, productive, working for unity among ourselves, with a new sense of political, social, and economic responsibility. . . . We must control our own destiny.[63]

When one reflects on the evangelistic inclusiveness that undergirded the phrase, "some mother's son and some father's daughter," one can observe an intergenerational and inter-gender basis for unity, a foundation for creative tension in the area of gender and sacred imagery. The dynamics of gender organization and of religious discourse in black churches operate at some times and under some conditions to include women and their experience under the umbrella of racial oppression and as a context illustrative of God's activity on behalf of people. Although the overall reality of the black church is *not* egalitarian, it does address the experience of women, and it does generate a subliminal level of consciousness that is integrative. It links men's issues and women's issues in the community's consciousness.

The phrase, "some mother's son and some father's daughter," represents an intergenerational and cross-gender linkage in people's consciousness and implies a common interest surrounding racial oppression in the lives of black women and men. Historically, it was "mothers' sons" who wrote the slave narratives and preached the sermons that described the special terrors of black women such as Hagar and her children. At the same time, it was "fathers' daughters" such as Ida B. Wells Barnett and Mary McLeod Bethune who struggled within the women's club movement with the problem of lynching, and who moved to positions of intellectual leadership at the height of the struggle against Jim (and Jane) Crow. An interesting social dilemma is created when the settings for women's discourse concerning men's issues exist outside of the black church pulpits, while men's ritual re-telling of women's terrors and troubles occur largely within those pulpits. The relative absence of men from church audiences implies that female leadership may be critically important for the re-inclusion and re-integration of men among the laity. Furthermore, the tales of black female hostility to women preachers become intelligible (although not excusable) in this context.

An additional and unstated aspect of the black religious ritual emerges in the form of aging congregations of mothers hearing assurances from their sons that they will carry forward their cherished traditions. Although currently dormant and under some stress, this intergenerational and inter-gender integration has in the past given rise to amazing levels of solidarity within the

Afro-Christian tradition. The Civil Rights Movement is one example. Historical accounts of the slave church suggest that its egalitarianism of necessity also created such a context.[64]

An examination of the wellsprings of Afro-American religious tradition must conclude that women are not outsiders to its social production. While the black religious experience is clearly patriarchal in most of its expression, and decidedly masculinist in much of its preaching, the cultural maxim, "If it wasn't for the women, you wouldn't have a church," rises up against male attempts to exclude, ignore, trivialize, or marginalize women in a number of capacities.

The biblical scholar Krister Stendahl commented, "I have come to think of heaven as the place where one can discuss one issue at a time."[65] For a scholar concerned with the intersection of gender and race in the problems of this society, this observation rings particularly true. The problems confronting members of our society cut across lines of race, ethnicity, and gender to such an extent that we must begin to think pluralistically about concrete expressions of racial oppression and gender inequity. In the face of such complexity, the study of the black religious experience as a vital aspect of social organization in the context of survival, rebellion, and cultural tradition comprises a number of tasks. The work of thorough description and explanation of the experience and its organization and interpretation of gender must precede the tasks of restructuring, of redress, and of recasting a tradition that has, in the words of testimony and song, "brought us from a mighty long way." Critical and creative thinking about the Afro-Christian tradition must reflect upon those historically derived strengths and potentials while it articulates a vision of change that fosters wholeness.

# 8

# "Sisters Who Can Lift a Community"

## Nannie Helen Burroughs,
## "The Slabtown District Convention,"
## and the Cultural Production
## of Community and Social Change

*We must have a glorified womanhood that can look any man in the face—white, red, yellow, brown, or black, and tell of the nobility of character within black womanhood.*

—NANNIE HELEN BURROUGHS

Historically, African-American women in the United States have produced and shaped diverse and critical models of leadership and community organization. Often their community and church work have been dismissed as simple responses to racial oppression. Recent womanist and black feminist scholarship has challenged us to probe more deeply the roles of African-American women in shaping black churches, communities, movements for social change, and distinctive ethical perspectives on social justice and human liberation. While the labeling of black women's ideas as "black feminist" and "womanist" thought or theorizing is relatively recent,[1] black women have a long history of asserting their understandings about how black people should act within their communities and in addressing the problems and oppressive structures that need to be changed. At critical points and junctures in African-American history, certain creative, activist women have emerged as heroes because of their actions, ideas, and organizational innovations. In the history of African-American church women, Nannie Helen Burroughs was one such woman. Not only was she a leader of church women, but she was an activist, educator, and a writer who shared her ideas in ways that fostered the vision of racial uplift she shared with women in the National Baptist Convention and the National Association of Colored Women's Clubs.[2]

In order to highlight the life and work of Nannie Helen Burroughs and her importance in developing critical models of community leadership, models we would now call womanist or black feminist, this chapter explores and analyzes a play, a musical comedy, that Burroughs wrote: "The Slabtown District Convention."[3] Burroughs's play comically represented and criticized various dimensions of African-American religious culture and consciousness during the early twentieth century. In her play, Burroughs not only offered prescriptions for the roles and relationships of educated women in their communities, but she criticized the misbehavior of male leaders and the collaboration of women in that misbehavior. The importance of her play is not only in the dramatic content, but also in the place of her work within the institutional framework of the black experience as a pedagogy of the oppressed that was widely communicated through the central institutions of the black community, namely, the churches. In spite of the early twentieth-century representations of the play, the play was still being performed in churches in the last decade of the twentieth century. Burroughs's activist career was related to the play's text, especially in her emphasis on religion and education. Burroughs's work provided an important case study of the way black women shaped African-American culture to their purposes, not only through their organizational involvements but also through their ideas.

Burroughs's ideas are an important example of the multiple consciousness that shaped the foundation of womanist or black feminist thought and theorizing.[4] Nannie Helen Burroughs's life and work and their relationship to her stage play point to the importance of connecting such terms as "womanist," "black feminist," and "cultural worker."[5] Furthermore, women such as Burroughs challenge sociologists to focus on the intersection of biography, history, and social structure, what C. Wright Mills identified as the interrelated starting points of a critical sociology.[6] Such an approach allows for an analysis of the role of outstanding leaders and their contributions to social change, without ignoring their embeddedness in and consequences for a larger community. This particular chapter focuses on the cultural basis on which subordinate/oppressed groups construct and shape leadership roles and from which these groups confront dominating segments of society.

### African-American Women's Agency in a Culture of Resistance

Minna Caulfield's concept of a "culture of resistance" captures one of several dimensions of life in oppressed communities.[7] In addition to combatting the damage imposed on their communities, oppressed people often try to develop and instill values that differ drastically from those communicated by the dominant culture, especially when they recognize the role that values play in the social world of their oppressor. Sometimes oppressed people must create roles that do not exist in the societies that oppress them, and sometimes they must radically reorganize the content of roles that already exist. In the African-American experience, such innovation and resistance has been a response to the constant pressure to devise "a way out of no way."

Culture is a historically informed way of life or life-style. Culture is composed of people's collective and cumulative efforts at prescriptions for human behavior. Cultures of resistance are no different, except that they are constructed in opposition to a more powerful dominant culture. In order to construct oppositional ways of thinking and acting, people must be able to idealize their oppositional alternatives. They must be able to point to people who embody those roles in order to be socialized or to socialize others. Cultural change occurs when significant constituencies advocate and adopt new ways of acting and thinking. The actors in these new or refashioned roles are charged with maintaining an alternative, critical worldview within a community under pressure to conform to dominant ways in spite of its conflicting interests. This countercultural process involves the construction of new social knowledge and is the most important product of cultural agency. Activist and church woman Nannie Helen Burroughs exemplifies this kind of cultural agency. She took seriously the importance of women's leadership in the social construction of new social knowledge within the African-American community.

Burroughs was active and educated during one of the most significant periods in African-American women's history, and her work and activities weave together many of the diverse political, cultural, and religious threads of that period. Her play prescribes heroic role models for women with explicit ideologies concerning the form and content of women's leadership. The play also asserts the importance of women's leadership in settings considered to be largely the public stage of male leaders. Burroughs also confronted the problem of elitism and criticized styles of spirituality and their relationships to political and communal values. The play explicitly addressed several historical cultural dilemmas African Americans have faced. Through her play, Burroughs made choices that reflected controversies among competing constituencies within the black community of the late nineteenth and early twentieth century, controversies that remain sources of individual and group tensions today. Burroughs's work facilitates an understanding of a distinct black feminist or womanist tradition within the United States.

Burroughs's play takes place in the black church, the most important setting for cultural production. Plays, pageants, and oratorical programs have been an important source of motivation and public affirmation of group values, particularly for young people. For the vast majority of African Americans, the church was the setting for their first exercise in public speaking, reciting the "Easter piece" or the "Christmas piece" or playing a part in the Sunday School pageant. There is a long-standing recognition of the importance of religious settings in shaping and supporting social movements within the black community. The most acknowledged aspect of this importance has been the focus on the leadership provided by the clergymen.[8] Although the role of women is acknowledged in background support and overwhelming membership, their direct impact in the constitution of the church setting and the production of its distinctive expressive styles is understated or ignored. The role of women leaders is usually examined with reference to movements and activities outside of the churches, and their centrality and indispensability to the church setting is masked.

Paula Giddings demonstrates the importance of women to the uplift of the community and to the success of its social movements, with some mention of the relationship between black women and their churches.[9] Brooks's work on Baptist women between 1880 and 1900 points out that women were pushed out of traditional roles of spiritual and political leadership:

> Although marginal to the American politico-economic mainstream, the Black Baptist male and female leadership reiterated time and again the necessity of having an educated pulpit and an educated laity. . . . These leaders, as witnessed by the men and women of the American National Baptist Convention, considered themselves to be the political, social, and spiritual voices of Afro-American Baptists. Of equal importance, Black Baptist women, who added to the feminist theological literature of the late nineteenth century, expressed pride in their own mental competence and challenged sexism from the standpoint of biblical criticism and interpretation. The feminist theology of Black Baptist women had significant implications for their future religious work. It buttressed women's demands for greater participation and infused their expanding ranks with optimism about woman's destiny at the dawn of a new century.[10]

From the cultural tensions emerging within the African-American community during Reconstruction, it is clear that women lost ground as churches "regularized," attempted to become more assimilated, and as part of that process attempted to suppress women's leadership voices. Their roles as cultural producers, what Bernice Johnson Reagon calls "cultural workers," and as agents of socialization remained central, largely through the women's own enterprising opposition to their exclusion and suppression. Cornel West, a political philosopher concerned with traditions and practices of public activism within black America, identified three interrelated traditions, Christian, womanist, and socialist, as significant social forces combining ideas and action to promote social change.[11] West separated the role of women and the role of the church and identified the organized activities of African-American women as the earliest *national* articulation of prophetic practices. The women active in the anti-lynching, suffrage, and club movements of the nineteenth and twentieth centuries were active in the churches as members of local congregations and denominational women's organizations, in spite of their blocked access to pulpits *as preachers and pastors*. Since they were denied the prominent role of "the black preacher" most visible to white society, it is more difficult to identify the way in which women's voices shaped the prescriptive dimensions of African-American culture as leaders within their churches.[12]

Burroughs's "Slabtown" provided a snapshot of the black community that brought women's agency in the process of cultural production into the foreground and detailed the ways women shaped prescriptions that affected men as well as women within religious settings. Burroughs's activities and stage play point to the process by which confrontation and integration between women and men undergird the process of African-American activism. Since the importance of male-female solidarity is one of the most critical issues that divide black and white women who are self-identified feminists,[13] Burroughs's work illuminates the distinct cultural reality undergirding African-American women's perspectives on church and community.

## Burroughs, Church, and Community

The beginning of Nannie Helen Burroughs's activist career and the beginning of the twentieth century were dramatically intertwined. Nannie Helen Burroughs (1883-1961) was an indomitable Baptist church woman, educator, school founder, club woman, and activist; she participated in nearly every African-American political and cultural effort of the early twentieth century. She was an important example of what sociologist Howard Becker called a "moral entrepreneur"[14]—someone who consciously, at times militantly, sought to define and clarify appropriate values and modes of behavior within the black experience. As an activist Burroughs publicly combined perspectives on "raising women" with the "uplift" of the entire black community.

According to several sources Burroughs was the granddaughter of slaves who became landowning freedpeople.[15] An eager student with an interest in literature, she wanted to become a school teacher. Unable to secure employment in the Washington, D.C., school system (probably because she was too young), she went to work as a bookkeeper and editor. Moving from Washington, D.C., to Louisville, Kentucky, she went to work for the National Baptist Convention as "a bookkeeper, stenographer, and editorial secretary." Early in her life, Burroughs was situated as a member of the professional staff of the largest black religious organization in the United States. The National Baptist Convention, until 1915 the only national body representing the majority of black Christians, today remains the largest. In spite of the growth of other black religious organizations, the majority of black Christians remain Baptist. Burroughs, in a key position of influence if not authority, was in a position of real power.

Apparently, she was also a precocious leader and possessed an educator's vision. When black Baptist women formed the Women's Auxiliary of the National Baptist Convention in 1900, Burroughs was only 17 years old. According to Daniel:

In 1900 she attended the annual meeting of the National Baptist Convention, Richmond, Virginia, and delivered an address that electrified the assembly. Her subject, "Hindered from Helping," was based on the following Biblical words, "Ye entered not in yourselves and they that were entering ye hindered." One result of her speech was her election to secretaryship of the Woman's Auxiliary. . . . At this meeting . . . the vision caught was world wide; the goal set was to reach and lift every woman.[16]

By 1901 Burroughs was the corresponding secretary for the group and responsible for communicating policy under its president. It was during this year that, according to Barnett, Burroughs proposed "that a special committee be appointed to advise with our Board to devise plans for the beginning of the Training School."[17] Shortly thereafter her organizing skills helped to transform the Women's Auxiliary into one of the most effective fundraising organizations in the black community.

Over the next thirty years Burroughs achieved prominence as she acted upon her feminist tendencies through her position as corresponding secretary. As one response to the repression against women's leadership, Burroughs nationalized the idea of Women's Day, presenting it as a day for women's missionary work, all the while believing that women needed a forum within the church to speak up for themselves. Decrying the tendency to use Women's Day primarily as a fundraising day, she insisted that it was a day to "raise women."[18] As corresponding secretary, Burroughs took it upon herself to distribute speeches to women in the churches who were shy or inexperienced public speakers. Her evangelical zeal was tied to her unswerving belief that women were responsible for and capable of preaching the gospel.

By 1907 she had begun the process for forming the National Training School for Women and Girls. According to Barnett, she conceived of the school as a place for women of all faiths.[19] Daniel asserted that Burroughs advanced the radical ideal of educating African women to be missionaries in their own countries.[20] In 1909, the school opened with Burroughs as president. According to Barnett, "The institution was called the School of the three B's for the importance placed on the Bible, bath, and broom as tools for race advancement."[21] According to Barnett's description:

[T]he National Training School attempted to speak concretely to the material conditions surrounding black women. American society demanded that the black woman work no less than her man for survival, while for many decades both sexes were for the most part limited either to agricultural work in the South or domestic service in rural and urban areas throughout the nation. . . . Stressing the importance of thorough domestic training at the National Training School for Women and Girls, Nannie Burroughs reasoned that "the Negro girl must be taught the art of home-making as a profession, because 98 percent of them must keep their own homes without any outside 'help' and, according to present statistics, 58 percent of the women who work out are cooks, nurse-maids, etc."[22]

Burroughs enlisted church women, church men, club women, and whole communities in her project and was able to boast of building a school whose foundations were built entirely on black philanthropy.[23]

Burroughs was a prominent club woman and "race" woman. In the process of building her school she enlisted the aid of other club women like Maggie Lena Walker, Mary McLeod Bethune, and Mary B. Talbert. Burroughs herself organized several clubs, including "the National Association of Wage Earners, in order to attract public attention to the plight of the black working woman."[24] She also belonged to and worked with the National Association of Colored Women and the International Council of Women of the Darker Races. Considering the issues dealt with by both groups, it is clear that Burroughs was a black feminist thinker of that period. Not only was she focused on the problem of uplift for "the race" in the United States, but her work with the Council indicates a clear critique of American imperialism. According to Barnett:

> By forming local study groups in order to analyze conditions in specific areas, e.g., Africa, Haiti, and India, the women hoped to broaden their own cultural knowledge and also gain recognition for the study of women of color as an accepted field.
>
> The concern of these women for the darker races of the world—the Third World, as it is commonly known today—coincided with the period of European and American imperialism. The growth of international finance capital, as well as its export into areas in Africa, Asia, and the islands culminated in the colonial subjugation of peoples of color throughout most of the world. Although the International Council of Women did not address itself to the issue of national liberation struggles, it nonetheless represented a positive thrust.[25]

Racial pride was another important dimension of Burroughs's contribution. Barnett points out:

> There was no more staunch advocate of racial pride and heritage than Nannie Burroughs. She was a life member of the Association of Negro Life and History. . . . [At the 1927 convention] Burroughs shared the platform with noted scholars Carter G. Woodson and Alain Locke. . . . Her speech, "The Social Value of Negro History," was recounted in the *Journal of Negro History* as follows: "By a forceful address Miss Nannie H. Burroughs emphasized the duty the Negro owes to himself

to learn his own story and the duty the white man owes to himself to learn of the spiritual strivings and achievements of a despised but not an inferior people."[26]

Burroughs believed passionately that black people had a significant social role and an alternative worldview that came from their experience of suffering. According to Burroughs's thinking, internal self-development would not only benefit black people materially, but would also empower black people to speak forthrightly and critically to the nation, transforming and redeeming black and white people. Her racial pride was one of the reasons why she sought to build the Training School without the help of the major, white-controlled philanthropic funds of her day (e.g., American Baptist Home Mission Society, Slater Fund, Phelps-Stokes). "To her, the goal of economic self-reliance was the only guarantee for racial uplift and independence."[27]

To get her ideas across, Burroughs wrote articles in various publications, including the *Southern Workman*. She gave speeches at churches around the country and at national meetings. She insisted that an oration on African-American history be a graduation requirement from her *industrial* training school, and each year, after competition, the two best orations were presented publicly. She was a militant anti-segregationist at the same time she was critical of the self-denigrating behaviors she saw as black people's attempts to assimilate. In the process of communicating her ideas about racial uplift, group pride, America's racist idolatry, male-female responsibilities and obligations, education, self-reliance, and international affairs, Burroughs wrote plays, pageants, articles, and speeches. She utilized traditional and popular settings in the black community to communicate the central ideas and issues of her time. In some ways Burroughs was singularly brilliant and precocious. However, she was a cultural worker *par excellence*, insisting that ideas had to be wedded to action and were without merit and value unless they served the community rather than self.

"The Slabtown District Convention" is an example of her philosophy and its importance to the larger community. The play also points to the role of women in the cultural production of religious settings. Today, churches still use plays, public speaking, and pageants as vehicles for socialization and leadership training. Her play is part of a larger tradition in which the political and cultural tensions within black communities are aired publicly, through a variety of performance traditions. Through both the content of the play and its intended audiences, Burroughs points to the importance of community gatherings such as national and regional conventions and convocations to the process of cultural production.[28] These settings have been important primary contexts in which group solidarity, cultural identity, and group values have been communicated and reaffirmed beyond the boundaries of a local community, fostering a "common sense" of national black community.

## "The Slabtown District Convention"

Part of Burroughs's description of the play signals that the play, although "A Comedy in One Act," is not simply for entertainment. "Everybody Laughs the Evening Through at Slabtown/ But everybody gets the point." The play is actually a musical comedy in which the actors are expected to reproduce the meeting of an annual district-level Baptist Convention in a deprived area of the rural South. The songs to be sung are primarily traditional Negro spirituals.

The plot is quite simple. In the setting of a district convention, the delegates arrive, they call the meeting to order, they approve the agenda of the meeting and then follow that agenda through to its conclusion. Throughout this process, Burroughs peppers the dialogue with stinging critiques highlighting leadership styles, the relationship between spirituality and social action, the relations between male and female leaders, individualism, and materialism—all pet peeves of hers. Within the convention, in a manner similar to the use of public meetings and conventions by Frances Ellen Watkins Harper in her novel *Iola LeRoy*, Burroughs includes carefully crafted discourse on the most prominent issues facing black Americans and her observation of the most effective solutions to their problems. In the discourses on social issues, Burroughs represents not only her own views, but presents for public understanding an explicitly black feminist or womanist ideology on leadership and achievement. The fact that the play's most important constructive statements concerning leadership and community relations come from the mouths of women is Burroughs's subtle way of presenting her black feminist or womanist position.

The play opens with the arrival of the delegates—delegates who represent the diverse range of classes, styles, and political orientations within southern black communities. Some of the names, particular of the clergy characters, are clearly satirical: the pastor is "Rev. Napoleon Socrates Stepandfetchit, D.D.," and the convention's visiting preacher is "Rev. J.B.H. Bigjohn, A.B., L.L.D., C.B.B."[29] As we meet the characters, Burroughs alerts us to the diverse personal styles bound together in a context of shared spiritual enthusiasm. For instance, there is the stereotypical sanctified "shouting" sister who refuses to tip adequately the young man (child) who carried her overly heavy luggage. When the delegates are seated, an agenda, which reads like the topics of concern of the National Association of Colored Women or the International Council of Women of the Darker Races, is presented. The program, after its "welcome," "response to the welcome," and president's annual address, is to include the following topics: "What Are We doing in Our Community?"; "What We Have Done for Africa"; "The Training of Children"; "An Appeal for the Redemption of Slabtown." After the delegates vote to approve the program, the play continues following the format of the approved program.

Within the rest of the play, Burroughs does several things. First, she embeds "grassroots" criticisms of religious leaders in her dialogue and in the "audience's" comments. She also lays down important conventions or normative guidelines for heroic role models among women. In the financial reports, she criticizes the self-serving behavior of the delegates and the convention hosts/hostesses that reduces the resources available for philanthropy. Burroughs places all of these criticisms and complaints in the mouths of ordinary people. In this, she does not so much create characters as communicate complaints and issues that African-American intellectuals of the early twentieth century shared concerning the church; at the same time, she utilizes the wisdom of the grassroots to offer alternative models that offer real "progress" for the race. At the climax of the play, a moving speech for the redemption of Slabtown, Burroughs offers several conclusions for both the ideology and practice of racial uplift. She affirms the centrality of education as a strategy for survival, mobility, and development. Burroughs places that strategy in the context of both external institutional constraints (racism, powerlessness, and lack of political representation) at the same time she criticizes the divisiveness of the social distance related to class and status differences. She concludes by tying the issues of public education and leadership to issues of moral education. For Burroughs, the appropriate leader works with the people, presenting appropriate models of cultural biography.[30]

## Prescriptions for Legitimate Leadership

One character in particular, Mrs. Flannelette Jonesbury, almost derails the convention before it has a chance to get started. When the president presents the motion to approve the convention program, Mrs. Jonesbury shouts "not ready" and demands assurances that people like her will be heard throughout the convention. Mrs. Jonesbury shouts:

> Not ready. I is from Sunflower. We give' that school in this district a whole barrel of herrons, and sent fo'bits to the National Secretary for books and papers, and we got them, and we is entitled to recognitions, and we ain't got it, and I'se not ready.

Mrs. Jonesbury points out that Sunflower is not included in the program. She announces, "I is tired, I is. We do de wo'k, we do de givin', you do all de bossin' and get all de hono'. We done come here to get ou' rights and we ain't goin' to let yawl budge 'til we is recognized on this program." The convention is forced to confront the issue that she raises concerning relationships between the elites and masses in the community. After much discussion of the problem, a discussion in which Mrs. Jonesbury's point is conceded, she concludes the discussion by stating, "We are goin' to put these honor seekers out of business in this very meeting."

Burroughs then uses the chaplain of the women's group as a foil for criticizing the role of the preacher. Although the preacher's discourse actually comes later, Burroughs first presents a chaplain who takes care of business by addressing very briefly and very forcefully the importance of their work in relationship to God. "He sho' ain't got not time for hypocrits." Later in the play, Rev. Bigjohn will present the annual sermon. It is full of aphorisms, irrelevancies, and malapropisms. His performance, his style, is quite moving and he delights the audience. Without saying a word directly, Burroughs presents the preacher as an anti-hero. She is arguing that there may be more illusion than reality in the intellectual leadership of many black preachers. Her critique is consistent with the issues concerning the clergy that were expressed over and over again by women's groups within the churches and within the concerns of the National Association of Colored Women. The intellectual underdevelopment of men within the clergy, the exclusion of qualified women from the clergy, and the importance of women's intellectual development and leadership regardless come through clearly in these characterizations. The chaplain with her folksy style says more in her little "opening" than the preacher—*Rev. Bigjohn!*—in his dramatic closing.

In other characterizations, Burroughs offers the criteria for prominence, leadership and influence she feels are important within the community. "Miss *Florida* Knobb" presents the welcome because, in an unveiled similarity to Mary McLeod Bethune and her introduction to the National Association of Colored Women, "her *work* has brought her to the front in our convention."[31] During the president's address, Burroughs stresses the importance of self-education as a task of leadership:

You women who don't study and keep yourselves up to date with new ideas have no business trying to lead anybody. I have gone to societies where the women have not a piece of literature of any kind. If you women do not study you cannot know, and if you do not know you cannot lead. The blind cannot lead the blind, and people who have sight are not going to let the blind lead them. There is no excuse for ignorance in this day.

The competence of women as leaders is also asserted. Burroughs presents the problem of mission societies and their relationships to their pastors as a problem in male-female relations. Complaining about the use of missionary funds to pay church debts and pastoral salaries, President Crabtree exclaims:

The Bible asks, "Will a man rob God?" I answer, yes. A man will not only rob God, but he will get the women to help him. . . . To these brethren who come to these conventions to tell the sisters what to do and how to vote, I want to say to you that you are welcome to our meetings, and if you will appreciate the courtesy extended to you by this association, you will go down from this place without any mark of displeasure upon you. But if you come here to use some of these sisters as tools . . . we want you to look to the Lord and be dismissed right now. The way some of the men carry on, it seems to me that men ought to mend their own meetings. Remember, this is a Woman's Convention and not a men's sermon show. We run our homes every day in the year and we certainly can run a little old District Convention three days in a year.

This particular discourse reflects several realities within the black community, the most important of which is the philosophy behind the black women's club movement. At the very end of the nineteenth century, Josephine St. Pierre Ruffin made it clear that a women's movement involved leadership and decision-making by women, but that it was not separatist in that the movement welcomed the participation and involvement of men. Burroughs echoes these same themes and then argues that the work of women in their homes and the organizational skills involved in running their homes equips them for independent leadership and management of their organization. Ultimately, the criteria for women's leadership is found in President Crabtree's conclusion: "We want women who can think for themselves and think straight."

Burroughs's characterizations point to several important dimensions of leadership. Legitimate leadership is based on the involvement of all those who work. It is an anti-elitist notion that confers legitimate voice on the basis of action. She subtly points out that failure to involve the grassroots will eventually lead to their exercising a veto power for progress. She also points to the legitimacy of women as leaders and affirms as more effective their less showy but no less legitimate style. Burroughs, consistent with African-American tradition and current black feminist and womanist ideologies, affirms male-female solidarity while insisting on the independence and competence of women leaders. Finally, she insists, explicitly in the discourses and implicitly in her satire of the preacher, on the importance of education as a task and requirement for leadership. Eschewing an elitist notion of education, she points to the women's local groups as appropriate forums in which this education can take place.

## Burroughs's Critique of Elitism

An important dimension of Burroughs's thinking involved the growing divisions she observed in the black community. While her central concern was with and for the mass of black working women, she believed that progress for black people and progressive change for the entire nation was dependent upon the solidarity of black people across various differences. Indeed, one of her more famous publications was a 1904 essay titled "Not Color But Character." Burroughs was distressed by the behavior of those whom she saw as seeking to assimilate themselves into the dominant culture. In a perspective similar to James Baldwin's concern about integrating into a burning house, Burroughs saw black people's slavish emulation of white America as bad for the community and for the nation as a whole. Toward the end of her life, she opposed interracial marriage for these reasons, not for reasons of basic antipathy toward white people.

Burroughs made it clear that elitism was a serious stumbling block within the community and that the future depended upon a very real solidarity across the lines of class and color. President Crabtree concluded her speech with a pointed statement reflecting Burroughs's philosophy by saying, "I recommend that no woman shall become President of a missionary society who thinks herself too good to mix with the common people and help to improve their condition."

In a portion of the play that is really the ideological point, there is a speech titled "An Appeal for the Redemption of Slabtown." After the speeches focusing on community work, Africa, and children, a character from Slabtown stands to speak. Burroughs's point is that the most critical work for racial uplift begins in local communities. She makes this point through the mouth of a character who represents the articulate and commonsense grassroots. Mrs. Betsy Lizzard speaks for Slabtown and, for Burroughs, every local community where there are black folk in need:

> I come in behalf of the schools in our district. I ain't no educated woman, but I got plenty of mother wit and common sense, and I got plenty of old fashion pride. I know the value of education in building up people and in building up communities.

Sister Lizzard goes on to talk about the consequences of ignorance (disgrace, workhouses, and jails) and the role of teachers as moral educators for the community. She then describes the kind of teacher they don't want:

> Sisters, we just got to get the right kind of moral teachers who is properly educated, for the schools. We done had enough of that kind that thinks they are better than anybody else because they got a little education. That all they have got. They ain't got no common sense and they ain't got influence enough to change a run-down community. Anybody can put on airs. *We want teachers who can lift a community.*[32]

Sister Lizzard concludes by emphasizing the fact that "we want people who'll sociate with us; show us how to live; how to organize our community work." She finishes by describing "dear Miss Georgia," one of the teachers in Slabtown, a hardworking teacher with limited resources. It is a discourse that reflects the importance of cultural (auto)biography as ideological and practical prescription:

She's what I call educated. . . . She's a model. . . . Look how she meets us in our mother's meetings; look how she speaks to us when she meets us in the road or at the store. . . . We want teachers with souls, heads, and hands dedicated to the redemption of Slabtown.

Leadership for Burroughs is clearly relational. It is also found in the way in which it empowers others to survive and to be uplifted within a community. For Burroughs, individualism is not the value she upholds. In that, she is taking sides in an African-American cultural tension between individual achievement and group solidarity that reaches back into slavery. Utilizing her perspective on Slabtown, Burroughs offers a model that gives the community primacy over the individual, a radical and anti-elitist approach to professional and community life.

### Conclusion: The Moral Basis of Womanist Counterculture

Drama or staged and scripted behavior is one means of socialization. Within Western tradition, morality plays have been effective forms of communication for ideas, particularly ideas about ideal or heroic women and men. Burroughs's work is a morality play designed to utilize the moral force of humor within African-American tradition.[33] By laughing at particularly odious adaptations to oppression, Burroughs admonishes her listeners to attempt to embrace the folks—in the words of Alice Walker, to "love the folk"[34]— within community boundaries while at the same time challenging them to change.

Ideas and role models that figure prominently among groups with historical interest in creating change are clearly the product of human interaction and human enterprise. For oppressed groups in the United States, the persistent problems of inequality create an abiding interest in promoting social change. This interest in social change, especially for African Americans, is historic. Thus the problem of social action and social ideas demands an understanding of the interpersonal processes and social contexts in which ideas become shared and collective and contribute to a culture of resistance and challenge. Several recent sociological studies and journalistic and personal accounts of the civil rights movement have acknowledged the importance of changing ideas, what McAdam called "cognitive liberation," in the development of the movement.[35] Although there is a tendency to focus on the ideas of charismatic leaders and their consequences for the movement, several recent accounts have pointed to the importance of this process of "cognitive liberation" for the larger mass of people who supported the movement.

For subordinate groups in unequal societies, social change is a constant social problem as well as a desired end. Thus there exists what Minna Caulfield has termed a "culture of resistance."[36] Because change is such a routine and constant problem, the study of social movements does not adequately grasp the sources of ideas and the production of culturally prescribed role models. Collectively held ideas and philosophies as well as strategies and agents for making change are constructed from the materials that members of groups are able to perceive and utilize from both real and ideal models within and outside of the community. External dominant models are easy to identify because both dominant and subordinate groups tend to share these. They may be positive or negative, but both groups share an understanding of what they mean. Models indigenous to oppressed communities cannot be taken for granted within the community. They must be explicitly and constantly elaborated and illustrated because these oppositional models receive no support from the dominant culture, which seeks to contain or destroy any efforts at social change. Thus, indigenous art forms such as plays and other staged presentations become settings in which these alternative worldviews are elaborated and asserted. Within Burroughs's "Slabtown," traditional settings and styles of leadership are reworked and satirized in order to communicate the importance of conscious "cultural work" as a strategy for social change.

Bernice Johnson Reagon uses the term *cultural worker* to describe members of a community who "distanc[e themselves] from the culture in which [they live] and selecting things from that culture, organiz[e] them, and us[e] them to bring back information, positions, and political stances to the community that had created the material in the first place."[37] Reagon points to the role of women as critical and "central to the continuance of many of the traditional practices" that undergirded a culture firmly oriented toward survival in hostile circumstances and tranformation of both subordinate community and dominating society. Such women were "heads of their communities, the keepers of the tradition. The lives of these women were defined by their culture, the needs of their communities, and the people they served."[38] Pointing to the dialectical nature of their role, these cultural workers performed work that was both ideological and utopian. Reagon concludes:

> There is the element of transformation in all of their work. Building communities within societies that had enslaved Africans, they and their people had to evolve in at least dual realities. These women are best seen as a central part of the community structure and process. Their role was to resolve areas of conflict and to maintain, sometimes create, an identity that was independent of a society organized for the exploitation of natural resources, people and land.[39]

Other approaches to the African-American women's experience have focused on the combined importance of racial solidarity and feminist advocacy for black women.[40] One term increasingly utilized by a range of black women scholars, especially in theological and religious studies, to describe the distinctiveness of historical experience, cultural reality, and political role is Alice Walker's coined term "womanist."[41] Walker's conceptualization implies that representations of black feminist action and criticism must be grounded in the concrete historical experiences of black women as interpreted and handed down by black women in political and community tradition—traditions that include the family and spirituality as vehicles for social change.

The complex relationship between social knowledge and human action is important for understanding the process of social change. Studies of the civil rights movement have pointed to the critical relationship between the production of consciousness and group mobilization.[42] Recent accounts have pointed to the role of women such as Ella Baker, Fannie Lou Hamer, and Septima Clark in this process.[43] Exploring Nannie Helen Burroughs's musical comedy allows us to reach back before the civil rights movement to point to the importance of women's leadership and the self-conscious (black feminist, womanist, cultural autobiographical) models they themselves offered to the community. The leadership of women is traditional in settings usually understood as the preserve of male leaders, and it is important to account both for the historical depth associated with male-female solidarity in leadership and cultural work and for the periodic separatism that emerges in women's religious and political organizations. As a result, we are able to see the extent to which styles of leadership and models of change are products of black women's agency and assertive investment in the ideological and practical transformation of their total community.

# PART 4

# CRISES, CONFRONTATIONS, AND CONFLICTS

# 9

# "Liberated to Work Like Dogs!"

## *Labeling Black Women and Their Work*

The moral value of people and groups in society is expressed through their placement in a hierarchy of social statuses. The devaluation of some people and groups in society diminishes the degree of humanity and respect they receive. We call this moral placement *labeling*. This devaluation and labeling is a power contest in the form of a stigma contest[1] and a conflict over rules, the power to make rules, and the power to enforce rules that define the situations in which people exist.[2] It is a socio-political process in which losers are forced to survive in society with diminished moral claims on goods, services, political efficacy, social honor, and respect. This chapter focuses on the labeling of black women and their work and the consequences of that labeling for black women's definition of their situation in relation to self, work, the women's movement, and activities for social change.

### Labeling and Black Women

In a pluralistic society such as the United States, diverse groups find themselves faced with a variety of survival problems in the hostile interaction contexts that labeling produces.[3] Many groups, for example the mentally ill, the physically disfigured, and gay women and men, have experienced the impact of this labeling process. Labeled groups can be stripped of their legal personhood through the misuse of medical ideology and the manipulation of cultural images and stereotypes, socially discredited and pushed out of occupational settings, or victimized by extralegal violence and various forms of discrimination.[4]

Women and racial-ethnic groups are distinctive victims of labeling. Gender and race-ethnicity, along with class, are major sources of social inequality that have deep moral meaning. These moral meanings have serious consequences. In a culture of affluence, the poor are victimized by stereotypes labeling them lazy and profligate. In a culture of white-skin dominance and privilege, dark skin is associated with danger and degradation. And in the patriarchal culture of the United States, women are imaged as fragile, ineffective, and intellectually inferior to men. All groups who fall outside the norms of affluence, whiteness, and maleness encounter demeaning and sometimes hostile stereotypes which assign them to specific cultural roles with limited and limiting expectations. The labeling of such groups is intensified when, as Albert Murray pointed out with reference to black people, social scientists codify idealized and unrealized models of white norms and institutions which have no basis in reality by which they measure the conformity or nonconformity of black people.[5]

The moral relationship of women and minorities to the labor force is probably the most dramatic indication of their powerlessness and their moral devaluation. Indeed much of the rhetoric concerning affirmative action implies a normative hierarchy of access to jobs based on the assumption that all white[6] males should be employed before white women and before black women and men. Such problems of access are further complicated by the cultural assumption that good clean people should have good clean jobs and that bad, dangerous, and dirty people should have bad, dirty, and dangerous jobs, if any jobs at all. A good job is a high paying job and, historically, when traditionally dirty jobs were redefined as "good," black people were often excluded.

In an analysis of white women's place in contemporary society, Schur argued that "under the gender system as presently constituted women are subject to an enormous array of increasingly questioned, but still dominant norms."[7] This complex of "gender norms" governs women's presentations of self, marriage and motherhood, sexuality, criminality, and occupational choice. A "normal" woman is a warm, attractive, fragile, white wife, and willing mother with a decorous sexual image who refrains from permanent participation in the labor force. Any woman who falls outside of this narrow definition suffers from the general devaluation of things female and from the punishment meted out to those who stray beyond these demeaning boundaries of normal womanhood.

For "black women in white America"[8] there is a peculiar interaction of norms and expectations governing society's evaluation of their historical role as laborers. White institutions with their power to define have pointed to black women's work roles as evidence of their deviance. As Dill pointed out, the image of black women laborers as "beasts of burden" contradicts a dominant cultural image of white women that emerges as "fragile, white, and not too bright."[9] As laborers, black women must contend with stereotypes and images which have labeled them inferior and defective females. As victims of the labeling process, black women must collectively resist these negative definitions and a negative social identity while engaged in their so-called improper conduct in order to survive. Black women, slave and free, were exempted from the usual complex of gender norms,[10] punished for that exemption, and, as laborers, assigned to bad, dirty, and dangerous work. This additional burden of labeling shapes an extremely stressful situation for black women—perhaps the most stressful in America's racial-ethnic order.

These cultural and historical distinctions foster contrasting and often conflicting definitions of social reality among black women. Such conflicting perspectives have fostered an ambivalence on the part of black women towards "women's liberation." Attempts to explain this ambivalence have focused on hostility rooted in inequality,[11] on black women's lack of consciousness,[12] on their overall disadvantage compared to white women,[13] and on black women's concern with the problems of the total black community.[14] Andolsen identified explicit conflicts between white and black feminists over the issues of rape, work, beauty, and male-female solidarity.[15] These black feminist perspectives reflect black women's overall discomfort with the prevailing ideologies of American feminism.[16]

Black women's participation in the labor force and their involvement in the public affairs of community and society, historically, are important contrasts to the experiences of white women and, in addition to their experiences as family members, primary sources of their "definition of the situation." Black women's responses to the feminist movement include hostility, ambivalence, cautious acceptance, and complex theoretical criticism. Many black women attach such great importance to the distinctiveness of their experience, they embrace Alice Walker's term *womanist* to describe their black-woman-centered definitions of self, critiques of culture, and praxis.[17] Their responses are rooted in a sense of self that is historically grounded in their consciousness concerning their labor experience and in their experience of isolation, conflict, and devaluation stemming from the negative labeling of their selves and their work.

## The Research

In order to explore black women's "definition of the situation" with reference to work and to the women's movement, data are utilized which were gathered on twenty-five black women community workers in a northern city. These women were recognized by the local black community as its full-time activists and advocates. These women also worked as appointed and elected politicians and human service professionals. Each participant was recommended by members of the community as women who had "worked hard for a long time for change in the black community." They had also been similarly recognized by the black press at least eight years prior to the commencement of the study. Each woman provided a taped open-ended interview averaging two hours in length but ranging from forty-five minutes to six hours. The interviews explored childhood, educational, occupational, and

cultural experiences with special reference to their careers in community activities and their daily work lives—work lives that were thoroughly integrated
with their work for social change and community survival.[18]

Although the study did not focus primarily on the women's attitudes and
feelings toward the feminist movement, the women voluntarily expressed
their feelings when asked about their perception of the problems that contemporary black women face and about their experiences working with white
people. Additionally, women provided perspectives on their work and labor
histories during the narrative section of the interview in response to the question, "Tell me about yourself."

Although the sample is small, these women's perspectives are significant.
They are the most admired women in the local black community, and in
spite of their visibility and public honor, they represent the spectrum of the
black experience, in their class, ethnic, regional, and status origins. In spite of
their current white-collar, managerial, middle-class occupations and their great
prestige, their social networks involve the entire black community. Two of
the women were in their eighties and retired from full-time paid work. The
twenty-three younger women, ages thirty to sixty, were employed full time
in a variety of human service agencies where they integrated fully their roles
as professionals, advocates, and activists in order to advance the economic,
political, and social interests of the black community. Their definition of
"the black community" included not only the diverse, segregated, disproportionately poor urban community in Hamptonville (a pseudonym) but
also "wherever black people can be found" and "people of African descent."
All of these women were married at some point in their lives and had worked
full-time during the child-rearing and childbearing years. Although two
women were childless, they defined the importance of their work with reference to the community's children in precisely the same terms as those women
who were mothers.

## The Definition of the Situation

Perspectives on self, work, and the women's movement were expressed
with reference to the social and labor histories of black women. A typical
statement usually pointed to both history and contemporary reality: "I guess
I have to think about what I am and what I am is a black woman, living in
America, . . . and all that means historically and realistically." Realistically
and historically, the meaning of being a "black woman living in America" is
tied to the social history of black women in the world of work and political
conflict. These women's assessments of their situation demand an examination of the historical problems of black women and their work outside the
home for explanations of their attitudes toward the women's movement.
Although much of the concern of the feminist movement has been with
work, the movement has not spoken loudly to the conditions created for

black women through the interaction of their color, gender, and labor history, and the society's labeling of black women and their assertive management of their difficulties.

Black women have had a higher labor force participation rate at consistently lower wage and status levels than white women. This work has been a response largely to the demands for survival. The society's response to this work has been to generate a set of negative images and stereotypes that focus largely on the black woman laborer. Concrete expressions of this deviantizing or labeling are found in such labels as "Mammy," "Sapphire," and "matriarch" by which black women are depicted as bad women and dangerous mothers. Such labeling structurally and ideologically isolates black women from the experiences and problems of other women. The nature of black women's work, particularly domestic work,[19] is such that non-black women are often implicated in the deviantizing process. The moral isolation of labeling represents a victimization distinct from that experienced by white women. Although isolated from white women, the same process prompts black women to integrate themselves into the public affairs and social problems of the black community and fosters a tradition of political activism and autonomous women's movements. As Becker pointed out:

> Members of organized deviant groups of course have one thing in common: their deviance. It gives them a sense of common fate, of being in the same boat. From a sense of common fate, from having to face the same problems, grows a deviant subculture: a set of perspectives and understandings about what the world is like and how to deal with it, and a set of routine activities based on those perspectives. Membership in such a group solidifies a deviant identity.[20]

Keeping in mind that the "deviance" of black women is conferred upon them by the larger society, the realities of their work and community lives demand that they develop and communicate "a set of perspectives and understandings about what the world is like and how to deal with it."

Black women do have a distinct set of perspectives and understandings about the world concerning their social image, their work and contemporary feminism. The perspectives of these community workers are important because they shape and are shaped by the attitudes and concerns of the larger community. They sit on boards, attend meetings, and work in organizations and agencies which are highly visible. They are vitally connected to all segments of the black community and are crucial links to the realization of both community survival needs and aspirations for social change. As visible participants in all movements affecting black community life, these women are occupational, political, and social role models to other black women and men at all socio-economic levels of the black community. The honor and prestige accorded these women within the black community (and occasionally outside of it) places them in the position of trendsetters and contributors to the ideological perspectives and practical strategies extant within the black community at any given time.

Community workers volunteered perspectives on their relationship to the feminist movement in response to my question, "What are some of the most important problems that black women face today?" The women consistently referred to their powerlessness in the face of the racism that dictated the terms of employment of the black community in general and black women in particular. They emphasized the degraded and coerced circumstances of some of their past jobs, the problems of black family life, and the negative definitions attached to black women's working. They spoke plainly of the isolation that encouraged black women to develop an interdependent approach to their problems. Observing that adjustment to the problems of the labor force was a focal concern of white women, community workers insisted they had already adjusted. They were more concerned with black women's structural isolation at the bottom of the labor market and the emotional and social isolation that stemmed from the negative labels attached to black women's economic roles.

One elected official summarized the overall theme of community workers' perspectives on liberation and work. She stated flatly, "We've had the opportunity as black women to be forever liberated—to go out and work like dogs!" During her interview, she described her own work history. Her sense of working "like a dog" came from her early jobs in factories. She described her first job where she refused to be treated "like an animal." She said:

> Well, I remember that when I first went to work . . . right after the Second World War, . . . I was working in a meat packing factory and started smoking quite young. They would give us breaks, but I would get tired. I'd do my work but I'd go in the Ladies Room and have a cigarette. And the floor lady came telling me to stop doing it. Well I knew she was doing the same thing, so she'd say "stop" to me and I said to her, "You stop, and I'll stop." And I had no business saying that . . . but I just felt that if she had those kind of privileges, why couldn't I. And I didn't have to sit there like an animal! But I had a right to get up and rest myself if I was producing what I was supposed to produce.

After marriage and her first child in the early 1950s, she left the meat packing factory and sought a job in the garment industry. She encountered difficulties because "jobs were scarce":

> I went looking from place to place, for a job and everybody kept telling me that I didn't have any experience. I went into this one particular place and the man told me you don't have any experience. And I turned around and looked him dead in the eye and said, "How can I ever get any if nobody hires me!" and was walking out the door. So as I started

out, he said, "Hey, com'ere! You want a job?" I said, "Why do you think I came in here?" [He said,] "OK, I'll hire you."

She described her general feistiness in the labor force as the foundation for her public involvement. Her basic philosophy asked, "Why can't I do it?" when faced with a new opportunity. She said, "And I never hesitate to apply." Always involved in community activities as a volunteer, by the 1960s she said, "I was ready to come out of the factory." Another woman with similar experiences described how she fought and threatened legal action in order to gain admission to a clerical training program. After criticizing clerical work as demeaning, she explained her struggle to end her long career in factories by stating, "I was sick and tired of getting my hands dirty."

Regardless of their class origins, the women all complained about dirty work such as domestic service, sweat shops, and factories that they or their close friends had endured. Some complained openly about white female supervisors and employers and vividly recounted instances of direct conflict with them in early jobs. One elderly woman instituted a program in her women's club to teach fellow domestic workers how to be assertive about receiving the agreed-upon wages for their day's work. They all saw the problem of black women as the "overall level of work." One professional woman with middle-class origins said:

> The level of work is something that is a problem to black women. We are still found to be in the domestic jobs. . . . The other is if it is not domestic work that one is involved in, it is work that is considerably low paying.

Not only did community workers cite their disadvantaged structural position, but they described the injury caused by the labels attached to their work and their economic contributions to the families. The image of the matriarch was particularly burdensome isolating them from the larger society and from many black men who saw them as rivals and embarrassments to "the Race." A child welfare worker related her perception of black women's problems, saying:

> A really big problem for most of the black women I know is trying to find out where we fit in the social system, . . . particularly when the matriarchal system has been so stereotyped—trying to get out of the stereotypes. And getting help, being so isolated. . . . We've had to lean on each other a lot and that has made it more difficult for us to relate to any black males. . . . It's vicious a cycle.

Many other women also observed this conflict with black men and that it stemmed both from the misidentification of black women as matriarchs and from the specialized pressure racism placed on black men. They also complained that there seemed to be fewer black men, especially fewer who were sympathetic to the problems of black working women.

The social and emotional isolation from black men was cited as a recent problem. The two elder community workers, both widows, were concerned and puzzled by their observations of increasing conflict between black men and women and of a change for the worse in the situation of the black working women and their families. These elders had successfully combined paid work, long marriages, and child rearing. One had been a household domestic and the founder of numerous clubs and programs, some of which addressed the problems of household domestics directly. The other had been a successful businesswoman—at one time the owner of the largest black business in the Hamptonville metropolitan area. Both had been distinguished executives in the local NAACP. One said:

> I think a good many of the young [black] women of today have a hard time finding men who have the same ideas that they have and seem to want to cooperate with them enough. . . . I've noticed that and that's why a lot of them have broken marriages so much; most of the time I've found that it's been the women that are most progressive and, it seems, want to do more in making a home and preparing for the future.

The community workers' perspectives were linked to their present reality, their personal work histories, and their understandings concerning black women's history. Although two thought incorrectly that black women were doing better than black men, they all expressed a sense of victimization stemming from inequity, isolation, and the status degradation fostered by negative images and stereotypes. One woman shared the outline of a lecture that she had presented to black professional women. One prominent topic heading was, "Labels—aggressive, domineering, hardnosed." Another topic, referring especially to those black women "wearing two hats" as breadwinners and parents, described black women's victimization through labeling in similar terms. Describing their situation as "very difficult" she described the effects of labeling:

> You're footing two bills—being known as too aggressive and being professional and not being warm enough and womanly enough. . . . Black women perceived by the total community at large are the victims of a lot of superficial values of the society—more than white women, more than white men, more than black men or other minorities—because at this point [white and other minority] cultures dictate that [white and other minority] women take the position they have taken.

She insisted that the negative perception of black women as different came from black men as well as the dominant culture. Addressing labeling as "that syndrome," she concluded, "I just think that black women who [must] break out of that syndrome are beset with problems from 'Jumpstreet'."

The most prominent community worker openly criticized the ideology of the matriarchy in her discussion of problems confronting the black community. She said:

> When I first started to work in the NAACP, for example, . . . there was a certain kind of togetherness that we don't feel now. . . . We have allowed ourselves to become divided by white people's philosophies such as the matriarchal society—you know, black women have all the power [over] black men. . . . We've allowed all these divisions it seems to me to interfere in a way it didn't seem to me they interfered [before].

She perceived the problem of labeling in black women's lives and also recognized it as a problem in the black community's internal organization. She felt that the labeling of black women as matriarchs had increased the amount of disrespect in the political community and had undermined black women's ability to contribute to the efforts of the entire community without conflict. She was particularly conscious of the external pressure of the labels. She said:

> Well I see a real need for black women to do some kind of united [action]. I think black women have severe problems that have been put on us. . . . There's this put-down constantly of black women. I think of the little girls because . . . you look at the TV and I said, "What can little girls think of when they look at TV with this long flowing hair?" The image that's been put out there is not going to be happening for black women. . . . I think that black women have a problem in the kind of image that's been portrayed about them . . . that we've been cut off and set aside and kind of isolated. That there are certain myths about how black women can proceed.

She concluded with an insistence that black women of all age and occupational and professional statuses shared a common problem that required a collective response. She said, "I just think that it would be good if black women had some way of getting together across age lines, across professional lines and see that they have a common problem dealing with the kinds of put-downs."

The inequities in the labor force and the difficulties black women were facing in their communities were part of the consciousness with which black women viewed the concerns of the women's movement. One woman, who viewed the movement as important but problematic, argued that the movement seemed to be preoccupied with "some of the fluff." They were particularly unsympathetic to the problems of affluent white women who were seeking opportunities to enter the labor force. One woman, an elected official said, "I'd like to be able to stay at home and just get bored and want to go look for a job." There was, however, an overall rejection of simply aspiring towards the luxury of staying home. One woman actually quoted Linda LaRue[21] when she warned of the "trap of 'Miss Ann's warmed over throne.'" There was little sympathy, however, for those women who were actually denigrating the homemaker role.

One professional, who was very much involved in several national black women's organizations, provided some extended criticism of black women's relationship to the feminist movement. She said:

> I hate to keep using the same words but we've got to straighten out in our own minds who we are and what we're about. Some of us I think have gotten a little off track in being with quote unquote "women's liberation" in the narrowest sense—I'm talking about the middle class white world's interpretation of women's liberation. We need indeed to be about the business of the equal rights for all women. I really don't want to low-rate that part of it at all but some of that other esoteric intellectualization! I'd hate for us to get too far off in that ball game because we've got too much work to do within our own black communities, within our own families, within our own relationships with each other and if we've got extra energy we've got to invest it in our own communities. Now, for example, that business of reading skills: I think we'd better be about that than worrying too much about whether we're M-S or M-R-S or M-I-S-S.

Community workers recognized white America's moral evaluation of them as morally dangerous women and deviant mothers and of their work as dirty, degrading, and deviant. They also perceived this labeling as divisive for the whole community. This recognition when tied to their consciousness of black women's history fueled their criticism of the dominant society and its white feminist movement. For black women, the labeling of their persons and their work was the crowning blow of a history of economic exploitation, political victimization, and cultural assault.

### "Even in Slavery Times": History and Consciousness

The problems these women identify are historical in scope and they are conscious of that history. They refer to it and their sense of history is part of the definition of the situation. Work has been the defining element in black women's experience and the stereotypes with which these women feel battered are tied to their work history.

That work history includes slavery and rural southern peonage, experiences that institutionalized the "mammy" and "the bad black woman."[22] "Mammy" and "the loose black woman" were stock characters of the antebellum South and "the loose black woman" emerged as "Jezebel."[23] These stereotypes were much larger than reality.[24] Northern migration, urbanization, the civil rights movement, and black demands for empowerment modified these images but did not erase them. The newer images became the "castrating force of Sapphire"[25] and "the matriarchy."[26] Barbara Christian identified "the sapphire and the matriarch" as "two variations on the mammy image."[27] However, these images, both direct assaults on black working women, became publicly institutionalized during the 1950s and the poverty policy debates of the late 1960s. These debates became the vehicle through which the deviant image of black women was widely publicized and communicated through the culture, making the stereotypical images of black women more intractable and culturally pervasive than that of men.[28] The life and times of these stereotypes are tied to the role of black women laborers at specific times in the history of the United States.

As slaves black women participated fully in rural and urban work forces, beginning their history with 100 per cent labor force participation. Because of their sex, they were burdened with additional tasks as mothers and wives. Women who refrained from bearing children were often punished or sold, so the role of working mother was inescapable. The plantation system, with its preponderance of men, actually encouraged slave women's fertility resulting in one of the highest fertility rates at that time.[29] Slave women feigned sickness and weakness in order to prolong periods of lying-in.[30] As working wives and mothers, they confronted limited choices of survival strategies. Less than twenty percent of the runaways were women and the more famous female fugitives ran with their families or, as in the case of Harriet Tubman, had no children.[31]

One community worker pointed to these precise historical realities in describing the contemporary problems of black women. She said:

> Even in slavery times, the man could leave but the woman had to stay. Not only stay but take care of the children and the work. Very few black women would leave their children to that situation. And the same thing is true now, we still can't leave; we still have to stay in the struggle but I think we've been about the struggle at a most basic level and our realism and our pragmatism reflect that; and we still have ideals and we still have *lofty* ideals which we carry on in the form of culture bearers.

Her perspective was reflected in Angela Davis's analysis of black women's roles in the slave community—a role that involved the integration of "toiling under the lash from sun-up to sun-down" with the care of family yet "annulled as woman" so that she could "function as slave."[32]

This life stood in stark contrast to that of white women, who were deemed to be the quintessential definition of womanhood. The stereotypes that stripped black women of their feminine humanity became ideologies by which slave masters justified their sexual exploitation of slave women and further intensifying the "Jezebel," "bad," or "loose" image. Ironically this immoral woman also raised the master's children. As the large sexless mammy, black women's nurturant and biological capacities were exploited by the planter class, not only for the sake of their children's material welfare but also for the ideological defense of slavery. Although the actual number of "mammies" was small, they were the ideological and material base for the pedestal on which the planter class placed upper-class southern white womanhood. The *ideal* of white womanhood became *reality* where "mammy" existed.

Sociologically, "mammies" were imaged as the highest ranking slaves on plantations sharing the closest and most sentimental relationships with the master and mistress. They were invested with a false image of power. As deviant mother—a corollary of the "myth of the bad black woman," the white children's needs took precedence over the needs of these slave women's own. Masters used this reality to demonstrate the good will and love present within the "peculiar institution," and to negate the black woman's humanity and to emphasize the slave's lack of commitment to the family. This powerful image, what Du Bois called "a perversion of motherhood" in response to southerners' attempts to erect a bronze statue to "mammy" in Washington D.C., loomed large in popular culture.[33] This physically large woman remained the only role for which a black woman had every received an academy award [until Whoopi Goldberg received one in 1990].[34]

The "mammy" with her illusion of power performed all of the drudgery of the female world. The tasks of housekeeping and child care became "mammy's." Her white mistress was projected as dependent upon mammy's loyalty, devotion, and skills. The image of "mammy's" competence and her mistress's dependence was based on another dimension of deviant womanhood, strength—physical, emotional, and spiritual strength. Emotional stability and physical strength were required for capable management of mansions and planter class children. Emotional instability, vapors, and fragility were "privileges" reserved for upper-class women. By doing all of the dirty work of womanhood, mammy's labor supported and enhanced the ideal woman.

According to Everett Hughes, the moral enhancement of a profession and its exercise of power often depend on its ability to pass on its dirty, routinized, boring, and least rewarding tasks to workers under their control. These repugnant tasks are supposed to elevate the status of those lower in the hierarchy.[35] Mammy contributed to the elevation of white women in a similar way. The dirty work of elite home and child care were passed along to black women, creating a cultural milieu in which it was unseemly for white women to do it. Christian pointed to the implications of this arrangement:

> When the black woman first began to experience and understand the contradictions about motherhood among the southern planters, she must have been truly appalled. . . . [T]hat the planters could relegate

the duties of motherhood, a revered and honored state, to a being supposedly lower than human, reveals their own confusion about the value of motherhood. That they could separate spiritual aspects of motherhood, which they acknowledged in their religion, from the physical aspects and give the duties of childrearing to a "subhuman" gives us some indication about the value they placed on women's work.[36]

The enhancement of the status of white women depended upon the mistress's passing her dirty work on to black women. By raising "mammy" above the rest of the slaves and conferring upon her the ambiguous privilege of white women's dirty work, the white woman's status was protected, purified, and dignified. The black woman's status became the dialectical opposite of the white woman's.[37] Ultimately, the ideological stability of slavery rested on the perception of black women as deviants—bad and dangerous women and mothers who became the ideological centerpieces in the cultural institution of American racism.

An irony of slavery was the relative social equality between black women and men. This social arrangement elicited another set of stereotypes assaulting both women and men. After slavery, black women continued to work in large numbers, by the turn of the century at two and one half times the rate of white women and this work was targeted as further evidence of racial inferiority.[38]

As the labor force demanded more female labor,[39] white women increased their labor force participation and black women continued their participation at higher rates with more continuity and at lower economic and prestige levels. Every upward shift in the demand for female labor placed white women into job levels higher than those held by black women. This occupational pattern reflected social patterns of the women's world established during slavery. Black women, as deviant women, were denied access to many of the "female" occupations, especially those such as secretary and department store clerk where feminine image was involved. One community worker described her early job as the "first" black department store clerk in downtown Hamptonville as evidence of the problem. Anecdotes, such as that told by labor executive Addie Wyatt, indicate that black women, because of their "unfeminine" image, were occasionally sent to better paying male jobs. Addie Wyatt had applied for a job as a secretary and was sent to work in meat packing, a higher paying men's job that led to her achieving the rank of vice president of the international union. Such incidents point to the importance of employers' moral evaluations of black women. The rigidity of white over black in the women's labor market is so evident that equality between black and white women "is likely to take at least several generations to attain" and "one might well predict continuing discontent with American society among black women."[40] Although the negative stereotypes persist, black women do not retreat from the labor force. Within this context of economic inequality and moral denigration, organized black women, as is evident in the present sample, maintain a high level of race pride, political activism, and community uplift.

### "Lifting as We Climb": A Response to Labeling and Institutional Racism

Black women's response to their labeling, historically, has been organized, public, and national, "the first national articulation of black prophetic practices . . . [p]redating the National Urban League and the National Association for the Advancement of Colored People."[41] Black women organized the National Federation of Afro-American women partly in response to insults published in the white press calling black women prostitutes and liars as an attempt to undercut Ida B. Wells's anti-lynching efforts. The Federation merged with the Colored Women's League, to form the National Association of Colored Women after the two groups had held their 1896 national meetings in Washington, D.C.[42] These organizations provided the foundation for black women's energetic organizing on a variety of political, economic, and cultural issues and levels. Later when northern migration and urban politics had placed civil rights on the federal agenda, black women, under the leadership of Mary McLeod Bethune in 1935, brought these organizations together with many others under the umbrella of the National Council of Negro Women in 1935.

These efforts consistently stressed the problems of "the Race" and the special problems of black women at work and at home. Although this was an era of white feminism, the color line and the negative moral evaluations that white women themselves placed on black women fanned racial antagonisms. White suffragists exacerbated these antagonisms with their accommodation to lynch law, particularly, and racism generally.[43]

Prompted by the assaultive labels, organized black women concerned themselves with lynching, peonage labor, prisons, unionization, professional and industrial education, and many other problems affecting both men and women. They initiated surveys of black working women, sent organizers into areas with no clubs, organized economic cooperatives and mutual aid associations, and developed social services for poor black women and youth. In response to degrading moral attributions and stereotypes, the women worked to erase the situations among black women that fed these stereotypes. This meant organizing across economic and status boundaries. Educated black women did what feminist Audre Lorde identified as the most liberating thing one can do with one's privilege—acknowledge it in order to make it available for wider use.[44] They organized many clubs to include "women in industry"— factory workers, laundresses, and household domestics, and not just educated white-collar workers and professionals.[45]

Such inclusion resulted in the leadership training of women of all social classes. One elderly community worker was a former household domestic whose newspaper column during the 1940s focused on the club activities of black women in Hamptonville and its surrounding communities. At the time of her interview, she was the president of a club affiliated with the National Association of Colored Women whose projects and programs focused on black working women. She described the importance of her first "community service club":

> Well I learned a lot about leadership and all that and how to lead a club and how to deal with people and I was president two or three different times; and helped to write the by-laws, those kinds of things. And you learn what different people are like too—different women. . . . We had some women who were very very deprived and some of us who weren't quite as deprived were able to help them a great deal by example and how to really have the proper decorum and everything that some of them didn't have. And some of their habits changed, particularly those who would drink a little too much and use profane language a little too much. They learned that that just wasn't the thing to do and they'd curb themselves and they became a little bit better oriented. All those things were done, and it wasn't done for any sort of lessons or anything that anybody would put a person through. But they learned from association, from other kinds of women; they could see the difference and some of them became wonderful [leaders] and some of them couldn't understand any kind of parliamentary procedure and they started to learn things and after a while they became leaders. . . . So we had a wonderful club.

Examples like this illustrate Du Bois's observation that the distinguishing feature of the black women's club movement was the creation of networks and connections throughout the black community.[46] Black women understood the implications of their organizing for the entire community. They asserted that by working together for the material and ideological uplift of black women who were on the bottom, then it would follow that the whole race would rise. The National Association of Colored Women's motto, "Lifting as We Climb," reflected this belief. The activities of black women in the organizations of the National Council of Negro Women as well as their activities in the Young Women's Christian Association (YWCA) continued the basic philosophy of the National Association of Colored Women with a more professionalized political strategy that included lobbying and Congressional testimony.[47] Several community workers held volunteer and paid positions with the YWCA and underscored this historical importance. During the Depression and on through World War II, organized black women continued their concerns for southern rural women, urban women workers, domestic workers, professional women, the economic and social problems of the black family, birth control, juvenile delinquency, women and children under colonialism, and apartheid.

One can argue that organized black women are ahead of white women in their concerns, perhaps one of the reasons many black women prefer Alice Walker's term *womanist*.[48] These movements recognize that black women's special problems are tied to the economic, social, and political problems of an entire community. Black women recognize clearly that the negative stereotypes of them are tied to ideological assaults on black men. In spite of these labels, and perhaps partly because of them, black women work aggressively in the public affairs of the black community, using their autonomous organizations as a springboard to community-wide leadership. The formation and growth of these movements demonstrate that black women are not antagonistic to the ideals of contemporary feminism. Instead one must point to the labeling of black women and their work as that which isolated their potential contributions. This was indeed the case for many community workers in Hamptonville.

### "First and Foremost, Powerlessness": Debunking the Matriarchy

Community workers felt most abused by the label "matriarch." As part of an inept analysis of the historical role of black women, the "matriarch" legitimated the Sapphire stereotype in an unprecedented way. According to a report issued by the Johnson administration, black women violated the norms in "a society that presumes male leadership in public and private affairs. The arrangements of society facilitate such leadership and reward it."[49] In the process of addressing the problems of black poverty, family structure, and male unemployment, black women and their work became part of the black problem. It was implied that black male employment problems were exacerbated by the labor force participation of black women and that efforts to "insure equal employment opportunity for Negroes . . . have redounded mostly to the benefit of Negro women, and may even have accentuated the comparative disadvantage of Negro men."[50] Many analyses, especially Jacqueline Jackson's, demonstrate that the disadvantage of black men is purely relative to white men and that there is *no* black male disadvantage in the labor force *relative to black women*.[51]

The "matriarch" label undermined black women within their own communities. Pauli Murray described the consequences of the matriarch label at a more general level. She noted that *Ebony*, in a special issue on black women in 1966:

felt it necessary to include a full-page editorial to counter the possible effect of articles by women contributors. After paying tribute to the Negro woman's contributions in the past, the editorial reminded *Ebony*'s readers that "the past is behind us," that "the immediate goal of the Negro woman today should be the establishment of a strong family unit in which the father is the dominant person," and that the Negro woman would do well to follow the example of the Jewish mother "who pushed her husband to success, educated her male children first, and engineered good marriages for her daughters." The editors also declared that the career woman "should be willing to postpone her aspirations until her children, too, are old enough to be on their own."[52]

Some community workers in Hamptonville, heads of their own agencies, were asked, as one administrator told it, "to step aside and let a man take over. It looks bad for 'the Race.'"

Black women responded to this label, "matriarch," and its implications, by producing a spate of literature criticizing erroneous assumptions concerning black women's advantage in the labor market. They also explored the black female experience with reference to black men in order to correct distortions, battle myths, and to provide self-affirmation in spite of the labeling.[53] Inez Reid, in a national sampling of ideologies at the grass roots level, identified a deep discontent among black women with the matriarch label. Many felt that the label presented black women to black men in white middle-class terms and they repeatedly underscored black women's lack of access to black men. Writers and community workers alike emphasized the importance of black women defending themselves. As the white feminist movement was beginning, black women were forced to prove their femininity, to examine seriously their culpability in black male "emasculation," and yet at the same time to maintain their position in the civil rights/black power movements and in their communities. As Toni Cade [Bambara] described the situation:

> Unfortunately quite a few of the ladies have been so browbeaten in the past with the black Matriarch stick that they tend to run, leap, fly to the pots and pans, the back row, the shadows, eager to justify themselves in terms of ass, breasts, collard greens just to prove that they are not the evil, ugly, monsters of tradition.[54]

One community worker saw the matriarchy label as an extension of the southern myth of free white men and free black women. She challenged this label, insisting:

> The black woman is never a threat to a white man no matter what position she holds, and no matter how many of us come together in a group. . . . We can't define black womanhood . . . it's been defined for us [referring to the "matriarchy."] Black womanhood means first and foremost powerlessness. I think that that myth that the white male and the black female are the only ones who are free is manifestly absurd because you can't be free if you're powerless and there's no question that we're the most powerless group in the culture, in the society today. We

can't even protect our own children and that is the ultimate test of powerlessness as far as I'm concerned. We can't even protect our own children.

Ultimately, the designation of an activity in society as deviant is a political act. The status of a deviant group, or the effectiveness of a society's label, is determined through political conflict. Some viewed the matriarchy thesis as a purely political device that blamed the victims and weakened the national black community's political organizing by creating hostility towards black women.[55] In light of the history of black women's political movements, particularly their visibility as lobbyists and advocates in Washington, D.C. through the Women's Bureau of the Labor Department, it is not unreasonable to hypothesize a political motive in identifying black women as the matriarchs crippling the economic and political aspirations of black men. Labeling black women and their work a matriarchy intensified the moral devaluation that black women faced historically. At the height of change and transition within black communities, black women faced the need for a time-consuming and politically deflective response to this intensified labeling.

## Confronting the Politics of Isolation

Labeling also separates and isolates "bad" people from "good" people. For black women this isolation is heightened at the beginning of a new women's movement. Labeling adds to existing political and economic gaps, and undermines much of the potential for a racially unified women's movement. The labeling of black women and their work also isolates them, as black men view them through the prism of white definitions. Such isolation and conflict diverts black women's critical energies away from the hierarchies of injustice in the overall society. One community worker, an educator critical of the matriarch label and involved with white women's groups described the problems. She said:

There *are* white people in the world who understand the limitations of the dominant culture as it has manifested itself: . . . women in women's groups or women's movements who want to do serious studies about black women, and how black women are at the bottom, and [these white women] associate the socio-economic structure and all of that, [white women] who want black women to join the fight against sexism and see that there's no natural coalition unless you see those same [white] people fighting racism over here. They [white women] can't leave that [the fight against racism] to us and capitalize on the benefits and privileges of being white while still hoping that some of those [black] women will come in and help them fight their battles with their men which essentially a lot of that comes down to for some women.

That conflict with "their men" makes Black women cautious about applying the white feminist critique to Black men. One community worker cautioned:

"Many of our men labor under anti-African definitions of themselves and they can be as sexist as anybody and some of our internal structures reflect that including our families. . . . I think it's true that while black men suffer from racism and classism, that we [black women] suffer from racism, classism, and sexism, even within the group and that's a problem. [But] I don't think black men are the first people we need to direct our attention to."

In spite of their separation and critique of feminism, some middle-class black professional women did form black women's feminist organizations.[56] While disagreeing with white definitions of feminist issues, community workers maintained close working relationships with white women's organizations. Aware of the isolating effects of labeling, they also pointed to the practical considerations in explaining their involvement. One elected official argued, "We cannot permit the white woman to control the women's movement and to set the agenda. [Black women] have got to be in it in order to help direct that agenda."

The position of black women in society and their relationship to white feminism cannot be understood without reference to the moral isolation of labeling. Pointing to the structural isolation black women face in the job market, Lewis was optimistic about the feminist potential of black women, particularly as they face more and more sex discrimination. However, community workers and the organizational history of which they are a part demonstrate that black women espouse feminist or womanist ideologies within their organizations and movements and combine this with a collective historical self-consciousness in response to labeling. It is not only the structural isolation in the economic system that blunts black women's participation, but it is also the moral isolation of labeling.

As part of their response to labeling, black women examine every white organization critically. Their community and church experiences teach them to cherish their autonomy. My own data on black women community workers show that these women participate in a wide range of organizations simultaneously: labor, public educational groups, health organizations, traditional civil rights organizations, religious groups, churches, professional associations, party politics, and radical political organizations. These multiple affiliations are pragmatic and address acute survival problems all black people face. Community workers as women experienced in the work of the civil rights movement, local community organizations, and autonomous black women's organizations, are realistically critical of white feminist organizations. Until black women are freed from the deviant labels that are ideologies of domination and racism, they will continue to keep a cautious distance from many aspects of contemporary feminism.

Isolated by their conflicts with labels, black women are still forced to expend additional energy convincing the black community that their "deviant" contributions of time, money, energy, talent, and leadership are not a threat to the credibility and advancement of "the Race." These intragroup strains and stresses exacerbate the pre-existent economic and political antagonisms. The labeling of black women is a function of a society that is both racist and sexist in not only its institutional arrangements but also its moral hierarchy, placing additional burdens on black women. The labeling of black women and their work represents an additional barrier to be removed before a truly united and integrated movement for total human liberation can be achieved.

# 10

# The "Loves" and "Troubles"
# of African-American Women's Bodies

## The Womanist Challenge to Cultural Humiliation
## and Community Ambivalence

As part of the racial oppression that African-American people experience, cultural humiliation based on beauty norms has serious implications for the self-esteem of African-American women and men.[1] Such a concern may seem trivial in the face of drugs, violence, poverty, and social isolation, but many current social problems are often tied to low self-esteem or self-hatred. Self-hatred or damage and brokenness to our inner visions make it impossible for us to make and share effective "liberating visions"[2] for our community and our world. Self-hatred may be one of the deepest sources of conflict and turmoil within the African-American community. This may be especially true concerning women and their bodies. Damage and fractures to our inner visions surrounding women and their bodies show themselves when we are confronted with public events such as the Mike Tyson/Desiree Washington case or the Vanessa Williams/Miss America scandal. By focusing on that dimension of Alice Walker's womanist idea/ideal that emphasizes love of self, others, and the life-affirming aspects of community life, I hope to show the importance of confronting this cultural humiliation and its consequences within ourselves.

Cultural humiliation assaults black women by undermining their capacities for self-love. A womanist approach to life and living underscores the importance of self-love for celebrating and resisting in a hostile society. The loves and troubles of black women's bodies represent a very narrow dimension of experience that has accumulated a weighty cultural burden. In attempting to grasp this weighty cultural burden, I first try to show that a major component of racial oppression—cultural humiliation—is highlighted by the paradoxes and conflicted inner visions surrounding embodied experience, the loves and the troubles. I then explore the roots of the "loves" and "troubles" in terms of the importance and power of experience. I attempt to juxtapose these experiences with the power of society to insinuate itself at the roots of our trouble. I conclude by focusing on the truly revolutionary nature of the challenge Alice Walker presents through her womanist idea. The ethical challenge to live out the mandates of love in a hateful and hate-filled world is a constant struggle and demands an attitude of resistance that must be embraced through what bell hooks calls "a process of critical remembering."[3] It is such a process, most often seen in the testifying of religious experience, that transforms individual victories over stumbling blocks and the destructive fury of society into prophetic resources for the larger community. Such resources, I hope to show, are essential for the kind of ministries necessary to empower and equip African-American women for full resistance to dehumanization and for full participation in the project of a truly humane society and world.

## Cultural Humiliation and Conflicted Inner Visions

Complexity and diversity are the foundations of any truths to be told about African-American women in the United States. Both Alice Walker[4] and Mary Church Terrell have observed that African-American women collectively come from a "flower garden" full of "universalist" potential with families of people ranging through "brown, pink, and yellow, and our cousins are white, beige, and black." Black people generally and black women most specifically are arrayed across the entire spectrum of female difference. The experience of these differences enables women to offer insights on life that never take so-called female privileges for granted. African-American women are also able to assess the underside of the cultural privileges associated with physical appearance and body size in a way that women of other ethnic groups, particularly white women, are not challenged to do. While sometimes the physical differences among African-American women have been a source of conflict and tension, my own experience, my observations of politically active African-American women, and my intense study of recent public events persuade me that conflict with one another is not the most critical problem African-American women face.[5] The paradoxes of being African American and female, of crossing an entire spectrum of embodied experience, and of being able to compare the experiences of different body types, sometimes within one's own family, may have contributed more to women's solidarity and critical empathy than to their division.

The historically conditioned responses of white people to the differences among African-American women and their bodies have been more of a problem and reflect more accurately the sexist and racist pathologies of American culture. If the responses of white people were the only problems, things would be easy. The racialized sexism and the sexualized racism of the larger society have elicited a wide range of responses among black people themselves as they have constructed strategies for survival and politics of resistance and liberation. As a result, there is within the African-American community a history of ambivalence about issues of physical appearance.

This ambivalence may be the source of the most critical "troubles" that are stumbling blocks on the pathway toward a healthy self-love. The stumbling blocks of ambivalence are found everywhere. Women across the full spectrum of African-American experience, from the lightest to the darkest and from the largest to the smallest, contribute to a fund of knowledge that highlights the paradoxes, the loves and the troubles, of existing in a black and female body in America. In spite of the high premium placed on culturally exalted images of white female beauty and the comedic exploitation that surrounds the large black woman, many African-American women know that the most respected physical image of black women, within and outside of the community, is that of the large woman. Although it is respected, it is a culturally deviant image that is not necessarily loved. It is an image of power in a community where women need to be fortified and empowered. Yet some of the most powerless women in the community struggle with overweight and its unhealthy consequences. It is an asexual image[6] that sometimes permits escape from the constant harassment and sexual aggression, accurately called "hitting on," that disproportionately pervade the lives of those black women who most approximate white cultural ideals.[7] In the era of "fitness and health," that same image is officially labeled "obese" and makes every large black woman an immediately suspected case of bulimia.[8]

This essay borrows its title from a collection of Alice Walker's short stories titled *In Love and In Trouble: Stories of Black Women*. A friend, taking a final examination in an English class, was asked to discuss the loves and the troubles present in Walker's stories. That question made me realize that the characters of Walker's stories exhibit self-destructive stumbling blocks right alongside self-constructed inner resources as they seek to live an ethic of love and resistance and to sustain life and hope. Walker's characters reflect the larger African-American experience as they play out the consequences of conflicted inner visions, inner visions that are the personal sources of cultural ambivalence and a barrier to self-love.

In one story, "The Welcome Table," we see the way inner visions can be tangled in contradiction. An elderly black woman who precipitates an apoplectic and apocalyptical crisis in a segregated church one Sunday morning is strengthened by Jesus, whom she images as white, who meets her at the point of violent rejection, and walks with her and talks with her as she travels to glory. One observes the woman with wonder, strengthened and joyous in her meeting with Jesus, at the same time one wonders about the image fixed in her mind, an image from a picture stolen from her white lady's Bible.[9] Such conflicted inner visions are at the heart of the embodied experiences of African-American women.

Conflicted inner visions come from mixed messages and the world is full of mixed messages about being black and female. Where our bodies and our appearance are concerned, because of the many mixed messages from within and outside of African-American culture, we are loved and troubled almost constantly. If we deviate from the dominant culture norms by being to dark or too light, we suffer a myriad of assaults on our self-esteem at the same time that we may discover that our bodies are a peculiar refuge from some forms of destructions and humiliations. If we are light and European-looking, we may find it easier to become campus queens, wives, and girlfriends, but we may have trouble being taken seriously as leaders in our churches, organizations, and communities unless we are attached to a man. Our so-called European "good looks" also mean that our behavior is excessively scrutinized for flaws in our commitment to and solidarity with "the Folk" at the same time we hear echoes of envy and longing when someone mutters, "All that yellow wasted." If we are dark and full-featured we are often made to feel unloved and unlovable, and if we are light and fine-featured we find ourselves asking, like Alice Walker's Squeak/Mary Alice, "do you really love me, or just my color?"[10] If we are dark and full-featured, particularly if we are large, members of our community presume that we are ready to take charge of our church organizations and our little brothers and sisters before our childhoods are over. If we are women clergy who are dark and large, we are attacked for embodying a mammy stereotype; however, if we are light and thin we are told that we are "too pretty to preach."

Because we are African American, the assaults on our lives and bodies are historically molded and take on a more ominous character and meaning. We find that our history of racial oppression has always been sexualized. And that all sexism is racialized and often by homogenizing it we miss the peculiar ways sexism is able to reinforce racial privilege for some and sharpen the consequences of racial oppression for others. Racialized sexism, particularly in the form of the specialized sexism that assaults African-American women, compounds our own community's ambivalence about the meaning of being black and female in America. This ambivalence is a source of the "multiple jeopardy" that characterizes our experience of oppression.[11]

Sociologist Deborah King, in her analysis of "multiple jeopardy" as a context for consciousness and feminist potential, points out that African-American women are a highly diverse group of women. Part of that diversity is tied to the various resources and disadvantages associated with our varying class, educational, and other status positions. From a sociological perspective, status can include dimensions of physical appearance, for instance, color, size, and conformity to appropriate gender images combined with the limits and options for roles and rewards that society assigns to physical appearance. Because of the high premium placed on physical appearance in our society, the vulnerabilities associated with race, class, and gender are greatly affected by the options, barriers, and limits created by physical appearance.

More than anything else, the diversity of experience related to physical appearance alone exposes the limitations of terms such as *double whammy* or *double jeopardy*. In spite of their rhetorical convenience and their contributions to rendering African-American women more visible, King points out that terms like double and triple Jeopardy often obscure "the dynamics of multiple forms of discrimination." She argues:

> Unfortunately, most applications of the concepts of double and triple jeopardy have been overly simplistic in assuming that the relationships among the various discriminations are merely additive. These relationships are interpreted as equivalent to the mathematical equation, racism plus sexism plus classism equals triple jeopardy. . . . Such assertions ignore the fact that racism, sexism, and classism constitute three interdependent control systems. An interactive model, which I have termed multiple jeopardy, better captures those processes.[12]

As part of this multiple jeopardy, these simultaneous and interacting oppressions have a multiplier effect. The dynamism in King's model is intensified by the wide range of experiences that are possible in individual African-American women's lives, making possible a very broad context for black women's resistance. The ability to resist, however, is dependent on how widely perspectives on issues of struggle are shared. Damaged and conflicted inner visions limit that ability to build upon the multiple potentials for resistance implied in the multiple dimensions of oppression.

The contradictions surrounding African-American women's experiences shape both personal and communal perspectives on culture and social change. African-American women have opportunities throughout their lives to develop insights on black, white, male, and female experiences. These insights inform not only their strategies for survival in a hostile society but also the ideas and actions they use to challenge an oppressive society through social movements and through individual acts of resistance. Patricia Hill Collins describes African-American women as the "outsiders within,"[13] occupying statuses that differed mightily from those presumed appropriate for white women. Calling these statuses "contradictory locations," Collins identifies them as the source of "a peculiar marginality that stimulated a special African-American women's perspective." She explains that:

> Black women's position in the political economy, particularly ghettoization in domestic work comprised [a] contradictory location where economic and political subordination created the conditions for black women's resistance. Domestic work allowed African-American women to see white elites, both actual and aspiring, from perspectives largely obscured from black men and from these groups themselves.[14]

While on the one hand such women experienced, according to Collins, a "sense of self-affirmation" by "seeing white power demystified," they also experienced at a very basic level the fact that they could "never belong."[15] Not only is such knowledge, from Collins's perspective, a source of profound frustration, it is also a source of creativity. This self-understanding, often shared in the communal spaces of women's life—their churches, their clubs, and their beauty parlors—evolves into a standpoint from which African-American women's ideas about life and society develop into what she calls "a recurring humanist vision."[16] This vision is deeply implicated in a legacy of organized activism and personal resistance. Both King and Collins point to the diverse ways in which African-American women have participated in actions and movements that have challenged racial oppression and have opened the doors for other groups to launch similar challenges. However, it is the poetic vision of Alice Walker that has provided the most succinct and probative perspective on the critical power embedded within black women's history and experience and the need for certain stances to be taken within one's personal experience in order for that power to be realized.

## The Womanist Idea and Ideal

Walker's term *womanist* and the complex definition that accompanies it underscore the powerful critique of oppression and potential for human liberation that can emerge from reflection on being black and female in America. She takes a position. I think we do Walker a disservice when we use her term womanist as simply a label for black women feminists and their intellectual efforts in order to distinguish them from white women feminists and their efforts. Walker's idea of black feminism lays out very clear positions that black women ought to adopt based upon the best traditions ingrained in their legacy of struggle, survival, and the construction of African-American women's culture. It is an ethical evaluation of African-American women's history that extracts a set of principles that women may choose as their orientation to the world.

Clearly, by Walker's standards, not all black women are womanists, but the womanist potential is embedded in all black women's experiences. Her word is part of a dictionary-style definition that she wrote, according to Karen Baker-Fletcher, in response to her editors' queries regarding the existence and meaning of a term she had used in her essays and the title of her book. Her term touched a deep spiritual nerve among African-American women in a way that no other African-American artist or critic had been able to do.[17] Because of the term's spiritual implications, Walker has probably reached more ordinary women in the black community than any other black feminist thinker and writer. My own encounter with the term sparked a period of introspection and "critical remembering." Walker's perspective helped me to re-member the voices that had helped to shape my own inner vision. Through re-membering these voices, the personal emerged more forcefully as a didactic resource. Walker extracted the heroic consequences of difference and the process by which these consequences became elements of a *critical* consciousness.

For African-American women, the pain of simply being embodied—coping with others' responses to our hair, skin, and size—can overshadow the strengths and options. The pathetic dimension too often obscures the heroic possibilities. William H. Grier and Price M. Cobb early recognized the extremely negative implications of black women's experience.[18] Other observers, when attempting to make sense of black life and culture in a racist society, also dwell primarily on the deprivations. Walker insisted that the experience of suffering and oppression can be a resource for liberating vision and spiritual growth. Walker asserted through Celie that the voice of "poor colored women" can make a difference. When Celie shocked her friend Shug with her comments about God, Celie shouted, "Let 'im hear me, I say, If [God] ever listened to poor colored women the world would be a different place, I can tell you."[19] Celie, like Sojourner Truth and Harriet Tubman, discovers that her voice and her testimony of experience has the power to "turn the world right side up" and "to shake a nation." Walker makes the heroic and critical side of being black, female, poor, and oppressed most explicit in her definition of womanist. Where the tension between the pathetic and the heroic fosters ambivalence, Walker pushes us toward clarity.

Walker's idea contains a vision in which the ambivalences of African-American culture toward women, their roles, and their images, are resolved. Her perspective is historically and traditionally grounded. The appropriate heroic models for her are women like Harriet Tubman, Mary Church Terrell, and Josephine St. Pierre Ruffin. Without ever mentioning their names, she taps into the legacies of struggle and collective work each has left behind. She calls us to emulate the boldness and daring of Harriet Tubman, a woman who just could not leave her community behind as a runaway from slavery. She asks us to think like Mary Church Terrell who thought that African Americans should call themselves "colored" because the diversity of African Americans was so broad. Although "colored" achieved only limited success, Terrell's vision was one that included the most privileged and the most deprived and sought to affirm and embrace the full range of images from the darkest to the lightest. Walker sees important models in the assertive and premature adulthood of women such as Ida B. Wells-Barnett, who lied about her age in order to secure a teaching job as a teenager, and Nannie Helen Burroughs, who was serving the National Baptist Convention in an executive capacity by the age of eighteen. In the tradition of Josephine St. Pierre Ruffin, Walker clearly reasserts the validity of the definition of a "woman's movement" as a movement led by women for "the survival and wholeness of the entire people, male and female."

Not only does Walker point to the dimensions of difference among African-American women as a source of "universalist" humanism, but she centers love as the orientation women should have to the world around them. In her articulation of the "loves" that a good woman should express, and of course a womanist is a good woman, Walker emphasizes those things that make possible what has come to be called "the beloved community." As one reflects upon these loves, it becomes clear that these loves oppose directly the central hatreds of this age. We live in a society that hates poor people and yet Walker calls us to love "the Folk." We live in a society that hates challenges to rigid order and hierarchical authority in its religious life and yet Walker insists that we love "the Spirit." In a society that in its hatred of poor people and fat people has allowed the ethic that "a woman can be neither too rich or too thin" to rain down life-threatening terrors on women, Walker exalts "food and roundness." And most importantly, in a society that pulls its various cultural hatreds together in such a way as to destroy and victimize black women, Walker passionately emphasizes the importance of self-love. "Loves herself. *Regardless.*"

These loves are on a collision course with the troubles that comprise the cultural humiliation of African-American women. In this context of dehumanization, Walker's challenge to love creates a context of *re*humanization. These loves must be seen as ethical positions associated with a good womanist. Walker emphasizes those dimensions of African-American culture that have helped African Americans maintain their sanity and humanity under impossible circumstances: spirituality and those things most associated with its expression—music, dance, and the Spirit. These loves are interwoven with ideals that should be part of the fabric of a humane spirituality, love of "the Folk," love of "struggle," and the love of oneself, "*regardless.*"

## On Loving Food, Roundness, and the Self

Linked within this list of loves, almost like the germinal center of a beautiful flower, is the deceptively revolutionary insistence, "Loves love and food and roundness." These loves of love and roundness and food seem almost ethereal and apolitical until they are placed in the context of contemporary culture. In my personal encounter with Walker's *womanist*, I stopped there. As a large, full-featured, dark brown African-American woman, I recognized a revolution in her call to love. Walker's emphasis remembered for me my own struggles with community and culture. My own experience and my understanding of the history of cultural humiliation embedded in American racism made it abundantly clear that these are not only a source of celebration and bonding in a human community but also a protest against a culture that systematically assaults the self-esteem of African-American women.

Edwin Schur has pointed to the importance of "gender norms" in defining the position of women in our society. These norms include narrow European standards of beauty, a model of marriage and motherhood that enforces economic dependence, and social and intellectual subordination. Violation of these norms brings about the exclusion and punishment of women in a variety of ways. African-American women, by choice and by circumstance, violate nearly every dimension of American gender norms. Failure to meet society's beauty norms is in Schur's terms, "visual deviance." Visual conformity in the

United States, of course, is tied to an idolatry of whiteness. African-American women, in terms of their color alone, stand in opposition to the culture's idolatry of whiteness. For this opposition, they are assaulted from outside their communities. But African-American women who are too dark face an outrageous complex of attitudes and behaviors from within their own communities. Often the behavior of men and their stated preferences for lighter-colored women reflect the men's own self-hatred. In spite of changes brought about by the black power movement, Alice Walker is still able to lament, "If the present looks like the past, what does the future look like?"[20]

Physical, psychological, and emotional assaults against women are endemic. However, the culture's approach to African-American women, their images, and their life styles has been a central thrust in the continued humiliation of the entire African-American community. The assault on black women has been so effective that, in recent times, the African-American community has turned against its women as the source of its problems rather than as heroic resources in the constant struggle against racial oppression. As a result, African-American women have waged more struggle on behalf of men as part of their commitment to the entire community than I think black men have waged on behalf of women. Some would argue that women have done more for the men than women have done for themselves. They have also been forced to justify themselves within and to their communities—a distracting process that deflects energy from the real struggle.

Straight talk about the loves and troubles of our bodies is almost impossible because there is so much pain. Paradoxes become apparent in very strange ways. Recently, when speaking at a conference, I pointed out the ways in which we needed to engage in ministry that addressed the ways in which the culture responded differentially to little girls who were considered "pretty" and those who were considered "ugly." This "pretty"/"ugly" dichotomy is so taken for granted within black culture that it is almost never discussed. Girls not considered beautiful by white American standards, if they are part of families and communities who take education and achievement seriously, are groomed to be good students and to be leaders. The others may also be groomed that way, but unless they grow up in middle-class settings where certain protections are in place, they walk a very treacherous pathway to adulthood that may leave them educationally and professionally underdeveloped and very vulnerable targets for all sorts of sexual aggression and exploitation. The failures of African Americans to address this problem is evident in the sad and sorry history of black women in beauty pageants.

When I pointed to the problem of young African-American girls and their self-esteem, one man got up and expressed amazement that when he would stop little girls in the grocery store and ask them if they were going to grow up to be Miss America, the little girls would scowl at him. His point was that at a young age they already seemed to know they were rejected. I responded that although he meant well, he was not only being cruel to them by simply asking the question but failing to reckon with the problems embedded in these pageants that black people, because of their history in the United States, should intuitively recognize.

Until the early 1960s black women were not permitted to enter the Miss America Pageant.[21] Although many black fraternal organizations and most black colleges had contests, the college competitions and most fraternal pageants almost never involved any kind of swimsuit competitions and still do not. As one observer pointed out, the swimsuit competition has one purpose: to answer the question, "How does she look without any clothes?" Because of the withering feminist critique the Miss America Pageant has elicited, one need only watch annually to see the pageant's incremental response. Since the 1960s, scholarship, education, and ideologies of professionalism have gained greater prominence. In 1991 and 1992, program segments featured interviews with former contestants from various states and former Miss Americas describing the careers and family lives the scholarship aid had made possible. Because the swimsuit competition is particularly indefensible, it has been recast as a display of "fitness and health." One year the pageant organizers went so far as to eliminate the wearing of high heels with swimsuits. Although the contestants were in their bare feet, every one of the women walked across the stage on her toes. Two years after Vanessa Williams entered, won, and embarrassed the pageant, the scoring system was changed to make it possible to win without winning in the swimsuit competition.

African-American women winners at the state level and the four who have served as Miss Americas have had a powerful impact on the pageant's attempt to maintain its relevance. The Miss America Pageant, however, is a genteel upper-middle-class institution that masks and mystifies a more sinister culture of female sexual exploitation, abuse, and violence. The display, exploitation, and abuse of African-American women is probably at the genetic core of this institutionalized misuse of women.

African-American women were probably the first women in the United States to be displayed publicly without clothing. Slave auctions often drew crowds of observers because, in their display of women to be sold as slaves, they pandered to white prurient interests. Black women's bodies were the objects of intense public curiosity.[22] The sexual exploitation endemic to slavery was made possible by the violence and abuse. Women were flogged and tortured just like men. Angela Davis points out that women who participated in revolts or engaged in violence were sometimes killed more brutally than the men.[23] Where men were hanged, women were burned at stakes. It is almost as if the American cultural rituals of immolating black men during lynchings after slavery had their antecedents in their attempts to control black women during slavery. The sexual abuse and violence went hand in hand and sometimes choices about survival were made by weighing the option of nonviolent submission against near-suicidal attempts at resistance. Often survival was possible at a high personal cost. There were historical and cultural costs as well.

The abuse and degradation of slavery was the first step in a devaluation or labeling process that shaped attitudes and actions toward black women. These attitudes and actions are so specialized and so deep that they even carry over into pornographic depictions.[24] African-American women's status as degraded sexual objects during slavery was carried forward to argue for the necessity of segregation after slavery. Beliefs about the sexuality of African-American women fueled ideologies that supported the lynching of their men. Those sexual images helped to carry forward the Jezebel image that had become a fixed stereotype associated with slavery. Additionally the images associated with women's roles as workers also carried forward the deviant image of Mammy—the loyal faithful worker who was also large, loving, and asexual. The oppositional dichotomy between the light-skinned, sexy, and European-looking black woman and the large, loving one became a fixed feature of American culture. Within African-American culture itself, such images became lovingly lionized as the dichotomy between women "built for comfort" and those "built for speed." Indeed black popular culture became far more affirming of big women than white popular culture.[25]

All human experience is embodied experience and the consequences of cultural humiliation are most dramatically shown with reference to the body. Not only is experience embodied, but stereotypes, pernicious cultural representations of people, are also embodied images. All racial stereotypes are usually named images attached to an image of a body, and all of those named images are gendered. Distorted black images come in male and female form, so for the male Sambo image, there is the female Mammy image. For the image of "Zip Coon" there is Jezebel. Hollywood depictions often ally Mammy with Sambo and Jezebel with Zip Coon. Implied also are presumptions about sexuality and danger. The safe, emasculated, black male is paired with the large, highly respected, and loving Mammy. Her industriousness is often contrasted with his laziness. Their lack of apparent sexuality is tied to her enterprise and his economic ineffectiveness and laziness.

If stereotypes are any guides to actual social roles, it is a paradox that the most symbolically privileged image of white women, the fragile, blond beauty queen, is diametrically opposed to the most exploited image of black women, the large physically powerful "mammy." In her powerful exploration of the ethical implications of racism for American feminism—particularly in the form of racial and cultural privilege, Barbara Andolsen points to the victimization of African-American women by cultural definitions of beauty. She points out that while both men and women have been victimized, men's popular images have changed more radically and become more varied than have women's images. Indeed Andolsen argues that the differential impact of white beauty standards serves to maintain divisions among women, even black and white women who are both feminists.[26]

My own experience as a dark, plump, African-American woman informs my reading and hearing of Walker's call to love food and roundness. Her call also challenged me to examine the scripts of my childhood and see the sources of my own conflicted inner visions. I am not a woman who became plump as the years have passed, but I have been so my entire life. My childhood doctor, a very loving Armenian woman named Agnes Grace Israelian, vehemently warned me during one of the many times I tried to lose weight that I was never to attempt to drop below one hundred forty pounds. By insurance company standards that is still overweight for my height. My parents' marriage was the union between a family of little women and big men. My mother weighed only eighty-seven pounds on the day she married my ex-football player father. My father's genes are clearly dominant: I look like and am built like my dad. However since my mother had rickets as a child, her size may also be a function of some deprivations in early childhood.

My mother's lack of experience with fatness forced me to navigate the treacherous waters of American body culture without the compasses and maps that often make "becoming a woman" a taken-for-granted process, regardless of how painful and destructive. I was actually forced to think about myself and my size and where I fit in the community and the family as my friends at school thought up newer and more creative names for my size and as my mother and her relatives agonized over strategies to make me slimmer. My family's quest to keep me at the same size as my many smaller friends is a rich catalogue of tragicomical failures. I drank 1950s skim milk. I was given special candy as an appetite suppressant. I was enrolled in dance classes at a very early age and encouraged to practice at home. I was divested of my Easter baskets and relieved of my jelly beans by Easter Monday. No desserts were served with dinners until after my brothers were born, eight and nine years after me. My brothers of course were encouraged to grow "big!" like the men of my father's family. I can now laugh about the strategies they tried. As a result, I am a big woman who does not have a ravenous sweet tooth and can let chocolate candy sit in the refrigerator for months and years at a time. My mother would also control my ability to snack through careful rationing of money. When I did develop a taste for Dorothy Muriel sugar cookies, I had to choose between the cookie and my carfare home. Every stolen cookie required a two-mile walk to get home. A fairly healthy consequence is that I love to dance and to take long walks in urban areas.

As the cultural critiques embedded in feminist and womanist ideas have pointed out, becoming women in contemporary culture often means being shaped by painful experiences shaped lovingly and caringly by other women. The ideals embedded in Walker's idea highlight the ennobling and empowering dimensions of mother-daughter dialogues. These are meant to counter the demeaning and destructive exchanges that often shape our feelings about our bodies and our life styles. Because these dialogues continue throughout life, our experience as black women often entails over-hearing and assimilating a wide range of conversations among our mothers and "othermothers," all of which serve to build and shape our inner vision.

My mother wanted me to be a "normal" size and I am sure that the times I came home and cried about my friends' name-calling only spurred her on to greater efforts. However, her zeal to slim me down led to statements while eating such as "You're digging your grave with your fork!" I was repeatedly warned that "children have heart attacks too." Fortunately growing up in most black families provides many voices for our inner visions and our many mothers have "no clips on their lips." My great-aunt and grandmothers saw things differently, and said so. They thought my mother was too thin and told her so in front of me. They delivered a set of counter messages along with a dazzling array of delectably cooked dishes for their very special niece and grandchild. I may not have a sweet tooth, but no spare rib, chicken leg, or green vegetable is safe in my presence. My propensity to eat fried chicken with a knife and a fork was carefully cultivated with rewards of peach ice cream by my Savannah, Georgia-born grandmother.

My size, and my size alone, exposed me to a diverse set of voices during the formation of my cultural world. The smaller and shorter friends at school were quick to taunt me with a range of names. Their favorite was "Baby Huey." It was probably the most accurate since I was always so much taller. Since being large meant that I was also full-featured, there were occasional words about this as well. Ironically many of these same children liked to come home with me after school. We would play "school" and they would elect me teacher since I looked the oldest, *because of my size*. I was also allowed to preside and preach at pet funerals, probably for this same reason. The negative messages about size were also countered with positive messages from men and women at church who said I was simply a "big" girl. They worked hard to make me feel comfortable. At the same time my peers and my mother impressed me with my visual deviance, my peers, my family, and my church encouraged me to occupy leadership roles and to excel in other ways. The negative voices about my size often came from the same chorus as the positive voices about other aspects of myself. Fortunately I was in a structural position and an institutional setting where the positive voices had a greater opportunity to be heard.

Walker is insisting that African-American women must not hate themselves. In spite of the overwhelming storm of cultural humiliations we are faced with every day, especially regarding our bodies and our psyches, part of our struggle is to live the loves. In the context of a misogynist world that lies to women about not being too rich or too thin, Walker's insistence that a womanist "loves love and food and roundness" takes on the character of a revolutionary manifesto. For women like me, encountering the womanist ideal involved hearing a persistent and prophetic call to sift through the oppositional tensions among the voices of our inner vision and choose the heroic over the pathetic. "Regardless," of all else that may claim our energies and challenge our being, we are challenged to encourage the manifestation of self-love.

## Living the Loves in a Hateful World

African Americans' existential ambivalence about their bodies may be the most personally painful legacy of slavery and racial oppression in the United States. The consequences of that ambivalence for women may be the most dangerous and debilitating. Black men also have injured self-images but they are able to defend themselves from certain kinds of assaults and have almost nothing to fear in terms of assaults and sexual harassment from women. There are also lucrative outlets for black men to use their bodies while maintaining tremendous illusions of power and in some cases real power. Most women are as defenseless now as they were during slavery and in some ways they may be more so. Given the problems of poor urban neighborhoods, the large slave community may have been more effective at defending its members. Slave communities may also have been more unified. The womanist idea is a call to the kind of unity that creates a community climate that is nurturing and empowering. When all of its implications are examined, the womanist idea as defined by Walker is a call to healing, spiritual wholeness, celebration, and struggle. Taken with Walker's other writings, it is an unambivalent and unconflicted call for the affirmation of life and all that sustains a healthy life. Walker is insisting that we must repair our inner visions in order to live the loves in a hateful and troubling world. She believes, and I agree with her, that if we are able to live this ideal it will benefit our world, not just our community.

It is no accident that many white women feminists, from Sarah Evans to Hillary Rodham Clinton, point to specific black women as role models who freed them from the gilded prison of silence, physical fragility, and intellectual subordination. For many women in the civil rights movement, women such as Fannie Lou Hamer, Ella Baker, and Ruby Doris Robinson were voices and images that empowered. Marian Wright Edelman, her prominence enhanced by her mentoring role to Hillary Rodham Clinton, was also one of the women of the civil rights movement whose actions and choices provided models of strength and self-actualization. These women reflect the adjectives that emerge from Walker's description of a woman as someone who is serious, responsible, courageous, and mature. African-American women's history is full of revered women whose critiques and contributions placed them in direct conflict with the prevailing norms and conventions of womanhood in the United States. Walker has called us to maintain our connection with that history by adopting this revolutionary standpoint of womanism.

Walker's call and its application to the lives of African-American women are also challenges to a society whose evil is fractionated and diffuse. African-American women are not the only women who suffer from cultural definitions of beauty and body image. However they are the only group that must sustain itself independently of these ideals because of the ontological impossibilities surrounding the vast majority. It is ironic that the parents of the two darkest Miss Americas, Marjorie Vincent and Debbie Turner, actively discouraged their daughters in order to protect them. These two women, in my opinion, expanded the value of professional aspirations as competitive currency in the Miss America Pageant. The contestants in their cohort were older and more heavily representative of graduate and professional students. Vanessa Williams, ironically, had not entertained a thought of winning the pageant and basically competed because it was a summer job opportunity for a dance and theater major. Yet even in her downfall, she contributed to changes that served to devalue the swimsuit competition. The only parent who actively encouraged her daughter was Mrs. de Gaetano, Suzette Charles's mother, who herself had wanted to compete in the Miss America pageant but was prohibited by its "white only" rules.[27] All four black women who served as Miss Americas were in some way or another part of the world of ontological impossibility and because of their peculiar marginality, they changed dimensions of the pageant.

The sordid history of exploitation of African-American women and their bodies is not over. We are developing a contemporary roll call, names like Anita Hill, Vanessa Williams, and Desiree Washington, to remind us. Both the Vanessa Williams scandal and the Mike Tyson case point to the fact that black women are still peculiarly victimized by the cult of beauty and the culture of sexual exploitation, abuse, and violence it masks. *And* they are vulnerable *within* the community as well as in the society at large. Karen Baker-Fletcher notes that the National Baptist Convention's support of Mike Tyson, while remaining silent about (and actually tacitly supporting) Desiree Washington's victimization and vilification, disrespects the history of struggle waged by black women on behalf of the entire community and sidesteps the problem of sexual violence and abuse in our own communities.[28] This situation is a stark reminder that we are all victimized and therefore we must each be someone who, in Walker's words, "loves struggle." If, through loving ourselves "regardless" and repairing our inner visions, we save our own lives, we have taken the first step toward our "response-ability" to save our brothers and sisters. Self-love then is probably the most critical task we complete in establishing our commitment "to survival and wholeness of entire people, male and female."

# 11

# Ministry to Women

## Hearing and Empowering "Poor" Black Women

African-American women have had a significant impact on United States culture and society. On occasion their heroic responses to oppression have become visible enough to impress others of the value of their perspective. In 1866, during the Combahee River expedition, Harriet Tubman became the first woman ever to lead United States soldiers in battle. An editor writing to praise her exploits exclaimed, "The desperation of a poor black woman has power to shake a nation that so long was deaf to her cries."[1] In one of the most critical and pivotal theological conversations of the late twentieth century, novelist Alice Walker's Celie, responding to Shug's attempt to blunt her impending heresies and blasphemies, shouts, "Let 'im hear me, I say. If he [God] ever listened to poor colored women the world would be a different place, I can tell you."[2] Celie's and Shug's revision of their thoughts about God takes place during a lifetime of abuse and humiliation. They develop a love and admiration for each other as they rebel against their victimization by those closest to them. The perspectives of the novelist and the editor both tell a vital truth about the standpoint, perspective, or point of view of African-American women in the United States—that in a racist and sexist world, "poor" African-American women might possibly have a more realistic view of that world. Indeed, Celie's revelation points to something many activist women, especially African-American churchwomen of the late nineteenth and early twentieth centuries, have long suspected, that the wisdom that comes from the responses of African-American women to their sufferings, if taken seriously by God and society, has the power to transform the world. Yet in spite of Celie, Shug, Harriet Tubman, and so many others, the popular images of black women continue to signify their continued subordination, denigration, and silencing in this society.

There are many images of African-American women in the popular culture of the United States. There is one image, associated with the highly profiled, talented, and famous, such as Lena Horne and Oprah Winfrey, which exalts the successful black woman as a symbol of strength, vitality and liberation. Another image, associated with the covers of *Newsweek* and *Time*, is the image of the impoverished welfare mother, the resident of public housing projects, the teenage mother, and the neglectful, crack-addicted mother, usually rolled up into one monstrous body. Between these extremes of historically charged contemporary images exists a reality of diverse experiences for African-American women. That diverse reality has been a significant engine in religion and movements for social change.

Indeed the creative persistence of analysts and artists has given us new terms and phrases—such as "multiple jeopardy and multiple consciousness" and "womanist"—to use as we try to organize black women's experience into theoretical or practical portrayals.[3] The ability of African-American women's experience to defy portrayal in conventional terms is related to certain distinctive realities. African-American women have been the victims of the longest, most sustained cultural assault experienced by any racial-ethnic-gender group. They have been victimized by institutionalized racism as practiced in the United States in its tri-dimensional expression: economic exploitation, political exclusion, and cultural humiliation. The cultural humiliation of African-American women has been intensified by the moral evaluations attached to their economic and political roles. The cultural assaults mounted against the black community as a whole have burdened the institutions in which women take part. These institutional pressures are compounded by cultural assaults aimed directly at their "woman" experiences. These externally imposed crises are intensified by the cultural ambivalence African Americans themselves express toward the contributions of women when racism elicits explicitly sexist forms of self-hatred.

Among the crises facing African Americans today, and one that is following us into the 21st century, is the situation of poor women in our communities. Folk wisdom recognizes the importance of "the mothers" to the survival and health of the community and to the perpetuation of worthwhile dimensions of African-American culture. Christian ministry is defined ultimately by its service to, with, and on behalf of "the least of these." In the context of the African-American community, women constitute "the least of these" and the peculiarities of their situation has profound consequences for the entire community. William Julius Wilson pointed to the depth of the crisis more than a decade ago when he wrote:

> The problem for black female-headed families is not so much the absence of fathers, but that in an overwhelming majority of cases they are impoverished. Indeed, the poverty stricken nature of the underclass is symbolized by the female-headed family pattern. The main problem, to repeat, is that the lower-class black family is experiencing severe economic problems and the growing percentage of female-headed families is one of the symptoms, not the cause of that condition. In this connection, a program of economic reform, if it is to be meaningful, has to be

directed not solely at improving the economic opportunities of poor
black men, but also of improving the job prospects of poor black women.
It would even be wise to include in this reform program the creation of
publicly financed day care centers so that women can realistically pursue such opportunities when they arise.[4]

Wilson's distress was echoed by earlier sociologists like E. Franklin Frazier,
Kelley Miller, W. E. B. Du Bois, and Oliver Cromwell Cox, when they expressed similar concerns about urban black women. At no time in the African-American experience have women not been among "the least of these."
As the primary caretakers of children and as the first to feel the effects of
economic crisis, the deprivation of black women often *is* the deprivation of
the entire community.[5]

The terms *ministry* and *women* are currently charged with great meaning
as African-American churches face the challenges of the twenty-first century.
The current attention to women in the ordained ministries of Christian
churches has been part of a larger critique of culture that insists upon the
inclusion of women at all levels of public leadership. At the same time, popu-
list emphases in women's history remind us that the activities of women at all
levels of churches also constitute "ministry." Discussion of "ministry to
women" must be sensitive to both dimensions of concern. By *ministry* we
mean not only that associated with pastoral vocations but also we point to
the broad range of Christian service within and beyond church walls that is
aimed at spiritual, physical, and social regeneration and transformation.

Any discussion of ministry or service to women must also be historical in
nature. In the African-American experience, women have been central to the
emergence and development of religious traditions, congregations, and denominations. During slavery, women were key to the crystallization of religious and family institutions as sources of survival and of resistance to slavery's
dehumanizing effects. Women reinforced the importance of religion among
themselves through autonomous women's rituals, prayer groups, and leadership structures.[6] Their voices, the voices of "the least of these," were irrevo-
cably woven into the traditions and organizations that became central to the
community's response to changing social institutions and to economic and
political challenges. Historically, any change in the socio-economic status
and political organization and participation of black women has meant a transformation of the organizational fabric of black churches. While a comprehensive and exhaustive understanding of this is not possible here, in this
chapter we review and note highlights pointing to the women's traditions
that today are resources for reformulating the meaning and practice of "ministry" to meet the new and diverse problems black women face.

These selected historical highlights of African-American women's experiences suggest the importance of the interrelationships among black women,
their churches, and their families. Such an exploration also sketches the way
black women's concerns and consciousness have operated as social forces to

shape institutions and communal responses to social problems. Not only has the changing socio-economic status of black women shaped their demands on the churches and the churches' responses to them, but recent changes in the economy have affected black women's needs for ministry as well as the content of those ministries. As contemporary churches and communities explore ways to respond to crises affecting black women, it is important to explore the responses of the past that shaped the traditions that exist in the present and which may provide what Bernice Johnson Reagon calls "the key to turning the century with our principles and ideals intact?"[7]

First, I will review the ways in which major historical changes have affected African-American women and their relationship to their churches. Focusing on the aforementioned tridimensional reality of institutionalized racism, as my focus, I will then discuss ways to address the empowerment of African-American women. I will conclude by noting how the distribution of opportunities for women in professional ministry creates a contradiction for talented African-American women who feel called to address the problems of the masses in the African-American community through the offices of ordained Christian ministry. Effective ministry to African-American women as they confront crises and, by extension, to their families and communities, will depend on a massive reorganization of attitudes about women, about women in ministry, and about the meaning of ministry in black Christian churches.

### "Poor" Black Women

James Cone and others have pointed to the tripartite reality of institutional racism in the United States: economic exploitation, political exclusion, and cultural humiliation. African-American response to that racism has manifested itself in part in an adaptive self-hatred that accepts models defined by the dominant society as normative for their community. Existence in this society has involved a twofold struggle. One part consists of constantly challenging the dominant society; the other is an internal contest over roles, values, and strategies for survival as well as for social change. Women have been central to both sides of this struggle. Indeed it has been argued that the legal and cultural statuses of African women and their descendants have been central to the peculiarities of slavery and its aftermath in the United States.[8] Among women there exists a "multiple consciousness" in response to this "multiple jeopardy" that has been ever present in the history of African-American women in the United States.

In spite of the centrality of women's reality and roles and in spite of the legendary "sheroes,"[9] such as Harriet Tubman, Sojourner Truth, Ellen Craft, Milla Granson, and others, who emerge from slavery, African-American churches have not consistently empowered the voices of women. Perhaps it was in the slave churches where their voices were heeded most attentively.

Although white society recognized and empowered the black male preacher, even when he was a bondsman, it mostly ignored the women. Accounts of the slave community indicate that enslaved men and women did not ignore women. Deborah Gray White points to several instances where powerful women arose as spiritual leaders who were able to exercise authority over the community.[10] Webber argues that slave communities exhibited a real lack of sexism in their allocation of leadership, authority, and respect.[11]

The church's voice during slavery was a clear and unwaveringly prophetic one. It was a voice that insisted simultaneously on the overthrow of slavery and the humanity of enslaved women and men. Occasionally, that voice was found in the themes that undergird the slave revolts, most notably Nat Turner's. Webber points to the centrality of women in constructing, maintaining, and transmitting a world view whose cultural themes emphasized solidarity and religious faith. "Even women preachers appear often enough, though admittedly less frequently than male preachers, to suggest that there was no community prohibition against their filling this crucial role."[12] Biographies of nineteenth century evangelists and Toni Morrison's 1987 novel, *Beloved*, in the person of Baby Suggs, Holy, remind us that the voice of the preaching woman has been a significant force for psychic survival. Yet it was all too often ignored and hindered from attaining authority after Emancipation.

The suppression of women's voices within African-American churches coincides with what Gayraud Wilmore calls "the deradicalization of the Black Church" as the prophetic voices of people like Henry McNeal Turner and Harriet Tubman died out.[13] Around the beginning of the twentieth century, women lost ground in their access to platforms and pulpits. Churches were urged to "regularize" and regularized churches had male pastors in their pulpits. Some churches accommodated the religious zeal of women allowing them to lead worship and pray "from the floor" as missionaries and evangelists. According to Evelyn Brooks Higginbotham, a "feminist theology" emerged among Baptist women between 1885 and 1900 as they contested the masculinism that threatened then with silence and marginality.[14] Apparently, the work of these women as equals, first within the American National Baptist Convention and later within the National Baptist Convention, was delegitimized. Once they were, in the words of Nannie Helen Burroughs, "hindered from helping," these women formed the Women's Auxiliary Convention of the National Baptist Convention from which they wielded tremendous influence within the church and the community at large.[15] A number of women found places for their voices in the Holiness Movement of the late nineteenth century, and in the Pentecostal Movement of the early twentieth. Baptist and African Methodist women were recruited and "converted," became the pioneer educators of these new churches, and were also powerful evangelists and revivalists who "dug out" or founded urban churches when women and their work moved to the cities.

As their suppression within their churches progressed and the church became less prophetic and more priestly in its response to political realities, African-American Christian women created other avenues for their "ministry." One of these was a women's movement that culminated in the formation of the National Association of Colored Women. It is important *not* to view this club movement of the late nineteenth and early twentieth centuries primarily as secular. It is more accurately viewed as a movement of prophetic Christian women who fulfilled their calling in their responses to social issues and in their demands for social change. The club movement's motto, "Lifting as We Climb," reflected their sense of shared suffering and mission. These women rejected the notion of competitive American individualism in favor of a corporate mobility designed to liberate. Throughout the papers of these movements one repeatedly finds Christian themes. Often the women's church work and community work overlapped significantly. Mary McLeod Bethune, for instance, was a graduate of Moody Bible Institute and an experienced street preacher. When she was denied a missionary post in Africa, she claimed her Africa to be right next door and founded what is now Bethune-Cookman College.[16] Other black women's narratives, such as that of Mamie Garvin Fields, describe similar missionary motives.[17] Leaders such as Mary Church Terrell traveled the country exhorting church women to act on behalf of their communities. Others expressed a biblical hermeneutic that undergirded their worldviews and actions. In her novel *Iola Leroy or the Shadows Uplifted*, Frances Ellen Watkins Harper points to the church as a place to reconstitute the African-American community and to formulate strategies and ethics for social change.[18]

These women were part of a leadership class of "preachers and teachers."[19] In addition to being heroic educators, Lucie Campbell's hymn, "Something Within," hints that these "teachers" were also carriers of the gospel. "If anything characterizes the role of black women in religion in America, it is the successful extension of their individual sense of regeneration, release, redemption, and spiritual liberation to a collective ethos of struggle for and with the entire black community."[20] Historically, African-American women have argued for a collective approach to the community's suffering. Their advocacy has focused on the experience of men and children sometimes giving their own specific concerns less emphasis than they deserve. Yet every dimension of black women's experience cries out for a specific response from the church that needs to hear and empower the voices of "poor" black women.[21]

Novelist Alice Walker has offered the term *womanist*, along with a definition that organizes and interprets the heroic historical experience of African-American women with reference to their femaleness, their relationship to community, their strategies for change, and their cultural emphases.[22] What Walker has identified as holistic and universalist commitment to the community's survival, Patricia Hill Collins has described as a "recurrent humanist vision" among black women activists and writers.[23] Both Walker and Collins illuminate a consciousness that emerges from suffering and recognizes the suffering of others. Given the pivotal place of African-American women in the racial-ethnic, class, and gender hierarchies of American culture, a ministry that concentrates on their empowerment should benefit the entire community.

## Economic Empowerment

African-American women's work history is linked inextricably with their religious history. Their roles as workers defined their history and status in the United States. Many of their responses to that history have been dependent on their religious opportunities and spiritual resources. As enslaved and free women, their work has been inseparable from the well being of the entire African-American community. As wage earners, they have been the poorest, least protected, and most insurgent group of workers. Slave or free, these vulnerable women have been among the staunchest supporters and most enterprising participants in the religious life of their communities.

As enslaved women they were subjected to the same violence and exploitative working conditions as men. Angela Davis points out that the work roles of enslaved women set the foundations for a "new standard of womanhood" and established a different relationship between black women and the labor force. As a result:

[p]roportionately, more Black women have always worked outside their homes than have their white sisters. The enormous space that work occupies in Black women's lives today follows a pattern established during the very earliest days of slavery. As slaves, compulsory labor overshadowed every other aspect of women's existence. It would seem, therefore, that the starting point for any exploration of Black women's lives under slavery would be an appraisal of their role as workers.[24]

Their combined role as workers and mothers was pivotal to the formation of African-American consciousness. Men were often the chroniclers of exploitations specific to women. One such memoirist described his mother's impact by simply saying, "my mother was *much* of a woman."[25]

These working women were also expected to reproduce the African labor force in America. As the demand for slave labor rose, the system depended more and more upon natural increase and unparalleled legal repression to maintain itself. Deborah Gray White points out that force, fraud, and other inducements were used to make enslaved women the most fertile population in the world (at that time). Central to their situation was a need for more humane conditions for mothering. These concerns provided the basis for an extensive network of mutual-aid among women that was, she argues, the base upon which the legendary strength of slave women rested. By helping each other, they were able to cope with work and motherhood in ways that became enshrined in folklore. The network's mutual-aid included prayer meetings and religious leaders who healed, prayed, exhorted, and prophesied, displaying remarkable amounts of influence and authority within slave communities.[26]

At the end of slavery, people sought liberation from the sexual and material oppression of the rural South. Women were eager to work for themselves and their families. To do this they educated their daughters as well as their sons. The educational ethic among freedwomen and men contributed institutions and policies that benefited the entire South. On occasion, black southerners in some areas had higher school attendance rates than their white neighbors. Part of the community's educational strategy was to free women from the sexual exploitation that came with agricultural and domestic work. Educated daughters, they hoped, would not have to work in "the white man's kitchen." Even with this work ethic, black women disappeared from the fields immediately after slavery. Their former owners accused them of "playing the lady." Some have argued, however, that fear of sexual exploitation prompted this disappearance.[27]

Some of the most poignant descriptions of the work orientation of African-American women are found with reference to their religious and educational orientations. Women worked and saved and ran farms to educate husbands called to the ministry.[28] Women also found enterprising ways to earn extra money to educate children in church related schools and to support the missionaries who taught them. White female employers complained about the precedence church activities sometimes took over their own needs.[29] The investments of "Negro washerwomen," according to Carter G. Woodson, were the foundations of the great black insurance companies in the South. The economic enterprise of African-American women, when successful, as in the cases of Maggie Lena Walker, Madame C. J. Walker, and Mary Ellen ("Mammy") Pleasants, benefited the entire community. Pleasants, a Catholic, financially supported the founding of several black Protestant congregations in California. Woodson insisted that the least educated and hardest working women were the ones most eager to invest in religiously suffused mutual-aid associations, community uplift projects, and new small businesses.[30]

Black women's work in the South moved to the cities before the demand for male rural labor declined. This transformation was a significant force in urbanization. Women outnumbered men in the cities. These migrant women and eventually their families became the nuclei around which new urban congregations formed. Many of these new late nineteenth- and early twentieth-century churches were part of the Holiness and Pentecostal movements. Many congregations were organized by the women who then sent "home" for male pastors. At the same time that sociologists, such as E. Franklin Frazier, decried the cities as places of "destruction,"[31] women were transforming the organizational and cultural matrix of the African-American church. The urbanization of women's work not only produced new churches but also new music, contributing to another cultural transformation in which women's voices are significant, the emergence of gospel music. Urban churches represented a substantial economic investment on the part of women. That investment was so prominent that, according to Taylor Branch, Montgomery Improvement Association founder E.D. Nixon defined the civic responsibilities of Montgomery's pastors in terms of what they "owed" the "washerwomen." For Nixon, it was obvious that the religious leadership derived its salaries and prestige from working women.[32] The centrality of churchwomen to the Montgomery bus boycott movement and to the civil rights movement overall is a story that is only beginning to be told.[33]

In spite of their hard work and sustained participation in the labor force, black women remain poorly remunerated and, as an aggregate, fall behind white men, black men, and white women. Only college-educated black women, a disproportionately small group, approach or surpass white women's income levels. This seeming anomaly is a consequence of black women's continuous labor force participation and the disincentive to remain in the labor force that married college-educated white women experience because of the economic opportunities available to their husbands.[34] Currently, according to Rothenberg, the poverty rate of all *working* black mothers *equals* the poverty rate of white men who are *not* in the labor force (13%).[35] Elderly black women represent one of the poorest groups. And it is elderly African-American women who are responsible for the organizational integrity of black religious organizations.

African-American churches need to be in the forefront of movements and strategies to uplift African Americans economically. African-American women and their communities stand to benefit from advocacy for economic justice more than any other group of women. Assuming the role of advocate for economic justice for African-American women is essential to the ministry of churches. Recently some churches have confused the roles of evangelism and prophecy. In the zeal to attract men, these churches ignore their mission to call social institutions to account for their failures to people. The most glaring economic failure (of many) in this society is the historical failure to secure economic justice for black women. Nannie Helen Burroughs and other churchwomen in the club movement recognized this contradiction and saw the call to secure economic justice as an essential task for creating an ideal society for everyone.[36] This task still awaits the full energies of the church.

### Political Empowerment

It is in the area of political empowerment that the institutional discrimination of African-American churches most directly excludes women. "Get to the ministers!" is still an American political ethic, according to Charles V. Hamilton, when most white politicians are seeking the "black vote."[37] In urban politics, ministers are most likely to be approached when officials are seeking to represent the "voice" of the black community on civic boards and in appointive political office. The refusal of African-American churches, particularly Baptist churches, to include women in ordained and authoritative leadership directly excludes women from participating in the decision making process affecting the communities in which they comprise the majority population.

Today, women do not accept such exclusion. The traditions of women's community work have provided alternative pathways for women to public leadership. Sometimes the path involves a highly public secular career in human services or electoral politics. While black women, as congresswomen, mayors, state representatives, agency heads, and city or town council members, and as Republican and Democratic party workers, make a substantial contribution to what political empowerment black communities achieve, they are often isolated from the male religious enclaves that are accorded special privileges of access to white political powers. Since black churches remain the most important site for working- and middle-class people who vote and otherwise participate in traditional politics, women's exclusion from church leadership dilutes their influence in other public spaces.

Historically, African-American women have insisted upon participating in the political destiny of black people. The nineteenth and twentieth centuries are full of examples of such participation. One of black America's earliest political writers and the first woman of any race to speak publicly and leave existing manuscripts, Maria Stewart offered incisive political-theological perspectives on the plight of black people.[38] Harriet Tubman and Sojourner Truth both framed their activism in religious terms. Sojourner Truth once challenged Frederick Douglass by asking, "Is God dead, Frederick?" Her challenge reminded Douglass and their listeners that, regardless of how hostile the society, African Americans were not totally alone in their struggle. She also underscored the significance black people attached to biblical-theological frameworks of social justice. Mary McLeod Bethune's missionary zeal moved her from higher education to the political arena during the Depression. She became, as convenor of Roosevelt's black cabinet, head of the National Youth Administration, and president of the National Council of Negro Women, the most powerful black leader since Booker T. Washington.

The activities of African-American women during the Civil Rights movement, although extensive and crucial, have not been adequately documented or assessed. However, two women, Ella Baker and Fannie Lou Hamer, both exude a common spirituality in spite of their radically different social origins. Ella Baker, the daughter of a minister, became a traveling prophet for the National Association for the Advancement of Colored People (NAACP) as a field secretary before becoming the executive director of Southern Christian Leadership Conference (SCLC) and the organizer of Student Nonviolent Coordinating Committee (SNCC). Her speaking schedule, as portrayed in a film biography, provides documentation of the extensive network of churches open to organizers from the NAACP.[39] Hamer was explicitly theological in her calls for participation in the civil rights movement. The same energy and assertiveness that made her an effective song leader in her church made her an effective public speaker and advocate for black people's political empowerment.[40] White women feminists point to women like Hamer as catalysts for their own assertiveness and political growth.[41]

These specific examples highlight the models of political participation that women often provide for the community. Although churchwomen can be as hierarchical and authoritarian as any human beings, they are more willing to "mother" others toward developing effective political participation and leadership skills. My own research on urban community workers uncovered networks and other organized settings in which women who became empowered actively recruited and trained others for similar kinds of participation and leadership. One may argue that women are more willing to do this because they have been so often forced to do this, but my observation of women's organizations leads me to conclude that black women enjoy exercising power by guiding others in its exercise. Both church mothers and community mothers utilize this model of influence in their organizations.[42]

If the church follows through in its advocacy for women's political empowerment, as in economics, such empowerment would be another source of benefit for the entire community. W. E. B. Du Bois recognized this during his campaigns for woman suffrage from the pages of *The Crisis*. We now know that African-American women vote in patterns that contradict their actual socio-economic position in the society, in spite of their structural and social alienation. The enhanced empowerment of African-American women holds prophetic possibilities for the entire community. Including women in the institutional life of the church in such a way as to enhance their access to public power would enable the church to benefit from their skills and talents in a way that others outside the church and outside the black community already do. Many activist women who do not attend church regularly explain their absence in terms of the discrimination they perceive. The inclusion of women would also represent a significant affirmation to women and a balance for the demands that the dominant culture often places on the male role—demands that enhance the individual career sometimes at the expense of the community's collective interests.

### Cultural Empowerment

The attainment of economic and political justice are really matters of "simple justice." Addressing the cultural humiliation of African-American women is a challenge to the church that is perhaps the most complex, most significant, and least understood emergency, cultural humiliation and its consequences for self-esteem. *Cultural humiliation* is a term that addresses the way in which African-American images, traditions, values, and symbols are devalued and regarded as deviant by the dominant (white) society. Some have argued that the low self-esteem of African-American women and girls contributes to the behaviors that choke off their most significant opportunities. Where the male supremacist dimensions of the society provide a few opportunities for black men that support a positive self-esteem, that same male supremacist ethic exacerbates the alienation of African-American women.

African-American women, by choice and by chance, violate nearly every dimension of American gender norms. Edwin Schur has pointed to the importance of "gender norms" in defining the position of women in our society.[43] These include meeting certain standards of beauty, a model of marriage and motherhood that enforces economic dependence, and social deference. Violation of these norms brings about the exclusion and punishment of women in a variety of ways. Schur describes the failure to meet society's beauty norms as "visual deviance." African-American women, in terms of their color alone, stand out from and against the culture's idolatry of whiteness. Not only are they assaulted from outside their communities, but African-American women who are too dark face an outrageous complex of attitudes and behaviors from within their own communities. Often the behavior of men and their stated preferences for lighter women reflect black men's own self-hatred, but in spite of changes brought about by the black power movement, Alice Walker is still able to lament, "If the present looks like the past, what does the future look like?"[44]

Ironically, black churches are often pastored by men who are the most fiercely committed to the dominant culture's notions of beauty and do not see these notions as white, male supremacist. Those notions are affirmed and reaffirmed from the pulpit to the door, often in quite subtle ways. The prettiest and lightest little girls in the church are often encouraged in ways that allow them to discover that their visual status is a resource for success; they are socialized to be "cute" and to grow up to be beautiful. In contrast the darker and plumper girls are encouraged to be serious, develop leadership skills, and, above all, do well in school. Some black women have called this the "pretty/ugly" syndrome in black culture.[45] Although poets and black feminists have vocalized this issue, churches have been strangely silent on the "pretty-ugly" ethic that abounds in our communities. Both strategies hurt! Many "pretty" black women are intellectually underdeveloped in a community that offers relatively little protection to its girls. Unless they are specially protected by middle class organizations, such girls/women are subjected to inordinate amounts of sexual aggression. Michelle Wallace, though in my opinion expressing it badly, tries to point to this phenomenon in *Black Macho and the Myth of the Superwoman*, complaining that the "prettiest" little girls in ghettoes or inner cities seemed to be the most likely candidates for teenage pregnancy.[46] At the same time, many "dark" black women are excluded from feeling good about themselves by the withholding of those acts of ceremonial deference within their own communities which "honor" their womanhood.

Issues of beauty represent just one of the rocky areas of a complex and dangerous course that African-American women must negotiate in American culture. Issues of body image, sexuality, white and black cultural definitions of work and family roles, and the way in which black women's deviation from dominant cultural definitions reflects on the total community all combine to place an inordinate amount of pressure on black women. The "Mammy" image, particularly, as expressed in literature, movies, and television is an assault on black women's work roles. The highly publicized attempt of a crack-addicted mother in St. Louis, Missouri, to sell her infant for twenty dollars worth of crack cocaine may be a singular but dramatic indicator of the damage wrought through cultural humiliation. As Paula Giddings has noted, in the history of the community, black women have been materially worse off and at the same time exhibited far less social pathology.[47]

The church must take seriously its prophetic role in regard to women's self-esteem. Drug abuse, violence, and teenage pregnancy are all related to issues of low self-esteem. In many ways, both subtle and overt, the vast majority of females in African America are assaulted by stereotypes and ideologies that humiliate them (and, incidentally, humiliate by reflection those who use them in their dealings with black women). Although I personally find the sexism and patriarchalism of Islam objectionable, particularly in its African-American varieties, Islam is currently the only corporate religious voice that states categorically and loudly that American standards of beauty and fashion "shame" and humiliate African-American women. Without reverting to a more primitive and restrictive view of women, African-American churches must address the cultural humiliation of women.

Barbara Andolsen identifies four major areas where white feminists and black feminists disagree. Besides work, rape, and male-female solidarity, the issue of beauty and the racial privilege associated with it stands out as a source of tension. She notes that while the images of black males in the media have changed and become more diverse, the images of black women have not.[48] The Mammy and the Jezebel still dominate the culturally acceptable images of black women. Actresses who refuse to participate in roles which reinforce stereotypes and culturally demean simply do not work often and do not reap the economic rewards of those who do. How often do we see Ruby Dee, Esther Rolle, and Cicely Tyson in large budget motion pictures? How often do we see African-American actresses featured in nonstereotypical roles?

Refashioning social meanings and cultural definitions is an essential task for changing society. It is also one of the most controversial and difficult as the political correctness backlash of the 1990s demonstrates. Critiques of culture depend, for their thoroughness and prophetic insight, on the standpoints or points of view of their authors. If the church thoroughly carries through its challenge to the cultural humiliation of women, the Afro-Christian critique of culture should be the most penetrating and the most prophetic. The production of a humane cultural experience for all African-American women depends upon a radical cultural critique. The church must work to produce that humane experience. The uplift of the downtrodden involves an aggressive campaign to redefine those aspects of culture which demean and exclude and humiliate. Such a prophetic stance involves the call to black women, issued in Alice Walker's in her definition of a *womanist*, to be self-loving *"regardless."*[49]

## Contemporary Issues and Spiritual Empowerment

If confusion over mission and identity are of any importance in the ability of any group of people to resist oppression, the last decades of the twentieth century may be the worst for African Americans. In spite of the misery and suffering of slavery and the wholesale terror and assault that characterized the Jim Crow era, there was a unity of purpose and a sense of shared suffering that helped to mediate the conflicts between women and men. Within the current context of social fragmentation, underclass isolation, and theological diversity, the economic and political issues confronting women are compounded by confusion and conflict over scripturally prescribed roles for women and misperceptions about the actual status of African-American women in society. Many male pastors and other spokespersons believe falsely that African-American women are doing better than the men in their communities. It is an unfortunate distortion of the situation of a small proportion of professional women to argue this. The cultural context of the United States has consistently assaulted and punished the economic roles of black women and, through various public policies, engineered blame for the disadvantage of black men in the direction of black women.

The distorted images of African-American women's professional and economic successes provide further fuel to many men's belief that the ministry is still the only place where African-American men have access to influence and authority. As a result, resistance to women's ordination is still quite fierce among many African-American ministers. Currently, the largest black denomination (National Baptist Convention, U.S.A., Inc.) does not recognize the ordination of women at a level of national policy. Although the NBC leaves the issue of ordination to the local church and its associations, the overwhelming sentiment expressed by delegates has rejected efforts of leaders to encourage the acceptance of women's ordination. Contrary to the Baptist legacy of congregational autonomy and freedom of conscience, local and regional Baptist associations will go to great lengths to restrain churches and pastors from ordaining women. At times the struggle to maintain denominational power and public prominence seems to overshadow the response of these organizations to the current emergencies of public life. The black Methodist denominations, African Methodist Episcopal, African Methodist Episcopal Zion, and Christian Methodist Episcopal Churches, all ordain women. However, they elected no women bishops until the year 2000, when the Rev. Dr. Vashti Murphy McKenzie was elected a bishop of the

African Methodist Episcopal Church. Several Pentecostal denominations, including the largest, the Church of God in Christ, do not officially ordain women, while other denominations do. Several of those denominations have presiding bishops who are women. The picture for women in the ordained ministry *within the historically African-American denominations* is not good.

Ironically, there are two contradictions at work among black professionals and white churches. Other black professional men, particularly in male dominated professions such as medicine and law, have had no problem affirming the leadership of black women, electing them to the presidencies of the National Medical Association and the National Bar Association, as well as to the presidencies of other professional, clinical, and academic associations. Most mainstream white Protestant denominations, with the exception of the Southern Baptist Convention, do affirm white and black women in professional ministry. Episcopalians, United Methodists, Congregationalists, Presbyterians, and Disciples of Christ, Christian, ordain women without significant conflict. Episcopalians and United Methodists have elected women bishops. American Baptists and Presbyterians have elected black women as moderator or presiding officer. Ironically, the denominations most associated with upper- and middle-class white people or with poor and marginalized black people in the United States have provided the greatest access to ecclesiastical authority for black women. These churches are also more flexible in their approach to biblical interpretation. The churches with the greatest mass appeal in black communities facing great crises have thrown up the greatest barriers to women's empowerment in their national bodies and local congregations.

Churches in black communities are more female than their white counterparts. The more "mass" the church, the more female has been the congregation. Regardless of this skewing, Theressa Hoover offers us the overall figure of 75% to describe women's participation.[50] This figure masks a range that reaches past ninety percent in some congregations of the Sanctified Church. The full empowerment of the church to speak to the needs of all African-American people cannot be accomplished without the full empowerment of women at every level.

## Conclusion

This chapter cannot answer all of our questions about the church's mission to African-American women. One aim has been to identify several key ideas or themes that will make it possible not only to serve the needs of African-American women in a changing society but also to contribute to the solution of national problems from a strong, viable, and flexible religious tradition. I believe, in precisely the ways in which the black Christian club women—ministers truly—of the late nineteenth and early twentieth centuries believed when they adopted the motto, "Lifting as We Climb," that to struggle and push from the bottom of our communities will mean that the whole community will rise. Listening to and empowering "poor colored women"—economically, politically, or culturally "poor"—is essential to the material and spiritual redemption of African-American communities.

Our communities sit literally on the edge of cultural, political, and economic destruction. Significant segments of the African-American community are experiencing a relentless economic genocide.[51] Our central challenge is this: If the "Black Church" or the "African-American religious experience" or the "Afro-Christian tradition" (whatever we may wish to call it) is as strong as our sagas, legends, and sermons insist that it is, then the church must, in its best historical tradition, respond to this crisis with an internal ministry that addresses the needs of those who are suffering at the same time it projects an uncompromising prophetic force outward that demands and effects significant social, economic, political, and cultural change. In an 1886 speech before the colored clergy of the Protestant Episcopal Church at Washington, D.C., Anna Julia Cooper, insisted:

> *"I am my Sister's keeper!"* should be the hearty response of every man and woman of the race, and this conviction should purify and exalt the narrow, selfish and petty personal aims of life into a noble and sacred purpose.[52]

We still have not answered Cooper's challenge to become, as a community and as a nation and, most importantly, as a church, our "sister's keeper." The echo of that call to ministry still stands unanswered. Harriet Tubman, Alice Walker's "Celie," and Anna Julia Cooper all challenge us to heed the voices of "poor" colored women. It may not be an overstatement to say that the community's response to the historical roles of black women, particularly active/activist black Christian women within and outside of their churches may be the key to the moral and historical contributions of the entire black community to the twenty-first century.

# Notes

## Introduction

1. Linda J. M. LaRue, "Black Liberation and Women's Lib," in *Sociological Realities II: A Guide to the Study of Sociology*, ed. Irving Louis Horowitz and C. Nanry, 282-287 (New York: Harper & Row, 1971).

2. My initial research on the Sanctified Church was not begun with a specific emphasis on women. However, as soon as one engages church documents, the prominence and importance of women cannot be ignored. After having just completed research on community women, the connections between these women and the women of the Sanctified Church leaped from the page and the importance of women to the production of the sacred had to be placed in the foreground.

3. James E. Blackwell, *The Black Community: Diversity and Unity,* 2d ed. (New York: Harper & Row, 1985).

4. This sense of indispensability is not limited to women activists and churchworkers. I have heard testimonies in several black churches, with high degrees of affirmation from the congregation, in which congregants insist that the United States is fortunate that black people pray for their nation. It is almost as if ordinary black churchmen and churchwomen see themselves as the antidote to Thomas Jefferson's stated concerns for the nation when realizing that God is just. This sense that their prayers are indispensable to the nation's well-being needs to be explored more fully.

5. Toni Cade, *The Black Woman* (New York: New American Library, 1970).

6. The only white woman who I ever met who was familiar with Women's Day was in the Assemblies of God. Since that pentecostal denomination had its origins in the Church of God in Christ, I have come to see her as an exception that proved the proverbial rule.

7. Emile Durkheim, *The Elementary Forms of Religious Life*, trans. Karen Fields (New York: Free Press, 1995 [1915]), 167.

8. Robert Wuthnow, *Producing the Sacred: An Essay on Public Religion* (Urbana, Ill.: University of Illinois Press, 1994).

9. Angela Y. Davis, *Blues Legacies and Black Feminism: Gertrude "Ma" Rainey, Bessie Smith, and Billie Holiday* (New York: Pantheon Books, 1998).

10. W. E. B. Du Bois, "Of the Faith of the Fathers," in *The Souls of Black Folk: Authoritative Texts, Contexts, Criticism* (New York: W. W. Norton, 1999), 120.

11. Exemplary of this tradition of works on black male leadership are Peter Paris, *Black Leaders in Conflict: Joseph H. Jackson, Martin Luther King Jr., Malcolm X, Adam Clayton Powell Jr.* (New York: Pilgrim Press, 1978) and Robert Franklin, *Liberating Visions: Human Fulfillment and Social Justice in African-American Thought* (Minneapolis, Minn.: Augsburg Fortress Press, 1990). Gayraud Wilmore's now-classic *Black Religion and Black Radicalism: An Interpretation of the Religious History of*

*Afro-American People* (Maryknoll, N.Y.: Orbis Books, [1973] 1983, 1998) presents an account of African-American religious history whose basic theory, the radicalization and deradicalization of the black church at very specific periods, is an androcentric theory; the period of deradicalization that is often linked to the rise of the Sanctified Church (or black sects and cults) is also one of the most intensive periods of activism of black church women who were both agents of intense spirituality in the Sanctified Church and their missionary societies and political activism in their organizations affiliated with the National Association of Colored Women and later the National Council of Negro Women.

12. Jualynne Dodson and Cheryl Townsend Gilkes, "'Something Within': Social Change and Collective Endurance in the Sacred World of Black Christian Women," in *Women and Religion in America,* vol. 3, *The Twentieth Century,* ed. Rosemary Radford Ruether and Rosemary Skinner Keller (San Francisco: Harper & Row, 1986).

13. Lucie E. Campbell, "Something Within," reprinted in Dodson and Gilkes, "Something Within," 93-94.

14. Toni Cade Bambara, in short stories in *Gorilla, My Love* and *The Sea Birds Are Still Alive,* presents images of the dynamite sisters who challenge the oppression of black people in a myriad of ways. In the opening lines of one such story, we find a black woman activist pulling her car over to observe while the police stop and frisk a black man. Her interest begins with the question, "Is that a brother over there?"

15. Barney G. Glaser and Anselm L. Strauss, *The Discovery of Grounded Theory: Strategies for Qualitative Research* (Chicago: Aldine Publishing Company, 1967).

16. See Alice Walker's definition of *womanist* in *In Search of Our Mothers' Gardens: Womanist Prose* (New York: Harcourt Brace Jovanovich, 1983), xi-xii. See also Cheryl Sanders, "Roundtable Discussion: Christian Ethics and Theology in Womanist Perspective," *Journal of Feminist Studies in Religion* 5/2 (1989): 83-112. This article also contains responses to Sanders by myself, Katie Cannon, bell hooks, and others. See also my essay "Womanist Ways of Seeing," *Peacework: A New England Peace and Social Justice* 210 (July-August 1991): 5-6; reprinted in James H. Cone and Gayraud Wilmore, eds., *Black Theology: A Documentary History, Volume Two: 1980-1992* (Maryknoll, N.Y.: Orbis Books, 1993).

17. Vashti Murphy McKenzie, *Not without a Struggle: Leadership Development for African American Women in Ministry* (Cleveland, Ohio: United Church Press, 1996).

18. Barbara Hilkert Andolsen, *"Daughters of Jefferson, Daughters of Bootblacks": Racism and American Feminism* (Macon, Ga.: Mercer University Press, 1986).

19. C. Eric Lincoln and Lawrence Mamiya, *The Black Church in the African American Experience* (Durham, N.C.: Duke University Press, 1990).

20. See Cheryl Townsend Gilkes, "Plenty Good Room: Adaptation in a Changing Black Church," *The Annals of the American Academy of Political and Social Science* 558 (July 1998): 101-121.

21. Ibid., 114.

## PART 1
## THE COMMUNITY CONNECTION

### 1  "If It Wasn't for the Women . . . "

*An earlier version of this chapter was presented to the Center for Research on Women at Memphis State University during its May 1987 research institute. The author is grateful for the helpful comments of many participants in the institute, especially Bonnie Thornton Dill, Maxine Baca Zinn, Elizabeth Higginbotham, Evelyn Nakano Glenn, and Lynn Weber.*

1. Aldon Morris, *The Origins of the Civil Rights Movement: Black Communities Organizing for Change* (New York: The Free Press, 1984).

2. Stanford Lyman, *The Black American in Sociological Thought: A Failure of Perspective* (New York: G. P. Putnam and Sons, 1972).

3. Robert Blauner, *Racial Oppression in America* (New York: Harper & Row, 1972); William Julius Wilson, *Power, Racism, and Privilege: Race Relations in Theoretical and Sociohistorical Perspectives* (New York: Macmillan, 1973); Cheryl Townsend Gilkes, "The Sources of Conceptual Revolutions in the Field of Race Relations," in *New Directions in Ethnic Studies: Minorities in America*, ed. David Claerbaut, 7-31 (San Francisco: Century Twenty-One, 1980); Everett C. Hughes, "Race Relations and the Sociological Imagination," *American Sociological Review* 28 (1963): 879-890.

4. Toni Cade, *The Black Woman* (New York: New American Library, 1970); Mary King, *Freedom Song; A Personal Story of the 1960s Civil Rights Movement* (New York: William Morrow and Company, 1987); Cheryl Townsend Gilkes, "Liberated to Work Like Dogs: Labeling Black Women and Their Work," in *The Experience and Meaning of Work in Women's Lives*, ed. Hildreth Y. Grossman and Nia Lane Chester (Hillsdale, N.J.: Lawrence Erlbaum Associates, 1990), 165-188.

5. The data for this chapter are taken from my larger study, "Living and Working in a World of Trouble: The Emergent Career of the Black Woman Community Worker" (Ph.D. dissertation, Northeastern University, 1979). Similar studies of the Chinese American and Puerto Rican community also identify the critical roles of women community workers. See Miren Uriarte-Gaston, "Organizing for Survival: The Emergence of a Puerto Rican Community" (Ph.D. dissertation, Boston University, 1988) and Stacey Guat Hong Yap, "Gather Your Strength, Sisters: The Emergence of Chinese Women Community Workers" (Ph.D. dissertation, Boston University, 1983).

6. Earlier versions of this paper were presented to the Center for Research on Women, Memphis State University, Summer Institute, 1983 and 1986.

7. James E. Blackwell, *The Black Community: Diversity and Unity*, 2d ed. (New York: Harper & Row, 1985), xi.

8. Blauner, *Racial Oppression*. See also Aime Cesaire, *Discourse on Colonialism* (New York: Monthly Review Press, 1972 [1955]), and Manning Marable, *How Capitalism Underdeveloped Black America*: (Boston: South End Press, 1983).

9. Substantial insights for this discussion of racial oppression and internal colonialism are drawn from collaborative work with Bonnie Thornton Dill, Evelyn Nakano Glenn, Elizabeth Higginbotham, and Ruth Zambrana, sponsored by the Inter-University Working Group on Gender, Race, and Class.

10. Everett C. Hughes, *The Sociological Eye: Selected Papers on Work, Self, and the Study of Society* (Chicago: Aldine-Atherton, 1971), 313.

11. The importance of the extra time and work cannot be overstated. Bettylou Valentine, discussing the expanded time budgets of ghettoized African Americans in *Hustling and Other Hard Work: Life Styles in the Ghetto* (New York: The Free Press, 1978), considers this to be part of the social cost of their combined poverty and racial oppression. She not only identified "hustling" as the legal and extralegal strategies that Blackston residents used to produce and augment income, she also means

the term to apply to the extra work, the extra hustle, that must be packed into each day because of poverty and racial oppression.

12. When I began this research, people assumed I would be studying the African-American equivalent of the Junior League. Although the twenty-three women who were employed full-time were in middle-class occupations, their class origins were as diverse as those of the larger community. Women with poor and working-class origins had usually experienced their upward mobility in the process of acquiring more education in order to qualify for positions in human services that allowed them to do community work full-time, both as volunteers and as professionals. Calling it "going up for the oppressed," I explored this special kind of upward mobility in an earlier article. See Cheryl Townsend Gilkes, "Going Up for the Oppressed: The Career Mobility of Black Women Community Workers," *Journal of Social Issues* 39 (1983): 115-139.

13. Bernice Johnson Reagon, "My Black Mothers and Sisters or on Beginning a Cultural Autobiography," *Feminist Studies* 8 (Spring 1982): 81-96, especially 82-83. See also, Bernice Johnson Reagon, "African Diaspora Women: The Making of Cultural Workers," *Feminist Studies* 12 (1986): 77-90.

14. A pseudonym.

15. Deborah Gray White, *Ar'n't I a Woman?: Female Slaves in the Plantation South* (New York: W. W. Norton, 1985); Thomas L. Webber, *Deep like the Rivers: Education in the Slave Quarter Community, 1831-1865* (New York: W. W. Norton, 1978). See also Angela Davis, "Reflections on the Black Woman's Role in the Community of Slaves," *Black Scholar* 3 (December 1971) and the revision of that essay in her book *Women, Race, and Class* (New York: Random House, 1981).

16. Linda Perkins, "Black Women and Racial 'Uplift' prior to Emancipation," in *The Black Woman Cross-Culturally*, ed. Filomena Chioma Steady, 317-334 (Rochester, Vt..: Schenkman Books, 1981); Dorothy Sterling, *We Are Your Sisters: Black Women in the Nineteenth Century* (New York: W. W. Norton, 1984).

17. Paula Giddings, *When and Where I Enter: The Impact of Black Women on Race and Sex in America* (New York: William Morrow and Company, 1984); Marilyn Richardson, ed., *Maria W. Stewart, America's First Black Woman Political Writer* (Bloomington, Ind.: Indiana University Press, 1987).

18. Sterling, *We Are Your Sisters.*

19. Elizabeth Lindsey Davis, *Lifting as They Climb: A History of the National Association of Colored Women* (Washington, D.C.: Moorland Spingarn Research Center, 1933), 19.

20. One Urban League consultant stated that women emerged as presidents of local Urban League and NAACP chapters as often as men, although they did not preside over the national bodies. She concluded that the role of women as local Urban League presidents combined with their roles in Urban League Guilds (women's clubs that raised money for the Urban League) showed the importance of the unacknowledged power of women in community affairs.

21. The Urban League was formed through the merger of two organizations, one male and one female.

22. The organization was originally called the Association for the Study of Negro Life and History.

23. Gerda Lerner, *Black Women in White America: A Documentary History* (New York: Vintage Books, 1972); Perkins, "Black Women and Racial 'Uplift.'"

24. Carter G. Woodson, "The Negro Washerwoman," *The Journal of Negro History* 15 (1930): 269-277.

25. Elsa Barkley Brown, "The Womanist Consciousness of Maggie Lena Walker and the Independent Order of Saint Luke," *Signs: Journal of Women in Culture and Society* 14/3 (1989): 610-633; Giddings, *When and Where I Enter*.

26. W. E. B. Du Bois, *The Gift of Black Folk: Negroes in the Making of America* (Millwood, N.Y.: Kraus Thompson Organization, 1975 [1924]), 273.

27. Morris, *The Origins of the Civil Rights Movement*.

28. Carter G. Woodson, *The Mis-Education of the Negro* (New York: The Associated Publishers, 1933).

29. Carter Woodson founded Negro History Week in 1926 and chose the month of February because the birthdays of Frederick Douglass and Abraham Lincoln occurred at that time. The movements of the 1960s prompted the expansion of the celebration to a month and changed the name from Negro History to Black History.

30. Vine Deloria points out that the problems of powerlessness and empowerment are shared across communities of color even when the specificity of racial oppression each community experiences may be quite different. See Vine Deloria, *We Talk, You Listen: New Tribes, New Turf* (New York: Dell Publishing Company, 1970).

31. Marian Wright Edelman, *Families in Peril: An Agenda for Social Change* (Cambridge, Mass.: Harvard University Press, 1987).

32. Sadie Iola Daniel with Charles H. Wesley and Thelma D. Perry, *Women Builders* (Washington, D.C.: Associated Publishers, 1970 [1931]).

## 2  Exploring the Community Connection

*An earlier version of this chapter was presented to the North Central Sociological Society. The author is grateful for the helpful comments of James Geschwender and for the comments and editorial suggestions of Judith Lorber.*

1. Reeve Vanneman and Lynn Weber Cannon, *The American Perception of Class* (Philadelphia: Temple University Press, 1987).

2. Elizabeth Higginbotham, "Just Who Is Black and Middle Class?" (Paper presented to the Society for the Study of Social Problems, Toronto, Canada, 1981); Bart Landry, *The New Black Middle Class* (Berkeley and Los Angeles: University of California Press, 1987).

3. Bonnie Thornton Dill, "Race, Class, and Gender: Prospects for an All-Inclusive Sisterhood," *Feminist Studies* 9 (1983): 131-150.

4. Jacqueline Jones, *Labor of Love, Labor of Sorrow: Black Women, Work and Family from Slavery to the Present* (New York: Basic Books, 1985).

5. Ibid., 133.

6. Ibid., 328-329.

7. Septima Clark with Cynthia Stokes Brown, *Ready from Within: Septima Clark and the Civil Rights Movement* (Navarro, Calif.: Wild Trees Press, 1986); Paula Giddings, *When and Where I Enter: The Impact of Black Women on Race and Sex in America* (New York: William Morrow and Company, 1984); Mary King, *Freedom Song: A Personal Story of the 1960s Civil Rights Movement* (New York: William Morrow and Company, 1987); Aldon Morris, *The Origins of the Civil Rights Movement: Black Communities Organizing for Change* (New York: The Free Press, 1984); Jo Ann Gibson Robinson, *The Montgomery Bus Boycott and the Women Who Started It* (Knoxville, Tenn.: University of Tennessee Press, 1987).

8. Cheryl Townsend Gilkes, "Living and Working in a World of Trouble: The Emergent Career of the Black Woman Community Worker" (Ph.D. dissertation, Northeastern University, 1979); Cheryl Townsend Gilkes, "Going Up for the Oppressed: The Career Mobility of Black Women Community Workers," *Journal of Social Issues* 39 (1983): 115-139.

9. Cheryl Townsend Gilkes, "Together and in Harness: Women's Traditions in the Sanctified Church," *Signs: Journal of Women in Culture and Society* 10 (1985): 678-699; idem, "The Role of Women in the Sanctified Church," *Journal of Religious Thought* 43 (1986): 24-41.

10. Gilkes, "Going Up for the Oppressed."

11. Alice Walker, *In Search of Our Mothers' Gardens: Womanist Prose* (New York: Harcourt Brace Jovanovich, 1983).

12. Ibid., xi.

13. Joyce Ladner, *Tomorrow's Tomorrow* (Garden City, N.Y.: Doubleday and Company, 1971); Bonnie Thornton Dill, "The Dialectics of Black Womanhood," *Signs: Journal of Women in Culture and Society* 4 (1979): 543-555.

14. Walker, *In Search of Our Mothers' Gardens*, xi.

15. Robinson, *The Montgomery Bus Boycott*.

16. Deborah K. King, "Multiple Jeopardy, Multiple Consciousness: The Context of a Black Feminist Ideology," *Signs: Journal of Women in Culture and Society* 14 (1988): 42-72, esp. 49.

17. Ibid., 72.

18. W. E. B. Du Bois, *The Gift of Black Folk: The Negroes in the Making of America* (New York: Washington Square Press, 1970 [1924]), 65-140.

19. Anna Julia Cooper, *A Voice from the South by a Woman of the South* (New York: Negro Universities Press, 1969 [Xenia, Ohio: The Aldine Printing House, 1892]), 151.

20. W. E. B. Du Bois, *W. E. B. Du Bois: The Crisis Writings*, ed. Daniel Walden (Greenwich, Conn.: Fawcett Publications, 1972), 351.

21. Ibid., 340.

22. Cooper, *A Voice from the South*, 31.

23. Ibid., 134.

24. Jualynne Dodson and Cheryl Townsend Gilkes, "'Something Within'": Social Change and Collective Endurance in the Sacred World of Black Christian Women," in *Women and Religion in America*, vol. 3, *The Twentieth Century*, ed. Rosemary Radford Ruether and Rosemary Skinner Keller (San Francisco: Harper & Row, 1986), 88-89.

25. Ibid., 122, 125.

26. King, "Multiple Jeopardy, Multiple Consciousness."

27. Du Bois, *The Gift of Black Folk*, 149.

28. John Blassingame, *The Slave Community: Plantation Slavery in the Antebellum South* (New York: Oxford University Press, 1972); Elizabeth Fox-Genovese, *Within the Plantation Household: Black and White Women of the Old South* (Chapel Hill, N.C.: University of North Carolina Press, 1988); Eugene Genovese, *Roll, Jordan, Roll: The World the Slaves Made* (New York: Random House, 1975); Deborah Gray White, *Ar'n't I a Woman?: Female Slaves in the Plantation South* (New York: W. W. Norton and Company, 1985).

29. Margaret Creel, *A Peculiar People: Slave Religion and Community-Culture among the Gullahs* (New York: New York University Press, 1988); Albert J. Raboteau, *Slave Religion: The Peculiar Institution in the Antebellum South* (New York: Oxford

University Press, 1978); Mechal Sobel, *Trabelin' On: The Slave's Journey to an Afro-Baptist Faith* (Westport, Conn.: Greenwood Press, 1979).

30. Herbert G. Gutman, *The Black Family in Slavery and Freedom, 1750-1925* (New York: Pantheon Books/Random House, 1976); Thomas L. Webber, *Deep like the Rivers: Education in the Slave Quarter Community, 1831-1865* (New York: W. W. Norton, 1978).

31. Genovese, *Roll, Jordan, Roll*; Gutman, *Black Family in Slavery*.

32. Blassingame, *The Slave Community*.

33. Gutman, *Black Family in Slavery*.

34. Dill, "Race, Class, and Gender"; Gutman, *Black Family in Slavery*.

35. Webber, *Deep like the Rivers*.

36. Toni Morrison, *Beloved* (New York: Random House, 1987).

37. Middleton Harris, Morris Levitt, Roger Furman, and Ernest Smith, *The Black Book* (New York: Random House, 1974), 10.

38. Leon Litwack, *Been in the Storm So Long: The Aftermath of Slavery* (New York: Random House, 1979), 461-462; White, *Ar'n't I a Woman?*, 137-138.

39. Webber, *Deep like the Rivers*.

40. White, *Ar'n't I a Woman?*

41. Ibid., 119.

42. Ibid., 131-132.

43. Ibid., 120.

44. Ibid., 140.

45. Ibid., 141.

46. Dodson and Gilkes, "Something Within."

47. Giddings, *When and Where I Enter*.

48. bell hooks, *Feminist Theory: From Margin to Center* (Boston: South End Press, 1984), 11.

49. Dill, "Race, Class, and Gender"; Ladner, *Tomorrow's Tomorrow*.

50. E. Franklin Frazier, *Black Bourgeoisie* (New York: The Free Press, 1957).

51. Evelyn Brooks Barnett, "Nannie Burroughs and the Education of Black Women," in *The Afro-American Woman: Struggles and Images*, ed. Sharon Harley and Rosalyn Terborg-Penn, 97-108 (Port Washington, N.Y.: Kennikat Press, 1978); Evelyn Brooks, "The Feminist Theology of the Black Baptist Church, 1880-1900," in *Class, Race, and the Dynamics of Control*, ed. Amy Swerdlow and Hannah Lessinger, 31-59 (Boston: G. K. Hall, 1983).

52. Gilkes, "Together and in Harness."

53. Burroughs, in Dodson and Gilkes, "Something Within," 126-127.

54. Walker, *In Search of Our Mothers' Gardens*, xi.

55. Dodson and Gilkes, "Something Within."

56. Giddings, *When and Where I Enter*.

57. Barbara Hilkert Andolsen, *"Daughters of Jefferson, Daughters of Bootblacks": Racism and American Feminism* (Macon, Ga.: Mercer University Press, 1986).

58. Toni Cade, *The Black Woman: An Anthology* (New York: New American Library, 1970).

59. Audre Lorde, *Sister Outsider: Essays and Speeches* (Trumansburg, N.Y.: The Crossing Press, 1984), 126.

60. Rhetaugh Graves Dumas, "Dilemmas of Black Females in Leadership," in *The Black Woman*, ed. LaFrances Rodgers-Rose, 203-215 (Beverly Hills, Calif.: Sage Publications, 1980).

61. King, "Multiple Jeopardy, Multiple Consciousness"; Patricia Hill Collins, "Learning from the Outsider Within: The Sociological Significance of Black Feminist Thought," *Social Problems* 33 (1986).

# PART 2
# CHURCH WOMEN AND THEIR WORK

## 3 "Together and in Harness"

*Earlier versions of this article were presented to the Women's Studies in Religion Program of the Harvard Divinity School and to the* Signs *Communities of Women Conference, held February 18-20, 1983, at the Center for Research on Women, Stanford University. I wish to acknowledge the support of Boston University's Faculty Research Program, the Women's Studies in Religion Program of the Harvard Divinity School, the Inter-University Research Group on the Intersection of Gender and Race, and the Bunting Institute of Radcliffe College for their contributions at various stages of the research and writing. I also wish to thank Paule Verdet, Thomas Koenig, and two anonymous* Signs *reviewers for criticism and editorial suggestions.*

1. Teressa Hoover, "Black Women and the Churches: Triple Jeopardy," in *Black Theology: A Documentary History*, ed. Gayraud Wilmore and James Cone, 377-388 (Maryknoll, N.Y.: Orbis Books, 1979); James Tinney, "The Religious Experience of Black Men," in *The Black Male*, ed. Lawrence E. Gary, 269-276 (Beverly Hills, Calif.: Sage Publications, 1981); See also Pearl Williams-Jones, "A Minority Report: Black Pentecostal Women," *Spirit: A Journal of Issues Incident to Black Pentecostalism* 1/2 (1977): 31-44.

2. Bonnie Thornton Dill, "The Dialectics of Black Womanhood," *Signs: Journal of Women in Culture and Society* 4/3 (Spring 1979): 543-555.

3. On the dominant culture's devaluation of black women, see bell hooks, *Ain't I a Woman: Black Women and Feminism* (Boston: South End Press, 1981). On the role of black women in education, see Linda Perkins, "Black Women and Racial 'Uplift' prior to Emancipation," in *The Black Woman Cross-Culturally*, ed. Filomena Chioma Steady, 317-334 (Rochester, Vt.: Schenkman Books, 1985); Angela Y. Davis, *Women, Race, and Class* (New York: Random House, 1981); and Gerda Lerner, ed. *Black Women in White America: A Documentary History* (New York: Random House, 1971). On the "relative" economic dependence of black women, see Dill, "The Dialectics of Black Womanhood"; and Angela Davis, *Women, Race, and Class*. On the political organization of black women, see Perkins, "Black Women in Racial 'Uplift' prior to Emancipation,"; Angela Davis, *Women, Race, and Class*; and Cheryl Townsend Gilkes, "Living and Working in a World of Trouble: The Emergent Career of the Black Woman Community Worker" (Ph.D. dissertation, Northeastern University, 1979).

4. Perkins, "Black Women and Racial 'Uplift' prior to Emancipaton," 321

5. W. E. B. Du Bois, "Votes for Women," in *The Crisis Writings*, ed. Daniel Walden (Greenwich, Conn.: Fawcett Publications, 1972 [1912]), 339-340, esp. 340.

6. Elizabeth Lindsey Davis, *Lifting as They Climb: A History of the National Association of Colored Women* (Washington, D.C.: Howard University, Moorland Spingarn Research Center, 1933), 19.

7. Ibid.

8. Charles H. Pleas, *Fifty Years of Achievement (History): Church of God in Christ* (Memphis, Tenn.: Church of God in Christ Publishing House, n.d. [*circa* 1957]), 35.

9. James Shopshire, "A Socio-historical Characterization of the Black Pentecostal Movement in America" (Ph.D. dissertation, Northwestern University, 1975), 144-145.

10. Church of the Living God, Christian Workers for Fellowship, *Glorious Heritage: The Golden Book—Documentary and History* (n.p.: Church of the Living God, Christian Workers for Fellowship, 1976).

11. Church of God in Christ (COGIC), *Official Manual with the Doctrines and Discipline of the Church of God in Christ* (Memphis, Tenn.: COGIC Publishing House, 1973).

12. Lucille Cornelius, *The Pioneer History of the Church of God in Christ* (Memphis, Tenn.: COGIC Publishing House, 1975); Church of the Living God, *Glorious Heritage*; Pleas, *Fifty Years of Achievement*.

13. Judges 5:7, *The Holy Bible* (King James Version).

14. Church of God in Christ, *Official Manual*; Church of the Living God, *Glorious Heritage*.

15. Church of God in Christ, *Official Manual*.

16. Women's Department, Church of God in Christ, *Women's Handbook* (Memphis, Tenn.: COGIC Publishing House, 1980).

17. Priscilla Douglas, "Black Working Women: Factors Affecting Labor Market Experience" (Working Paper, Wellesley College, Center for Research on Women, 1980).

18. Cornelius, *Pioneer History*, 24. Oral tradition and interviews set the amount at a minimum of $10,000.

19. Elizabeth Lindsey Davis, *Lifting as They Climb*.

20. Women's Department (COGIC), *Women's Handbook*, 21.

21. Cornelius, *Pioneer History*, 27.

22. Ibid.

23. Women's Department (COGIC), *Women's Handbook*, 21.

24. James Tinney, "Black Pentecostals: The Difference Is More Than Color," *Logos Journal* 10/3 (1980): 16-19.

25. Church of the Living God, *Glorious Heritage*.

26. Jualynne Dodson, "Black Women as an Unknown Source of Organizational Change" (Providence, R.I.: Society for the Scientific Study of Religion, 1982), typescript.

27. Rosemary Radford Ruether and Eleanor McLaughlin, eds., *Women of Spirit: Female Leadership in the Jewish and Christian Traditions* (New York: Simon and Schuster, 1979), 16-17.

28. Tinney, "The Religious Experience of Black Men."

29. Dill, "The Dialectics of Black Womanhood"; Pauli Murray, "The Liberation of Black Women," in *Voices of the New Feminism*, ed. Mary L. Thompson (Boston: Beacon Press, 1970); idem, "Jim Crow and Jane Crow," in Lerner, *Black Women in America*, 592-599; hooks, *Ain't I a Woman*.

### 4   The Roles of Church and Community Mothers

*Support for the research on church mothers was provided by the Faculty Research Program of the Graduate School at Boston University. I gratefully acknowledge the helpful criticisms of Paule Verdet, Jualynne Dodson, and two* Journal of Feminist Studies in Religion *reviewers.*

1. Iva Carruthers, "War on African Familyhood," in *Sturdy Black Bridges: Visions of Black Women in Literature*, ed. Roseann P. Bell, Bettye J. Parker, and Beverly Guy-sheftall (Garden City, N.Y.: Doubleday-Anchor, 1979), 8-9.

2. Harold A. Carter, *The Prayer Traditions of Black People* (Valley Forge, Pa.: Judson Press, 1976); Queen Mother Moore, "The Black Scholar Interview: Queen Mother Moore," *The Black Scholar* 4/6-7 (1973): 47-55.

3. Cheryl Townsend Gilkes, "Black Women's Work as Deviance: The Sources of Racial Antagonism within Contemporary Feminism," working paper no. 66 (Wellesley, Mass.: Wellesley College Center for Research on Women, 1979); Willa Mae Hemmons, "The Women's Liberation Movement: Understanding Black Women's Attitudes," in *The Black Woman*, ed. LaFrances Rodgers-Rose, 285-299 (Beverly Hills, Calif.: Sage Publications, 1980); Jeanne Noble, *Beautiful, Also, Are the Souls of My Black Sisters: A History of the Black Woman in America* (Englewood Cliffs, N.J.: Prentice-Hall, 1978).

4. Along with Hemmons's "Understanding Black Women's Attitudes," see Geraldine Wilson, "The Self/Group Actualization of Black Women," in Rodgers-Rose, *The Black Woman*, 301-314; Carruthers, "African Familyhood"; Theressa Hoover, "Black Women and the Churches: Triple Jeopardy," in *Black Theology: A Documentary History, 1966-1979*, ed. Gayraud S. Wilmore and James H. Cone, 377-388 (Maryknoll, N.Y.: Orbis Books, 1979).

5. Ralph Ellison, "An American Dilemma: A Review," in *The Death of White Sociology*, ed. Joyce A. Ladner (New York: Random House, 1973); Ronald Taylor, "Black Ethnicity and the Persistence of Ethnogenesis," *American Journal of Sociology* 84/6 (1979): 1401-1423.

6. Stokley Carmichael and Charles V. Hamilton, *Black Power: The Politics of Liberation in America* (New York: Random House, 1967); Robert Blauner, *Racial Oppression in America* (New York: Harper & Row, 1971).

7. Melville Herskovits, *The Myth of the Negro Past* (Boston: Beacon Press, 1958 [1974]); John F. Szwed, ed., *Black America* (New York: Basic Books, 1979); Norman E. Whitten and John F. Szwed, eds., *Afro-American Anthropology: Contemporary Perspectives* (New York: The Free Press, 1970).

8. Cheryl Townsend Gilkes, "Living and Working in a World of Trouble: The Emergent Career of the Black Woman Community Worker" (Ph.D. dissertation, Northeastern University, 1979).

9. Hoover, "Black Women and the Churches."

10. Church of God in Christ (COGIC), *Official Manual with the Doctrines and Discipline of the Church of God in Christ* (Memphis, Tenn.: COGIC Publishing House, 1973), 159; James S. Tinney, "Black Pentecostals: The Difference Is More Than Color," *Logos Journal* 10/3 (1980): 16-19.

11. Gilkes, "Living and Working in a World of Trouble"; idem, "Black Women's Work as Deviance."

12. Kamene Okonjo, "The Dual-Sex Political System in Operation: Igbo Women and Community Politics in Midwestern Nigeria," in *Women in Africa: Studies in Social and Economic Change*, ed. Nancy J. Hafkin and Edna G. Bay, 45-58 (Stanford, Calif.: Stanford University Press, 1976).

13. Ibid.

14. Carruthers, "African Familyhood."

15. John W. Blassingame, *The Slave Community: Plantation Slavery in the Ante-Bellum South* (Oxford: Oxford University Press, 1972); Stanford Lyman, *The Black*

*American in Sociological Thought: A Failure of Perspectives* (New York: Capricorn Books, 1972).

16. Letitia Woods Brown, "Battles Won and Evil Overcome," in *The Black Woman: Myths and Realities*, ed. Doris J. Mitchell and Jewell H. Bell (Cambridge, Mass.: Radcliffe College, 1978), 4.

17. Ibid., 4-5.

18. Judith van Allen, "'Aba Riots' or 'Igbo Women's War'?: Ideology, Stratification, and the Indivisibility of Women," in Hafkin and Bay, *Women in Africa*, 68.

19. Ibid., 45.

20. Ibid., 53.

21. Ibid., 54.

22. Ibid.

23. LaFrances Rodgers-Rose, "Introduction," in Rodgers-Rose, *The Black Woman*, 17.

24. Gwendolyn Randall Puryear, "The Black Woman: Liberated or Oppressed?," in *Comparative Perspectives on Third World Women: The Impact of Race, Sex, and Class*, ed. Beverly Lindsay (New York: Praeger, 1980), 256.

25. Eva L. R. Meyerowitz, *The Divine Kingship in Ghana and Ancient Egypt* (London: Faber and Faber, 1960).

26. Raymond Gore Clough, *Oil Rivers Trader: Memories of Iboland* (London: C. Hurst and Company, 1972).

27. Concerning Queen Hatshepsut, see Cheikh Anta Diop, *The Cultural Unity of Black Africa: The Domains of Patriarchy and Matriarchy in Classical Antiquity* (Chicago: Third World Press, 1978 [1958]), 115-117; Wilson, "The Self/Group Actualization of Black Women," 310-311. On the role of Queen Nzinga, see Wilson, "The Self/Group Actualization of Black Women," 311-312; and Chancellor Williams, *The Destruction of Black Civilization: Great Issues of a Race from 4500 B.C. to 2000 A.D.* (Chicago: Third World Press, 1976), 273-289. Concerning Queen Mother Yaa Asantewaa, see Wilson, "The Self/Group Actualization of Black Women," 312-313.

28. Diop, *The Cultural Unity of Black Africa*, 56-57; Noble, *Beautiful, Also, Are the Souls of My Black Sisters*, 13.

29. Wilson, "The Self/Group Actualization of Black Women," 305. Colonialism caused a deterioration in the status of African women, particularly in those areas of West Africa where women had considerable authority. See Okonjo, "The Dual-Sex Political System"; van Allen, "'Aba Riots' or 'Igbo Women's War'?; Claire Robertson, "Ga Women and Socioeconomic Change in Accra, Ghana," in Hafkin and Bay, *Women in Africa*, 111-134. The imposition of indirect rule and British values on West Africa meant that men's roles were developed at the expense of women. See Minna Davis Caulfield's discussion of this problem in "Imperialism, the Family, and Cultures of Resistance," *Socialist Revolution* #20 4/2 (October 1974): 67-85.

30. Williams, *The Destruction of Black Civilization*, 272.

31. Angela Davis, "Reflections on the Black Woman's Role in the Community of Slaves," *Black Scholar* 3 (December 1971); idem, *Women, Race. and Class* (New York: Random House, 1981).

32. E. Franklin Frazier, *The Negro Family in the United States* (Chicago: University of Chicago Press, 1939); Jesse Bernard, *Marriage and Family among Negroes* (Englewood Cliffs, N.J.: Prentice-Hall, 1966).

33. Ida Wells Barnett, *Crusade for Justice: The Autobiography of B. Wells* (Chicago: University of Chicago Press, 1970); Elizabeth Lindsay Davis, *Lifting as They Climb:*

*A History of the National Association of Colored Women* (Washington, D.C.: Moorland-Spingarn Research Center, Howard University, 1933); Emma Fields, "The Women's Club Movement in the United States, 1877-1900" (Master's thesis, Moorland Spingarn Research Center, Howard University, 1948); Rackham Holt, *Mary McLeod Bethune: A Biography* (Garden City, N.Y.: Doubleday and Company, 1964); Gerda Lerner, *Black Women in White America: A Documentary History* (New York: Random House, 1972); Mary Church Terrell, "The History of the Club Women's Movement," *The Aframerican Woman's Journal* 1/2-3 (1940): 34-38.

34. Holt, *Mary McLeod Bethune.*

35. Davis, *Lifting as They Climb*; Fields, "The Women's Club Movement." The wide range of concerns that the National Council of Negro Women exhibited can be seen in this journal. *The Aframerican Woman's Journal* was published from 1940 through 1948. As the council's involvement in the United Nations grew, and with it the council's consciousness of the shared nature of black women's problems in the United States and the emerging nonaligned nations, the name of the journal was changed to *Women United.*

36. Davis, *Lifting as They Climb*, 19.

37. Because of a protection of human subjects agreement all names and places associated with community workers who were part of my research, "Living and Working in a World of Trouble," are pseudonyms.

38. This and other unattributed quotations are from data used for Gilkes, "Living and Working in a World of Trouble."

39. Carter, *The Prayer Tradition of Black People*, 77-79; Mamie Garvin Fields and Karen Fields, *Lemon Swamp and Other Places: A Carolina Memoir* (New York: MacMillan-Free Press, 1983), 36.

40. 1 Corinthians 11:11, *The Holy Bible* (King James Version); Charles H. Pleas, *Fifty Years Achievement (History): Church of God in Christ* (Memphis, Tenn.: Church of God in Christ Publishing House, n.d., [*circa* 1957]), 36.

41. Church of God in Christ, *Official Manual*, 158.

42. Pleas, *Fifty Years Achievement*, 39. Cf., J. O. Patterson, Rev. German B. Ross, and Mrs. Julia Mason Atkins, eds., *History and Formative Years of the Church of God in Christ with Excerpts from the Life and Works of Its Founder—Bishop C. H. Mason* (Memphis, Tenn.: Church of God in Christ Publishing House, 1969); Lucille Cornelius, *The Pioneer History of the Church of God in Christ* (Memphis, Tenn.: Church of God in Christ Publishing House, 1975).

43. Church of God in Christ, *Official Manual*, 159, 160.

44. Bishop O. T. Jones, in Pleas, *Fifty Years Achievement*, 35.

45. James S. Tinney, "Black Pentecostals: Setting Up the Kingdom," *Christianity Today* (December 5, 1975), 42-43.

46. Pleas, *Fifty Years Achievement*, 48.

47. "Dr. Mallory-King Appointed First Commissioner of Education," *The Whole Truth* 8/6 (1975): 1-2.

48. Tinney, "Black Pentecostals: Setting Up the Kingdom," 43.

49. Cornelius, *The Pioneer History.*

50. Ibid., 23, emphasis added.

51. Ibid., 27, emphasis added.

52. "Thousands Pass over Bier of Mother Bailey," *The Whole Truth* 9/1 (1976): 1.

53. Pearl Williams-Jones, "A Minority Report: Black Pentecostal Women," *Spirit: A Journal of Issues Incident to Black Pentecostalism* 1/2 (1977): 31-44.

54. James Maynard Shopshire, "A Socio-Historical Characterization of the Black Pentecostal Movement" (Ph.D. dissertation, Northwestern University, 1975), 144.

55. Ibid.; Joe Samuel Ratliffe, "The Enabling of a Local Pentecostal Congregation to Rethink the Role of Women in the Church" (D.Min. thesis, Interdenominational Theological Center, 1976).

56. Church of the Living God, Christian Workers for Fellowship, *Glorious Heritage: The Golden Book—Documentary and Historical* (n.p.: Church of the Living God, Christian Workers for Fellowship, 1967).

57. Ibid., 25.

58. Ibid., 26, 35.

59. Ibid., 35.

60. Shopshire, "The Black Pentecostal Movement," 91-92.

61. Arnor Davis, "The Pentecostal Movement in Black Christianity," *The Black Church* 2/1 (1972): 65-88.

62. Until well into the 1950s, black people used "the Race" to denote a national black community with shared social, economic, and political interests. In denotation and connotation, it is similar to the phrase "La Raza," often used among Chicanos in the American Southwest. For the traditional usage of "the Race," see St. Clair Drake and Horace Cayton, *Black Metropolis: A Study of Negro Life in a Northern City* (New York: Harcourt, Brace, and World, 1945).

63. This strategy of white politicians called "get to the ministers" is described in Charles V. Hamilton, *The Black Preacher in America* (New York: William Morrow and Company, 1972), 11-12.

64. Albert Murray, "White Norms and Black Deviation," in Ladner, *The Death of White Sociology.*

65. Thomas L. Webber, *Deep like the Rivers: Education in the Slave Quarters Community, 1831-1865* (New York: W. W. Norton, 1978).

## 5   The Role of Women in the Sanctified Church

1. Alice Walker, "womanist," in *In Search of Our Mothers' Gardens: Womanist Prose* (San Diego: Harcourt Brace Jovanovich, 1983), xi-xii.

2. Unattributed quotations are taken from statements recorded in interviews, field notes, and research diaries.

3. Bonnie Thornton Dill, "The Dialectics of Black Womanhood: Towards a New Model of American Femininity," *Signs: Journal of Women in Culture and Society* 4/3 (Spring 1979): 543-55.

4. Paula Giddings, *When and Where I Enter: The Impact of Black Women on Race and Sex in America* (New York: William Morrow and Company, 1984).

5. Dorothy Sterling, *We Are Your Sisters: Black Women in the Nineteenth Century* (New York: W. W. Norton, 1984).

6. Zora Neale Hurston, *The Sanctified Church* (Berkeley, Calif.: The Turtle Press, 1981).

7. Theressa Hoover, "Black Women and the Churches: Triple Jeopardy," in *Black Theology: A Documentary History, 1966-1979*, ed. Gayraud S. Wilmore and James H. Cone, 377-388 (Maryknoll, N.Y.: Orbis Books, 1979).

8. James Tinney, "The Religious Experience of Black Men," in *The Black Male*, ed. Lawrence E. Gary, 269-276 (Beverly Hills, Calif.: Sage Publications, 1981); Pearl Williams-Jones, "A Minority Report: Black Pentecostal Women," *Spirit: A Journal of Issues Incident to Black Pentecostalism* 1/2 (1977), 31-44.

9. Cheryl Townsend Gilkes, "'Together and in Harness': Women's Traditions in the Sanctified Church," *Signs: Journal of Women in Culture and Society* 10/4 (Summer 1985): 679. [Cheryl Sanders has rightly pointed out that this number is actually much larger. See Cheryl Sanders, *Saints in Exile: The Holiness-Pentecostal Experience in African American Religion and Culture* (New York: Oxford University Press, 1996); Wardell Payne, ed., *Directory of African American Religious Bodies: A Compendium by the Howard University School of Divinity* (Washington, D.C.: Howard University Press, 1991).]

10. Gilkes, "Together and in Harness," 680.

11. "DeLeon Richards," *People* 23/16 (October 14, 1985), 16, 51.

12. Thomas Webber, *Deep like the Rivers: Education in the Slave Quarters Community, 1830-1865* (New York: W. W. Norton, 1978), 149-150.

13. Leon F. Litwack, *Been in the Storm So Long: The Aftermath of Slavery* (New York: Vintage Books, 1979), 450-501.

14. Ibid., 461-462.

15. Sterling, *We Are Your Sisters*, 338-342.

16. W. E. B. Du Bois, *The Gift of Black Folk: The Negroes in the Making of America* (New York: Washington Square Press, 1970), 141-149.

17. This development is described in Nell Irvin Painter, *The Exodusters: Black Migration to Kansas after Reconstruction* (New York: W. W. Norton, 1976) and in Jacqueline Jones, *Labor of Love, Labor of Sorrow: Black Women, Work, and the Family from Slavery to the Present* (New York: Basic Books, 1985).

18. Relevant documents can be located in Elizabeth Lindsey Davis, *Lifting as They Climb: A History of the National Association of Colored Women* (Washington, D.C.: Howard University, Moorland Spingarn Research Center, 1933).

19. James Shopshire, "A Socio-historical Characterization of the Black Pentecostal Movement in America" (Ph.D. dissertation, Northwestern University, 1975), 144-145.

20. Gilkes, "Together and in Harness," 687.

21. Sterling, *We Are Your Sisters*, 204.

22. Church of God in Christ (COGIC), *Official Manual with the Doctrines and Disciplines of the Church of God in Christ* (Memphis, Tenn.: COGIC Publishing House, 1973).

23. Charles H. Pleas, *Fifty Years of Achievement (History): Church of God in Christ* (Memphis, Tenn.: Church of God in Christ Publishing House, n.d. [*circa* 1957]).

24. Lucille Cornelius, *The Pioneer History of the Church of God in Christ* (Memphis, Tenn.: Church of God in Christ Publishing House, 1975).

25. Pleas, *Fifty Years of Achievement*, 36.

26. Melvin Williams, *Community in a Black Pentecostal Church: An Anthropological Study* (Pittsburgh, Pa.: University of Pittsburgh Press, 1974).

27. Sister Ann Smith, National Recording Secretary, "Minutes: 24th Annual Convocation," *The Whole Truth* 18/1 (January 1942), 1.

28. Ibid.

29. Kelly Miller, "Surplus Negro Women," *Radicals and Conservatives and Other Essays on the Negro in America* (New York: Schocken Books, 1968).

30. Anthony Heilbut, *The Gospel Sound: Good News and Bad Times* (New York: Simon and Schuster, 1971, 1975).

31. The biography of Mary McLeod Bethune and the oral history of Mamie Garvin Fields attest to the fact that black women often turned their deferred missionary zeal

for Africa into service to their own communities. See Rackham Holt, *Mary McLeod Bethune: A Biography* (Garden City, N.Y.: Doubleday and Company, 1964) and Mamie Garvin Fields with Karen Fields, *Lemon Swamp and Other Places: A South Carolina Memoir* (New York: Macmillan-Free Press, 1983).

32. Davis, *Lifting as They Climb.*

33. Pleas, *Fifty Years of Achievement,* 39.

34. Smith, "Minutes, 1941," 1.

35. Simeon Booker, "Thirty Years Ago: How Emmett Till's Lynching Launched Civil Rights Drive," *Jet* 68/14 (June 17, 1985), 11, 13.

36. Ibid., 18.

37. Lillian P. Benbow, "It's Time to Stop 'the Dance,'" *Ebony* (October 1976), 52.

38. Ibid.

39. Ibid.

40. Shawn D. Lewis, "A World without Sight or Sound," *Ebony* (October 1976), 108.

41. Examples of such research can be found in Dill, "The Dialectics of Black Womanhood"; Giddings, *When and Where I Enter*; Jones, *Labor of Love*; Sterling, *We Are Your Sisters*; and *The Black Woman,* ed. LaFrances Rodgers-Rose (Beverly Hills, Calif.: Sage Publications, 1980).

42. Giddings, *When and Where I Enter.*

43. Ronald Taylor, "Black Ethnicity and the Persistence of Ethnogenesis," *American Journal of Sociology* 84/6: 1401-1423.

44. Edward Shils, *Tradition* (Chicago: University of Chicago Press, 1981).

45. Walter Brueggemann, *Tradition for Crisis: A Study in Hosea* (Atlanta, Ga.: John Knox Press, 1968).

## 6   The Politics of "Silence"

*Earlier versions of this paper were presented to the University of Utah, Department of History, Religion and Society Series, and a joint session of the Sociologists for Women in Society and the Association for the Sociology of Religion, San Antonio, Texas. The author would like to acknowledge the support of Boston University Faculty Development Research Program, Harvard Divinity School Women's Studies in Religions Program, the Bunting Institute of Radcliffe College, and the Dean of Faculty's Office of Colby College.*

1. Paula Giddings, *When and Where I Enter: The Impact of Black Women on Race and Sex in America* (New York: William Morrow and Company, 1984).

2. James Blackwell, *The Black Community: Diversity and Unity* (New York: William Morrow and Company, 1982).

3. Deborah K. King, "Multiple Jeopardy, Multiple Consciousness: The Context of Black Feminist Ideology," *Signs: Journal of Women in Culture and Society* 14/1 (1988): 42-73.

4. Bonnie Thornton Dill, "The Dialectics of Black Womanhood: Toward a New Model of American Femininity," *Signs: Journal of Women in Culture and Society* 4 (Spring 1979): 543-555.

5. John S. Mbiti, *African Religions and Philosophy* (Garden City, N.Y.: Doubleday and Company, Anchor Books, 1969); Cheikh Anta Diop, *The Cultural Unity of Black Africa: The Domains of Patriarchy and Matriarchy in Classical Antiquity* (Chicago: Third World Press, 1978 [1958]).

6. Diop, *The Cultural Unity of Black Africa*.

7. Deborah Gray White, *Ar'n't I a Woman?: Female Slaves in the Plantation South* (New York: W. W. Norton, 1985).

8. Thomas L. Webber, *Deep like the Rivers: Education in the Slave Quarter Community, 1831-1865* (New York: W. W. Norton, 1978).

9. Leon F. Litwack, *Been in the Storm So Long: The Aftermath of Slavery* (New York: Vintage Books, 1979).

10. Jacqueline Jones, *Labor of Love, Labor of Sorrow: Black Women, Work, and the Family from Slavery to the Present* (New York: Basic Books, 1985).

11. The importance of this shared suffering is discussed by Angela Davis in *Women, Race, and Class* (New York: Random House, 1981).

12. Giddings, *When and Where I Enter*, 33-39.

13. Letitia Woods Brown, "Battles Won and Evil Overcome," in *The Black Woman: Myths and Images Realities*, ed. Doris J. Mitchell and Jewell H. Bell, 4-7 (Cambridge, Mass.: Radcliffe College, 1975), 5.

14. The term "Afro-Baptist" is Mechal Sobel's. See Mechal Sobel, *Trabelin' On: The Slave's Journey to an Afro-Baptist Faith* (Westport, Conn.: Greenwood Press, 1979).

15. See Sobel, *Trabelin' On*, and also Albert J. Raboteau, *Slave Religion: The Invisible Institution in the Antebellum South* (New York: Oxford University Press, 1978).

16. Stanley Elkins, *Slavery: A Problem in American Institutional and Intellectual Life* (Chicago: University of Chicago Press, 1959).

17. La Frances Rodgers-Rose, *The Black Woman* (Beverly Hills, Calif.: Sage Publications, 1980), 16.

18. Judith van Allen, "'Aba Riots' or Igbo 'Women's War'?: Ideology, Stratification, and the Invisibility of Women," 59-85, in *Women in Africa: Studies in Social and Economic Change*, ed. Nancy J. Hafkin and Edna G. Bay (Stanford, Calif.: Stanford University Press, 1976), 68.

19. Kamene Okonjo, "The Dual-Sex Political System in Operation: Igbo Women and Community Politics in Midwestern Nigeria," in Hafkin and Bay, *Women in Africa: Studies in Social and Economic Change*, 45.

20. Ibid., 53.

21. Eva L.R. Meyerowitz, *The Divine Kingship in Ghana and Ancient Egypt* (London: Faber and Faber, 1960), 196.

22. Geraldine Wilson, "The Self-Group Actualization of Black Women," in Rodgers-Rose, *The Black Woman*, 301-314.

23. Davis, *Women, Race, and Class*, 23.

24. Angela Davis, Bonnie Thornton Dill, and Deborah Gray White all describe models of womanhood that diverge from and at times are critical of the dominant culture's approach. See Davis, *Women, Race, and Class*; Dill, "The Dialectics of Black Womanhood"; White, *Ar'n't I a Woman?*

25. Davis, *Women, Race, and Class*, 29.

26. Ibid.

27. See White's discussion of the Jezebel stereotype in *Ar'n't I a Woman*; Cheryl Townsend Gilkes, "From Slavery to Social Welfare: Racism and the Control of Black Women," in *Class, Race, and Sex: The Dynamics of Controls*, ed. Amy Swerdlow and Hannah Lessinger, 288-300 (Boston: G. K. Hall, 1983); Gerda Lerner, *Black Women in White America: A Documentary History* (New York: Random House, 1971).

28. Linda M. Perkins, "Black Women and Racial 'Uplift' prior to Emancipation," in *The Black Woman Cross-Culturally*, ed. Filomena Chioma Steady, 317-334 (Rochester, Vt.: Schenkman Books, 1981), 321.

29. Rosalyn Terborg-Penn, "Discrimination against Afro-American Women in the Woman's Movement, 1830-1920," in *The Afro-American Woman: Struggles and Images*, ed. Sharon Harley and Rosalyn Terborg-Penn, 29-34 (Port Washington, N.Y.: Kennikat Press, 1978).

30. Ibid., 34.

31. Webber, *Deep like the Rivers*.

32. Harold A. Carter, *The Prayer Tradition of Black People* (Valley Forge, Pa.: The Judson Press, 1976); Weptonomah W. Carter, *The Black Minister's Wife* (Elgin, Ill.: Progressive Baptist Publishing House, 1976).

33. Cheryl Townsend Gilkes, "Cultural Constituencies in Conflict: The Sanctified Church and the Reorganization of Community, 1890-1950" (Paper presented to a joint session of the Association of Black Sociologists and the Society for the Study of Social Problems, Detroit, Michigan, 1983); Cheryl Townsend Gilkes, "Institutional Motherhood in Black Churches and Communities: Ambivalent American Sexism or Fragmented African Familyhood" (Boston, Massachusetts, 1981, unpublished manuscript).

34. Sarah Evans, *Personal Politics: The Roots of Women's Liberation in the Civil Rights Movement and the New Left* (New York: Vintage Books, 1980); Giddings, *When and Where I Enter*.

35. Giddings, *When and Where I Enter*, 301.

36. Howard Thurman, *With Head and Heart: The Autobiography of Howard Thurman* (New York: Harcourt Brace Jovanovich, 1979).

37. Ibid., 283; Mary King, *Freedom Song: A Personal Story of the 1960s Civil Rights Movement* (New York: William Morrow and Company, 1987).

38. Mechal Sobel, *Trabelin' On*; Herbert Gutman, *The Black Family in Slavery and Freedom, 1750-1925* (New York: Random House, 1976).

39. Davis, *Women, Race, and Class*; Giddings, *When and Where I Enter*; Harry A. Ploski and Roscoe C. Brown, *The Negro Almanac* (New York: Bellwether Publishing Company, 1967).

40. Evelyn Brooks, "The Feminist Theology of the Black Baptist Church, 1880-1900," in Swerdlow and Lessinger, *Class, Race, and Sex: The Dynamics of Control*, 31-59.

41. Jualynne Dodson, "Preaching Women in the AME Church" (Unpublished paper, Union Theological Seminary, New York, 1982).

42. Litwack, *Been in the Storm So Long*.

43. Ibid.; Carter G. Woodson, *The History of the Negro Church* (Washington, D.C.: Associated Publishers, 1972 [1921]).

44. Thurman, *With Head and Heart*.

45. Giddings, *When and Where I Enter*, 52.

46. Ibid.

47. Dorothy Sterling, *We Are Your Sisters: Black Women in the Nineteenth Century* (New York: W. W. Norton, 1984), 157.

48. Giddings, *When and Where I Enter*, 53.

49. Sterling, *We Are Your Sisters*; Marilyn Richardson, ed., *Maria W. Stewart, America's First Black Woman Political Writer* (Bloomington, Ind.: Indiana University Press, 1987).

50. Giddings, *When and Where I Enter*, 33.

51. Ibid.

52. Brooks, "The Feminist Theology."

53. Ibid. [This analysis is further developed in her later volume, Evelyn Brooks Higginbotham, *Righteous Discontent: The Women's Movement in the Black Baptist Church, 1880-1920* (Cambridge, Mass.: Harvard University Press, 1993).]

54. Brooks, "The Feminist Theology," 33.

55. Ibid., 39.

56. Dill, "The Dialectics of Black Womanhood."

57. Elizabeth Lindsey Davis, *Lifting as They Climb: A History of the National Association of Colored Women* (Washington, D.C.: Moorland-Spingarn Research Center, 1933).

58. Ibid., 19.

59. W. E. B. Du Bois in *W.E.B. Du Bois: The Crisis Writings*, ed. Daniel Walden (Greenwich, Conn.: Fawcett Publications, 1972), 340.

60. Brooks, "The Feminist Theology"; Jualynne E. Dodson and Cheryl Townsend Gilkes, "'Something Within': Social Change and Collective Endurance in the Sacred World of Black Christian Women," in *Women and Religion in America*, vol. 3, *The Twentieth Century*, ed. Rosemary Radford Ruether and Rosemary Skinner Keller, 80-128 (San Francisco: Harper & Row, 1986).

61. Evelyn Brooks Barnett, "Nannie Burroughs and the Education of Black Women," in *The Afro-American Woman: Struggles and Images*, ed. Sharon Harley and Rosalyn Terborg-Penn, 97-108 (Port Washington, N.Y.: Kennikat Press, 1978).

62. Burroughs's pamphlet, "Who Started Women's Day," is quoted in its entirety in Dodson and Gilkes, "Something Within."

63. Ibid.

64. Ibid.

65. Angela Davis, *Women, Race, and Class*.

66. James Harvey Robinson, "Some of the Fruits of Historical Study," in *Readings in Sociology*, ed. Jerome Davis and Harry Elmer Barnes, 3-6 (Boston: D. C. Heath and Company, 1927).

## PART 3
## WOMANIST CULTURE

### 7  "Some Mother's Son and Some Father's Daughter"

*Earlier versions of this paper were presented to the Society for the Study of Black Religion and to the Center for Research on Women, Memphis State University. I wish to acknowledge the support of Boston University Department of Sociology and of the Summer Visiting Scholar Program of the Center for Research on Women, Memphis State University, for their contributions at various stages of the research and writing.*

1. Margaret Andersen, *Thinking about Women: Sociological and Feminist Perspectives* (New York: Macmillan, 1983), 208.

2. Ibid., 219-223.

3. Ibid., 227. Andersen's use of Hegel parallels a similar and earlier usage by Angela Davis in her important work "Reflections on the Black Woman's Role in the Community of Slaves," *Black Scholar* 3 (December 1971), 2-15.

4. Andersen, *Thinking about Women*, 231-32.

5. Linda M. Perkins, "Black Women and Racial 'Uplift' prior to Emancipation," in *The Black Woman Cross-Culturally*, ed. Filomena Chioma Steady, 317-334 (Rochester, Vt.: Schenkman Books, 1981), 321.

6. Paula Giddings, *When and Where I Enter: The Impact of Black Women on Race and Sex in America* (New York: William Morrow and Company, 1984).

7. Davis, "Reflections on the Black Woman's Role, 8. Davis reworks and expands some of this analysis in her book *Women, Race, and Class* (New York: Random House, 1981), especially in the first chapter, "The Legacy of Slavery: Standards for a New Womanhood."

8. Charles H. Pleas, *Fifty Years Achievement (History): Church of God in Christ* (Memphis, Tenn.: Church of God in Christ Publishing House, n.d. [*circa* 1957]), 35.

9. Ibid., 36.

10. Ibid.

11. Ibid., 37.

12. Ibid., 38-39; Lucille Cornelius, *The Pioneer History of the Church of God in Christ* (Memphis, Tenn.: Church of God in Christ Publishing House, 1975), 38-39.

13. Jualynne E. Dodson and Cheryl Townsend Gilkes, "'Something Within': Social Change and Collective Endurance in the Sacred World of Black Christian Women," in *Women and Religion in America*, vol. 3, *The Twentieth Century*, ed. Rosemary Radford Ruether and Rosemary Skinner Keller (San Francisco: Harper & Row, 1986), 107-112.

14. Randall Collins, *Sociological Insight: An Introduction to Nonobvious Sociology* (New York: Oxford University Press, 1982), 37.

15. The Combahee River Collective, "A Black Feminist Statement," in *But Some of Us Are Brave*, ed. Gloria T. I. Hull, Patricia Bell Scott, and Barbara Smith (Old Westbury, N.Y.: The Feminist Press, 1982), 16.

16. Harriet Pipes McAdoo, ed., *Black Families* (Beverly Hills, Calif.: Sage Publications, 1981). McAdoo discussed her subjects' use of the spirituals as practical ideologies in a discussion following a paper she presented to the American Sociological Association annual meeting, New York, 1984.

17. Cheryl Townsend Gilkes, "The Roles of Church and Community Mothers: Ambivalent American Sexism or Fragmented African Familyhood?" *Journal of Feminist Studies in Religion* 2 (Spring 1986), 41-59.

18. James Cone uses the phrase "cultural humiliation" to characterize one of the unique features of racism in the culture of the United States and the experience of black people. See *For My People* (Maryknoll, N.Y.: Orbis Books, 1982).

19. Zora Neale Hurston, *Their Eyes Were Watching God* (New York: J. B. Lippincott, 1937), 236.

20. Mamie Garvin Fields with Karen Fields, *Lemon Swamp and Other Places: A Carolina Memoir* (New York: Macmillan-Free Press, 1983). References to practices during slavery abound throughout the narrative.

21. Cheryl Townsend Gilkes, "'Together and in Harness': Women's Traditions in the Sanctified Church," *Signs: Journal of Women in Culture and Society* 10 (Summer 1985), 687-689.

22. Dodson and Gilkes, "Something Within," 93-96. See also Paula Giddings, *When and Where I Enter,* for more extended discussions of these and many other women.

23. Carter G. Woodson, "The Negro Washerwoman," *The Journal of Negro History* 15/3 (1930), 269-277.

24. Giddings, *When and Where I Enter,* 52.

25. Thomas Webber, *Deep like the Rivers: Education in the Slave Quarter Community, 1830- 1865* (New York: W. W. Norton, 1978); Deborah Gray White, *Ar'n't I a Woman?: Female Slaves in the Plantation South* (New York: W. W. Norton, 1985); Giddings, *When and Where I Enter*; Dorothy Sterling, *We Are Your Sisters: Black Women in the Nineteenth Century* (New York: W. W. Norton, 1984).

26. Vincent Harding, *There Is a River: The Black Struggle for Freedom in America* (New York: Harcourt, Brace, and Jovanovich, 1981).

27. Campbell's hymn is reprinted in Dodson and Gilkes's article in Ruether and Keller, *Women and Religion in America*, 93-94.

28. Saunders Redding, *The Lonesome Road: A Narrative History of the Black Experience* (Garden City, N.Y.: Anchor Press/Doubleday, 1973), 60-66.

29. Phyllis Trible, *Texts of Terror: Literary-Feminist Readings of Biblical Narratives* (Philadelphia: Fortress Press, 1984).

30. In a sermon titled "What Ails You?" (Princeton University, 1982), Rev. Dr. Arlene Churn made particularly effective use of this term, "as mother used to call it, this 'outside child,'" in paralleling the experience of Hagar with black women generally, and with black women ministers particularly. Rev. Dr. Churn's sermon was inspired by a lecture about Hagar that Delores Williams gave on that same day; Williams's discussion is contained in her book, *Sisters in the Wilderness: The Challenge of Womanist God-Talk* (Maryknoll, N.Y.: Orbis Books, 1993).

31. Langston Hughes, *Not without Laughter* (New York: Collier Books, 1969); E. Franklin Frazier, *The Negro Family in the United States* (Chicago: University of Chicago Press, 1939).

32. From a feminist perspective, Jephthah's daughter is a highly problematic role model; she is a willing accomplice in her own destruction. Year after year, thousands of women in the Order of the Eastern Star celebrate this woman as an example of faithfulness. Since most feminists are not members of Eastern Star, they fail to perceive the depth to which this woman is revered in one of the most patriarchal and explicitly and exclusively patrilineal organizations to which Anglo-American and Afro-American women belong.

33. Suzan D. Johnson, "God's Woman," in *Those Preachin' Women: Sermons by Black Women Preachers*, ed. Ella Pearson Mitchell, 119-126 (Valley Forge, Pa.: Judson Press, 1985); Frances Ellen Watkins Harper, "Vashti," in *Black Sister: Poetry by Black American Women, 1746-1980*, ed. Erlene Stetson (Bloomington, Ind.: Indiana University Press, 1981), 27-29.

34. Audio recordings (vinyl record albums) are helpful in that they represent what is popular and accessible. They do not provide a full range of what is representative. Few women pastors command the resources and institutional support to enter the market of recorded sermons. Recorded sermons, however, do provide excellent examples of the use of tradition.

35. Virginia Ramey Mollenkott's discussion of "God Our Ezer," in *The Divine Feminine: The Biblical Imagery of God as Female* (New York: Crossroad Publishing Company, 1983), enables one to comprehend the irony of patriarchal and masculinist male preachers calling on God as a female.

36. Howard Thurman describes this phenomenon in his autobiography, *With Head and Heart: The Autobiography of Howard Thurman* (New York: Harcourt, Brace, Jovanovich, 1979).

37. C. L. Franklin, "The 100th Psalm (The Lord Is Good)," Sermon no. 62 (Englewood, N.J.: Chess Records).

38. Wyatt Tee Walker, *Somebody's Calling My Name: Black Sacred Music and Social Change* (Valley Forge, Pa.: Judson Press, 1979).

39. C. L. Franklin, "Nothing Shall Separate Me From the Lord," Sermon no. 16 (Englewood, N.J.: Chess Records).

40. The war referred to in the sermon is most likely the Viet Nam War.

41. Bishop P. A. Brooks and Charles Hawthorne, *Understanding Bible Doctrine as Taught in the Church of God in Christ* (Detroit, Mich.: Church of God in Christ, First Jurisdiction, Michigan, 1981). It is important to realize that missionaries in the Church of God in Christ would be considered ministers and preachers in other denominations; as of this writing [1986] the Church of God in Christ still does not officially ordain women to the titles pastor, elder, or bishop.

42. Franklin, "Nothing Shall Separate Me."

43. Jasper Williams Jr., "He's the Best I've Ever Seen (Jesus' Trial)" (Atlanta, Ga.: Church Door Records, 1984).

44. C. L. Franklin, "The Eagle Stirreth Her Nest," Sermon no. 21 (Englewood, N.J.: Chess Records).

45. C. L. Franklin, "The Lord Is Good."

46. Harold Carter, *The Prayer Tradition of Black People* (Valley Forge, Pa.: Judson Press, 1976).

47. Webber, *Deep like the Rivers*, see, for example, 43-58, 80-90, 157-179, 191-206.

48. Fields, *Lemon Swamp*, 36.

49. Jasper Williams Jr., "Didn't It Rain? (Mount Carmel)" (Atlanta, Ga.: Church Door Records, 1980).

50. James Baldwin, *Go Tell It on the Mountain* (New York: Dell Publishing Company, 1965 [1953]).

51. Hughes, *Not without Laughter.*

52. Rosemary Radford Reuther, *Sexism and God-Talk: Toward a Feminist Theology* (Boston: Beacon Press, 1983), 74.

53. W. Herbert Brewster, "Our God Is Able," in *Golden Gospel Songs: Volume 1* (Chicago: Martin Morris Music, 1975 [1949]), 1. The arranger for Brewster was Virginia Davis. According to the late Olden "Pop" Jones of Memphis, Tennessee, Brewster also collaborated with Isabella Jones on some of his songs (Interview with Herbert Plummer Jones, July 18, 1986). It is not unreasonable to think that Brewster's relationships with women had some bearing on the appeal of his songs to female singers and the inclusive nature of the language and imagery.

54. Anthony Heilbut, *The Gospel Sound: Good News and Bad Times* (New York: Simon and Schuster, 1975), 98.

55. Ibid., 100.

56. Ibid., 252. Additional words have also been transcribed from "Surely God Is Able," The Young Hearts, Alabama State University, The National Black College Gospel Workshop (Nashville, Tenn.: Reed Records, Nashboro Record Company, 1978). [I provide a more extended discussion of the importance of this imagery and its embeddedness in gospel music in Cheryl Townsend Gilkes, "'Mother to the Motherless, Father to the Fatherless': Power, Gender, and Community in an Afrocentric Biblical Tradition," *Semeia: An Experimental Journal for Biblical Criticism* 47 (1989): 57-85.]

57. Extended discussions of the importance of gospel music for the overall religious tradition can be found in Heilbut, *The Gospel Sound*; Walker, *Somebody's Calling My Name*. [See also my discussion of Mary and Martha in Cheryl Townsend Gilkes, "'Go and Tell Mary and Martha': The Sprituals, Biblical Options for Women, and Cultural Tensions in the African American Religious Experience," *Social Compass: International Review of Sociology of Religion* 43 (December 4, 1996): 563-581.]

58. Williams, "Didn't It Rain?"

59. See Bonnie Thornton Dill's article on the importance of sisterhood among black women and its importance for feminist theory. Bonnie Thornton Dill, "'On the Hem of Life': Race, Class, and the Prospects for Sisterhood," in *Class, Race, and Sex: The Dynamics of Control*, ed. Amy Swerdlow and Hanna Lessinger (Boston: G. K. Hall, 1983), 173-188. [For an additional discussion of the value of testimony to black mental health see Cheryl Townsend Gilkes, "The Black Church as a Therapeutic Community: Suggested Areas for Research into the Black Religious Experience," *The Journal of the Interdenominational Theological Center* 8/1 (Fall 1980): 29-44.]

60. Pauli Murray, "The Liberation of Black Women," in *Voices of the New Feminism*, ed. Mary L. Thompson (Boston: Beacon Press, 1970), 354-55; idem, "Jim Crow and Jane Crow," in *Black Women in White America*, ed. Gerda Lerner, 592-599 (New York: Random House, 1972).

61. C. L. Franklin, "The Meaning of Black Power," Sermon no. 45 (Englewood, N.J.: Chess Records).

62. Ibid.

63. Ibid.

64. Harding, *There Is a River*; Webber, *Deep like the Rivers*; Mechal Sobel, *Trabelin' On: The Slaves' Journey to an Afro-Baptist Faith* (Westport, Conn.: Greenwood Press, 1979); Albert Raboteau, *Slave Religion: The Invisible Institution in the Antebellum South* (New York: Oxford University Press, 1978).

65. Krister Stendahl, *The Bible and the Role of Women: A Case Study in Hermeneutics* (Philadelphia: Fortress Press, 1966), 2.

## 8 "Sisters Who Can Lift a Community"

*Earlier versions of this paper were presented to the American Sociological Association Session titled "Race, Gender, and the Social Construction of Knowledge" and to the University of Connecticut and Howard University. A portion of it was published as "Keeping Faith with the People: Reflections on Ethics, Leadership, and African American Women's Historical Experience," in* The Stones That the Builders Rejected: The Development of Ethical Leadership from the Black Church Tradition, *ed.* Walter E. Fluker, 73-81 *(Harrisburg, Pa.: Trinity Press International, 1998).*

1. The terms "black feminist thought," "womanist," and "black feminist theorizing," are developed in the following volumes: Patricia Hill Collins, *Black Feminist Thought: Knowledge, Consciousness, and the Politics of Empowerment* (Boston: Unwin Hyman, 1990); Alice Walker, *In Search of Our Mothers' Gardens: Womanist Prose* (New York: Harcourt Brace Jovanovich, 1983); Stanlie M. James and Abena P. A. Busia, *Theorizing Black Feminisms: The Visionary Pragmatism of Black Women* (New York: Routledge, 1993).

2. See Evelyn Brooks Higginbotham, *Righteous Discontent: The Women's Movement in the Black Baptist Church, 1880-1920* (Cambridge, Mass.: Harvard University

Press, 1993); Evelyn Brooks Barnett, "Nannie Burroughs and the Education of Black Women," in *The Afro-American Woman: Struggles and Images*, ed. Sharon Harley and Rosalyn Terborg-Penn, 97-108 (Port Washington, N.Y.: Kennikat Press, 1978); Evelyn Brooks, "Religion, Politics, and Gender: The Leadership of Nannie Helen Burroughs," *Journal of Religious Thought* 44 (Winter/Spring 1988): 7-22.

3. Nannie Helen Burroughs, "The Slabtown District Convention: A Comedy in One Act" (Washington, D.C.: Nannie Helen Burroughs School, n.d. [22d ed. 1979]).

4. Patricia Hill Collins, "Learning from the Outsider Within: The Sociological Significance of Black Feminist Thought," *Social Problems* 33/6 (1986): S14-S32; Walker, *In Search of Our Mothers' Gardens*; Deborah King, "Multiple Jeopardy, Multiple Consciousness: The Context of Black Feminist Ideology," *Signs: Journal of Women in Culture and Society* 14/1 (1988): 42-72.

5. Bernice Johnson Reagon, "African Diaspora Women: The Making of Cultural Workers," *Feminist Studies* 12/1 (1986): 77-90.

6. C. Wright Mills, *The Sociological Imagination* (New York: Oxford University Press, 1959).

7. Minna Caulfield, "Imperialism, the Family, and Cultures of Resistance," *Socialist Revolution* 20 (1974): 67-85.

8. Charles Hamilton, *The Black Preacher in America* (New York: William Morrow and Company, 1972).

9. Paula Giddings, *When and Where I Enter: The Impact of Black Women on Race and Sex in America* (New York: William Morrow and Company, 1984).

10. Evelyn Brooks, "The Feminist Theology of the Black Baptist Church, 1880-1900," 31-59 in *Class, Race, and Sex: The Dynamics of Control*, ed. Amy Swerdlow and Hanna Lessinger (Boston: G. K. Hall, 1980), 50.

11. Cornel West, *Prophetic Fragments* (Trenton, N.J.: Africa World Press, 1988).

12. Blocked access should not be read as absolutely no access. Black women did and do preach and pastor. See Bettye Collier-Thomas, *Daughters of Thunder: Black Women Preachers and Their Sermons, 1850-1979* (San Francisco: Jossey-Bass, 1998), for a detailed portrait of significant black women preachers in the nineteenth and twentieth centuries.

13. Barbara Hilkert Andolsen, *"Daughters of Jefferson, Daughters of Bootblacks": Racism and American Feminism* (Macon, Ga.: Mercer University Press, 1986).

14. Howard Becker, *Outsiders: Studies in the Sociology of Deviance* (New York: The Free Press, 1973).

15. Barnett, "Nannie Burroughs and the Education of Black Women"; Sadie Iola Daniel with Charles H. Wesley and Thelma D. Perry, *Women Builders* (Washington, D.C.: Associated Publishers, 1970 [1931]); Gerda Lerner, *Black Women in White America: A Documentary History* (New York: Random House, 1972).

16. Daniel, *Women Builders*, 115-116.

17. Barnett, "Nannie Burroughs and the Education of Black Women," 98.

18. Nannie Helen Burroughs, "Who Started Women's Day?" (Washington, D.C.: Nannie Helen Burroughs School, n.d.).

19. Barnett, "Nannie Burroughs and the Education of Black Women."

20. Daniel, *Women Builders*.

21. Barnett, "Nannie Burroughs and the Education of Black Women," 99.

22. Ibid., 99-101.

23. Ibid.; Daniel, *Women Builders.*

24. Barnett, "Nannie Burroughs and the Education of Black Women," 101.

25. Ibid., 103.

26. Ibid., 105.

27. Ibid., 105.

28. In her book *Righteous Discontent,* Evelyn Brooks Higginbotham forcefully discusses the role of the black church and the annual convention of the National Baptist Convention in constituting the black public sphere. Burroughs's play extends that analysis to regional and local meetings and the relationships between these smaller meetings and the larger national scene.

29. Later in the play, Burroughs lets us know that C.B.B. stands for "Can't Be Beat!"

30. Bernice Johnson Reagon, "My Black Mothers and Sisters or on Beginning a Cultural Autobiography," *Feminist Studies* 8/1 (1982): 81-96.

31. Emphasis added.

32. Emphasis added.

33. Zorah Neale Hurston, *Their Eyes Were Watching God* (New York: J. B. Lippincott, 1937) points out that African-American laughter has a thousand reasons and motivations. Mel Watkins also provides thick historical description of humor as a moral and cultural force in *On the Real Side: Laughing, Lying, and Signifying—The Underground Tradition of African American Humor That Transformed American Culture from Slavery to Richard Pryor* (New York: Simon and Schuster, 1994).

34. Alice Walker, "womanist," *In Search of Our Mothers' Gardens: Womanist Prose* (San Diego: Harcourt Brace Jovanovich, 1983), xi-xii.

35. Doug McAdam, *Political Process and the Development of Black Insurgency, 1930-1970* (Chicago: University of Chicago Press, 1982).

36. Caulfield, "Imperialism, the Family, and Cultures of Resistance."

37. Reagon, "African Diaspora Women," 77.

38. Ibid., 78.

39. Ibid., 79.

40. Collins, *Black Feminist Thought;* King, "Multiple Jeopardy, Multiple Consciousness"; Andolsen, "Daughters of Jefferson."

41. Walker, "womanist," *In Search of Our Mothers' Gardens,* xi-xii.

42. Doug McAdam, *Freedom Summer* (New York: Oxford University Press, 1984); Aldon Morris, *The Origins of the Civil Rights Movement: Black Communities Organizing for Change* (New York: The Free Press, 1984).

43. Joanne Grant, *Ella Baker: Freedom Bound* (New York: John Wiley and Sons, 1998); Cynthia Stokes Brown, ed., *Ready from Within: Septima Clark and the Civil Rights Movement* (Navarro, Calif.: Wild Trees Press, 1986); Chana Kai Lee, *For Freedom's Sake: The Life of Fannie Lou Hamer* (Urbana, Ill.: University of Illinois Press, 1999); Kay Mills, *This Little Light of Mine: The Life of Fannie Lou Hamer* (New York: Dutton, 1993); Belinda Robnett, *How Long? How Long? African-American Women in the Struggle for Civil Rights* (New York: Oxford University Press, 1997); Vicki L. Crawford, Jacqueline Anne Rouse, and Barbara Woods, eds., *Women in the Civil Rights Movement: Trailblazers and Torchbearers, 1941-1965* (Bloomington, Ind.: Indiana University Press, 1993 [1990]); Darlene Clark Hine and Kathleen Thompson, *A Shining Thread of Hope: The History of Black Women in America* (New York: Broadway Publishers, 1998).

## PART 4
## CRISES, CONTRONTATIONS, AND CONFLICTS

### 9   "Liberated to Work like Dogs!"

*Earlier versions of this paper were presented to the American Sociological Association, 1979 Annual Meeting, and distributed as Working Paper No. 66 of the Wellesley College Center for Research on Women. Support for research and various stages of writing were provided by the National Fellowships Fund and the Minority Fellowship Program of the American Sociological Association. Blanche Geer, Joan Arches, Carol Owen, and Murray Melbin provided valuable comments on this paper.*

1. Edwin M. Schur, *The Politics of Deviance: Stigma Contests and the Uses of Power* (Englewood Cliffs, N.J.: Prentice-Hall, 1980).

2. Howard S. Becker, *Outsiders: Studies in the Sociology of Deviance* (New York: The Free Press, 1973 [1963]).

3. Earl Rubington and Martin S. Weinberg, *Deviance: The Interactionist Perspective*, 5th ed. (New York: Macmillan, 1987).

4. Becker, *Outsiders*, 35-36; Erving Goffman, *Stigma: Notes on the Management of Spoiled Identity* (Englewood Cliffs, N.J.: Prentice-Hall, 1963); Thomas J. Scheff, *Being Mentally Ill: A Sociological Theory* (Hawthorne, N.Y.: Aldine Publishing Company, 1966).

5. Albert Murray, "White Norms, Black Deviation," in *The Death of White Sociology*, ed. Joyce A. Ladner (New York: Random House, 1973).

6. Although I use the term "white," I am aware that the dominant racial category is socially constructed and does not exclude all men and women of color with equal hostility. The focus of this paper is on the problems of black women within a racial-ethnic community of black people located in a racist society, and therefore, who share with black men many of the hostilities and stereotypes reserved exclusively for people of African descent native to the United States.

7. Edwin M. Schur, *Labeling Women Deviant: Gender, Stigma, and Social Control* (New York: Random House, 1984), 51.

8. Gerda Lerner, ed., *Black Women in White America: A Documentary History* (New York: Random House, 1972).

9. Bonnie Thornton Dill, "The Dialectics of Black Womanhood: Towards a New Model of American Femininity," *Signs: Journal of Women in Culture and Society* 4/3 (Spring 1979): 543-555.

10. Angela Davis, *Women, Race, and Class* (New York: Random House, 1981).

11. Mae C. King, "The Politics of Sexual Stereotypes," *The Black Scholar* 4/6-7 (1973); Linda J. M. LaRue, "Black Liberation and Women's Lib," in *Sociological Realities II: A Guide to the Study of Society*, ed. Irving Louis Horowitz and Charles Nanry, 282-287 (New York: Harper & Row, 1971); Jeanne Noble, *Beautiful, Also, Are the Souls of My Black Sisters: A History of the Black Woman in America* (Englewood Cliffs, N.J.: Prentice-Hall, 1978); Inez Smith Reid, *"Together" Black Women* (New York: Emerson Hall, 1972).

12. Michelle Wallace, *Black Macho and the Myth of the Superwoman* (New York: Dial Press, 1978).

13. Jacquelyn Johnson Jackson, "But Where Are the Men?," *The Black Scholar* 3/4 (1971); idem, "Black Women in a Racist Society" in *Racism and Mental Health*,

ed. Charles V. Willie, Bernard Kramer, and Bertram Brown, 185-258 (Pittsburgh, Pa.: University of Pittsburgh Press, 1973); idem, "The Mythological Black Woman, She Ain't Nowhere to Be Found," in *The Black Woman: Myths and Realities*, ed. Doris J. Mitchell and Jewel H. Bell (Cambridge, Mass.: Radcliffe College, 1978); King, "The Politics of Sexual Stereotypes"; Diane K. Lewis, "A Response to Inequality: Black Women, Racism, and Sexism," *Signs: A Journal of Women in Culture and Society* 3/2 (1977): 339-361; Mitchell and Bell, *The Black Woman: Myths and Realities*.

14. Toni Cade [Bambara], *The Black Woman: An Anthology* (New York: New American Library, 1970); Angela Davis, "Reflections on the Black Woman's Role in the Community of Slaves," *Black Scholar* 3 (December 1971); Davis, *Women, Race, and Class*.

15. Barbara Hilkert Andolsen, *"Daughters of Jefferson, Daughters of Bootblacks": Racism and American Feminism* (Macon, Ga.: Mercer University Press, 1986), i.

16. Delores Williams, "The Color of Feminism," *Journal of Religious Thought* 43/1 (1986).

17. Alice Walker, *In Search of Our Mothers' Gardens: Womanist Prose* (San Diego: Harcourt Brace Jovanovich, 1983), xi-xii.

18. Cheryl Townsend Gilkes, "Successful Rebellious Professionals: The Black Woman's Professional Identity and Community Commitment," *Psychology of Women Quarterly* 6/3 (Spring 1982); Cheryl Townsend Gilkes, "Going Up for the Oppressed: The Career Mobility of Black Women Community Workers," *Journal of Social Issues* 39/3 (1983).

19. Bonnie Thornton Dill, "The Means to Put My Children Through," in *The Black Woman*, ed. LaFrances Rodgers-Rose (Beverly Hills, Calif.: Sage Publications, 1980); Bonnie Thornton Dill, "Making Your Job Good Yourself: Domestic Service and the Construction of Personal Dignity," in *Women and the Politics of Empowerment*, ed. Ann Bookman and Sandra Morgen (Philadelphia: Temple University Press, 1988); Judith Rollins, *Between Women: Domestics and Their Employers* (Philadelphia: Temple University Press, 1985).

20. Becker, *Outsiders*, 38.

21. Linda LaRue, "Black Liberation and Women's Lib."

22. Lerner, *Black Women in White America*.

23. Barbara Christian, *Black Women Novelists: The Development of a Tradition, 1892-1976* (Westport, Conn.: Greenwood Press, 1980); Deborah Gray White, *Ar'n't I a Woman?: Female Slaves in the Antebellum South* (New York: W. W. Norton, 1985).

24. Eugene Genovese, *Roll, Jordan, Roll: The World the Slaves Made* (New York: Random House, 1974), 327-365; Jessie Parkhurst, "The Role of the Black Mammy in the Plantation Household," *Journal of Negro History* 23 (1970): 349-369.

25. Jean Carey Bond and Pat Peery, "Is the Black Male Castrated?," in Cade, *The Black Woman: An Anthology*, 113-118.

26. Lee Rainwater and William L. Yancey, *The Moynihan Report and the Politics of Controversy* (Cambridge, Mass.: M.I.T. Press, 1967); William Ryan, *Blaming the Victim* (New York: Random House, 1971); Robert Staples, "The Myth of the Black Matriarchy," in *The Black Family: Essays and Studies* (Belmont, Calif.: Wadsworth Publishing Company, 1971); Robert Staples, *The Black Woman in America* (Chicago: Nelson Hall, Publishers, 1973).

27. Christian, *Black Women Novelists*, 77.

28. Andolsen, *Daughters of Jefferson*, 99.

29. White, *Ar'n't I a Woman?*, 65-70.

30. White, *Ar'n't I a Woman?*; Genovese *Roll, Jordan, Roll.*

31. Ibid.

32. Davis, "The Black Woman's Role," 7.

33. W. E. B. Du Bois, "The Black Mother," in *The Crisis Writings*, ed. Daniel Walden (Greenwich, Conn.: Fawcett Publications, 1972 [1912]), 41.

34. Edward Mapp, "The Black Woman in Films," *The Black Scholar* 4, 6/7 (1973); Jeanne Noble, *Beautiful, Also, Are the Souls of My Black Sisters: A History of the Black Woman in America* (Englewood Cliffs, N.J.: Prentice-Hall, 1978), 77.

35. Everett C. Hughes, *The Sociological Eye* (Chicago: Aldine Publishing Company, 1971).

36. Christian, *Black Women Novelists*, 11.

37. Dill, "The Dialectics of Black Womanhood."

38. See W. E. B. Du Bois, "The Damnation of Women," in *Darkwater: Voices from Within the Veil* (New York: Schocken Books, 1969 [1920]), 163-192. He pointed to what he called the "harem like" ideals of the dominant culture. Others emphasized the economic necessity of black women's work: Oliver Cromwell Cox, "Sex Ratio and Marital Status among Negroes," *American Sociological Review* 5 (1940): 937-947; E. Franklin Frazier, *The Negro Family in the United States* (Chicago: University of Chicago Press, 1939); Kelley Miller, "Surplus Negro Women," in *Radicals and Conservatives and Other Essays on the Negro in America* (New York: Schocken Books, 1968 [1905]).

39. Valerie Oppenheimer, "Demographic Influence on Female Employment and the Status of Women," in *Changing Women in a Changing Society*, ed. Joan Huber, 184-199 (Chicago: University of Chicago Press, 1973); Valerie Oppenheimer, *The Female Labor Force in the United States: Demographic and Economic Factors Governing Its Growth and Changing Composition* (Westport, Conn.: Greenwood Press, 1970).

40. Joe R. Feagin, "Black Women in the American Work Force," in *The Family Life of Black People*, ed. Charles V. Willie, 23-35 (Columbus, Ohio: Charles E. Merrill Publishing Company, 1970), 31-33.

41. Cornel West, "The Prophetic Tradition in Afro-America," in *Prophetic Fragments* (Grand Rapids, Mich.: Eerdmans; Tremont, N.J.: Africa World Press, 1988), 38-49, especially 45.

42. Ida B. Wells Barnett, *Crusade for Justice: The Auto-biography of Ida B. Wells*, ed. Alfreda Duster (Chicago: University of Chicago Press, 1970); Elizabeth Lindsay Davis, *Lifting As They Climb: A History of the National Association of Colored Women* (Washington, D.C.: Moorland-Spingarn Research Center, 1933); Emma L. Fields, "The Women's Club Movement in the United States, 1877-1900" (Master's thesis, Moorland Spingarn Research Center, Washington, D.C., 1948); Paula Giddings, *When and Where I Enter: The Impact of Black Women on Race and Sex in America* (New York: William Morrow and Company, 1984); Rackham Holt, *Mary McLeod Bethune: A Biography* (Garden City, N.Y.: Doubleday and Company, 1964); Lerner, *Black Women in White America*; Mary Church Terrell, *A Colored Woman in a White World* (Washington, D.C.: Ransdell Publishing Company, 1940); Mary Church Terrell, "The History of the Club Women's Movement," *The Aframerican Woman's Journal* 1/2-3 (1940): 34-38. The Colored Women's League, organized by Mary Church Terrell in 1893, represented the interests of members of the black elite who were allies of W. E. B. Du Bois and his arguments regarding the "talented tenth." The National Federation of Afro-American Women, organized by

Josephine St. Pierre Ruffin and Margaret Murray Washington (Mrs. Booker T.), was composed of elite and mass black women. Both groups held their national conventions in Washington, D.C., in the summer of 1896. Each organization formed a committee of seven that was responsible for hammering out the details of the merger of the two groups. Mrs. Terrell, a founder of the League, was on the Federation's Committee; Mrs. Fannie Jackson Coppin, a founder of the Federation, was on the League's committee.

43. Andolsen, *Daughters of Jefferson*; Barnett, *Crusade for Justice*; Giddings, *When and Where I Enter*; Rosalyn Terborg-Penn, "Afro-Americans in the Struggle for Woman Suffrage" (Ph.D. dissertation, Howard University, 1977); S. Jay Walker, "Frederick Douglass and Woman Suffrage," *The Black Scholar* 4/6-7 (1973).

44. Audre Lorde, *A Burst of Light* (New York: Thunders Mouth Press, 1987), 130.

45. Elizabeth Lindsey Davis, *Lifting as They Climb*, provides a helpful sampling of these organizations.

46. W. E. B. Du Bois, *The Gift of Black Folk: The Negroes in the Making of America* (New York: Washington Square Press, 1970 [1924]).

47. Lerner, *Black Women in White America*.

48. Walker, *In Search of Our Mothers' Gardens*.

49. Rainwater and Yancey, *The Moynihan Report*, 45.

50. Ibid.

51. Jacqueline Jackson's discussions all emphasize this point: "But Where Are the Men?"; "Black Women in a Racist Society"; "The Mythological Black Woman."

52. Pauli Murray, "The Liberation of Black Women," in *Voices of the New Feminism*, ed. Mary L. Thompson (Boston: Beacon Press, 1970), 354-355; idem, "Jim Crow and Jane Crow," in Lerner, *Black Women in White America*, 592-599.

53. Cade, *The Black Woman*; Josephine Carson, *Silent Voices: The Southern Negro Woman Today* (New York: Dell Publishing Company, 1969); Pat Crutchfield Exum, *Keeping the Faith: Writings by Contemporary Black Women* (Greenwich, Conn.: Fawcett Publications, 1974); Toye L. Lewis, "The Imbalance of Black Males and Black Females: Implications for Black Family Structure," in Mitchell and Bell, *The Black Woman: Myths and Realities*, 61-64; Reid, *"Together" Black Women*.

54. Cade, *The Black Woman*, 163.

55. Gwen C. Patton, "Black People and the Victorian Ethos," in Cade, *The Black Woman*, 143-148; King, "The Politics of Sexual Stereotypes."

56. Lewis, "A Response to Inequality," 339-340.

## 10 The "Loves" and "Troubles" of African-American Women's Bodies

*The author gratefully acknowledges the support of the W. E. B. Du Bois Institute for African American Research and Colby College in the writing and production of this paper.*

1. For an expanded discussion of beauty as conformity or deviance from social norms, see Edwin Schur, *Labeling Women Deviant: Gender, Stigma, and Social Control* (New York: Random House, 1984). I depend heavily on Schur's perspective in my own analysis of African-American women's deviance in terms of their labor history. See Cheryl Townsend Gilkes, "'Liberated to Work Like Dogs!': Labeling Black Women and Their Work," in *The Experience and Meaning of Work in Women's Lives*, ed. Hildreth Y. Grossman and Nia Lane Chester (Hillsdale, N.J.: Lawrence Erlbaum Associates, 1989).

2. For the different kind of "liberating visions" that emerge from our various life histories, see Robert Michael Franklin, *Liberating Visions: Human Fulfillment and Social Justice in African American Thought* (Minneapolis, Minn.: Augsburg Fortress Press, 1990).

3. bell hooks [Gloria Watkins], "Loving Blackness as Political Resistance," in *Black Looks: Race and Representation* (Boston: South End Press, 1992), 19.

4. Alice Walker, "womanist," in *In Search of Our Mothers' Gardens: Womanist Prose* (San Diego: Harcourt Brace Jovanovich, 1983), xi-xii.

5. Some black feminist critics see African-American women's anger at one another as one of black women's biggest problems. While it is sometimes a problem, it is not *the* problem. For some more pessimistic discussions, see bell hooks, *Black Looks*, and Audre Lorde, *Sister Outsider* (Trumansburg, N.Y.: Crossing Press, 1984), especially her essay, "Eye to Eye: Black Women, Hatred, and Anger."

6. On the asexuality of the "Mammy" image associated with the large black woman, see Barbara Christian, *Black Feminist Criticism: Perspectives on Black Women Writers* (New York: Pergamon, 1985), and Deborah Gray White, *Ar'n't I a Woman?: Female Slaves in the Plantation South* (New York: W. W. Norton, 1985).

7. Michelle Wallace tried to talk about this disparity in her book *Black Macho and the Myth of the Superwoman* (New York: Dial Press, 1978). She had difficulty making herself understood, however, because she uncritically used the term "prettiest" to talk about the problems of teenagers in the ghetto whose appearance most conformed to white norms.

8. This is not to ignore the very real risks that African-American women face. In her introduction to Georgianna Arnold's essay "Coming Home: One Black Woman's Journey to Health and Fitness," Evelyn C. White, editor of *The Black Women's Health Book—Speaking for Ourselves* (Seattle, Wash.: Seal Press, 1990), points out that as "American women have gotten increasingly heavier," the problem has been "even greater for black women." Not only do we have increased risks of heart disease, diabetes, and high blood pressure, but we also may be more victimized by our social circumstances. According to White, "Researchers believe that social factors including self-image, career and marital expectations, education, images in the media and role models can influence weight gain."

9. Alice Walker, *In Love and in Trouble: Stories of Black Women* (New York: Harcourt Brace Jovanovich, 1973).

10. Alice Walker, *The Color Purple*, 10th anniversary ed. (New York: Harcourt Brace Jovanovich, 1992), 92.

11. Deborah K. King, "Multiple Jeopardy, Multiple Consciousness: The Context of a Black Feminist Ideology," in *Black Women in America: Social Science Perspectives*, ed. Micheline R. Malson, Elisabeth Mudimbe-Boyi, Jean F. O'Barr, and Mary Wyer, 265-295 (Chicago: University of Chicago Press, 1988).

12. Ibid., 270.

13. Patricia Hill Collins, "Learning from the Outsider Within: The Sociological Significance of Black Feminist Thought," *Social Problems* 33/6 (1986): 14-32. See also idem, "The Social Construction of Black Feminist Thought," *Signs: Journal of Women in Culture and Society* 14/4 (1989); idem, *Black Feminist Thought: Knowledge, Consciousness, and the Politics of Empowerment* (Cambridge, Mass.: Unwin Hyman, 1990).

14. Collins, *Black Feminist Thought*, 11.

15. Ibid.

16. Ibid., 37-38.

17. Karen Baker-Fletcher, "Womanism: It's More Than Blush," *Que Pasa? Information by Racial/Ethnic Clergywomen* [Louisville, Ky.: Women's Ministry Unit, Presbyterian Church {U.S.A.}] (February 1993), 1.

18. William H. Grier and Price M. Cobb, "Achieving Womanhood," in *Black Rage* (New York: Bantam Books, 1968), 32-45.

19. Walker, *The Color Purple*, 187.

20. See Walker's essay by this same title in *In Search of Our Mothers' Gardens*, 290.

21. Lois W. Banner points out that the Miss America Pageant, beginning in 1921, "made a national ritual of the . . . powerful notion that the pursuit of beauty ought to be a woman's primary goal." For a general history of beauty that includes the Miss America Pageant as a pivotal social institution, see Lois Banner, *American Beauty: A Social History through Two Centuries of the American Idea, Ideal, and Image of the Beautiful Woman* (New York: Random House, 1983). My general observations on the Vanessa Williams affair are drawn from my own extensive and uncatalogued collection of clippings on the subject of African-American women and beauty pageants. [Since this essay was first written, an additional African-American woman has served as Miss America, bringing the total to five.]

22. Some of the more egregious examples of this can be found in Sander L. Gilman, "Black Bodies, White Bodies: Toward an Iconography of Female Sexuality in Late Nineteenth-Century Art, Medicine, and Literature," in *"Race," Writing, and Difference*, ed. Henry Louis Gates Jr., 223-261 (Chicago: University of Chicago Press, 1986).

23. Angela T. Davis, *Women, Race, and Class* (New York: Random House, 1981).

24. Alice Walker offers a forceful analysis of this in her essay "Coming Apart," in *You Can't Keep a Good Woman Down* (New York: Harcourt Brace Jovanovich, 1981), 41-53.

25. I am grateful to Deborah King, who provided examples from her popular collection, particularly references to songs such as "Big Leg Woman with a Short Mini-Skirt" (Israel Tolbert on Warren Records, Stax Records Distributor, 1970).

26. Barbara Hilkert Andolsen, *"Daughters of Jefferson, Daughters of Bootblacks": Racism in American Feminism* (Macon, Ga.: Mercer University Press, 1986).

27. Ironically, "Charles" is Suzette de Gaetano's stage name. Her father, who is white, understood the culture of sexual exploitation and abuse well enough to insist that his daughter never be photographed out of his presence. The Rev. Samuel D. Proctor, in a sermon before the National Convention of Gospel Choirs and Choruses in 1984, pointed out that the history of white America's response to our "little light girls with funny eyes" should have prompted more surveillance of Vanessa Williams's employers on the part of her father. Vanessa Williams herself later pointed out that other well-known actresses had shared stories of their own exploitation by photographers.

28. Karen Baker-Fletcher, "Tyson's Defenders and the Church of Silence," *New York Times* (March 29, 1992), Opinion section, 17.

## 11 Ministry to Women

1. Quoted in Milton C. Sernett, "On Freedom's Threshold: The African American Presence in Central New York, 1760-1940," in *The African American Presence in New York State: Four Regional History Surveys*, ed. Monroe Fordham, 51-78 (Albany, N.Y.: The New York African American Institute, 1989).

2. Alice Walker, *The Color Purple,* 10th anniversary ed. (New York: Harcourt Brace Jovanovich, 1992), 187.

3. See Deborah K. King, "Multiple Jeopardy, Multiple Consciousness: The Context of Black Feminist Ideology," *Signs: Journal of Women in Culture and Society* 14/1 (1988), 42-72; and Alice Walker, *In Search of Our Mothers' Gardens: Womanist Prose* (San Diego: Harcourt Brace Jovanovich, 1983).

4. William Julius Wilson, *The Declining Significance of Race: Blacks and Changing American Institutions* (Chicago: University of Chicago Press, 1980), 161.

5. Prathia Hall Wynn has identified sexism as an oppression visited on the *entire* black community. She points out, and rightly so, that the critical involvement of women in the material survival of the community and its institutions (church and family) means that women's poverty and degradation extends to the entire community (unpublished paper).

6. Deborah Gray White, *Ar'n't I a Woman? Female Slaves in the Plantation South* (New York: W. W. Norton, 1985).

7. Bernice Johnson Reagon, "Coalition Politics: Turning the Century," in *Home Girls: A Black Feminist Anthology,* ed. Barbara Smith (New York: Kitchen Table Press, 1983), 363.

8. Paula Giddings, *When and Where I Enter: The Impact of Black Women on Race and Sex in America* (New York: William Morrow and Company, 1984), 35; Anna Julia Cooper, *A Voice from the South by a Woman of the South* (New York: Negro Universities Press, 1969 [Xenia, Ohio: The Aldine Printing House, 1892]), 31.

9. This is a term offered by Katie G. Cannon.

10. White, *Ar'n't I a Woman?,* 119-141.

11. Thomas L. Webber, *Deep like the Rivers: Education in the Slave Quarter Community, 1831-1865* (New York: W. W. Norton, 1978).

12. Webber, *Deep like the Rivers,* 149.

13. Gayraud Wilmore, *Black Religion and Black Radicalism: An Interpretation of the Religious History of Afro-American People,* 2d ed. (Maryknoll, N.Y.: Orbis Books, 1983).

14. Evelyn Brooks Higginbotham, *Righteous Discontent: The Women's Movement in the Black Baptist Church, 1880-1920* (Cambridge. Mass.: Harvard University Press, 1993).

15. Higginbotham, *Righteous Discontent.*

16. Rackham Holt, *Mary McLeod Bethune: A Biography* (Garden City, N.Y.: Doubleday and Company, 1964).

17. Mamie Garvin Fields with Karen E. Fields, *Lemon Swamp and Other Places: A Carolina Memoir* (New York: Macmillan-Free Press, 1983).

18. Frances Ellen Watkins Harper, *Iola Leroy or the Shadows Uplifted* (Boston: The Beacon Press, 1987 [1893]).

19. Evelyn Brooks Higginbotham in *Righteous Discontent* calls the women of this group the female half of the talented tenth.

20. Jualynne Dodson and Cheryl Townsend Gilkes, "'Something Within': Social Change and Collective Endurance in the Sacred World of Black Christian Women," in *Women and Religion in America,* vol. 3, *The Twentieth Century,* ed. Rosemary Radford Ruether and Rosemary Keller, 80-130 (San Francisco: Harper & Row, 1986), 81.

21. I use the term "poor" not only as a designation for those whose incomes place them below the poverty line, but in a way similar to the way in which James Cone

uses the term "black"—as a label designating those who stand in solidarity with the least of these, and, for the purposes of this discussion, the least of these are "poor" black women.

22. Walker, *In Search of Our Mother's Gardens,* xi-xii.

23. Patricia Hill Collins, "The Social Construction of Black Feminist Thought," *Signs: Journal of Women in Culture and Society* 14/4 (1989).

24. Angela Davis, *Women, Race, and Class* (New York: Random House, 1981), 5.

25. Jacqueline Jones, *Labor of Love, Labor of Sorrow: Black Women, Work and the Family from Slavery to the Present* (New York: Basic Books, 1985).

26. White, *Ar'n't I a Woman?*

27. For extended discussions of this phenomenon, see Nell Irvin Painter, *The Exodusters: Black Migration to Kansas after Reconstruction* (New York: Random House, 1977), and Jones, *Labor of Love.*

28. Dorothy Sterling, *We Are Your Sisters: Black Women in the Nineteenth Century* (New York: W. W. Norton, 1984).

29. Jacqueline Jones, *Labor of Love.*

30. Carter G. Woodson, "The Negro Washerwoman," *The Journal of Negro History* 15/3 (1930), 269-277. See also, Giddings, *When and Where I Enter.*

31. E. Franklin Frazier, *The Negro Family in the United States* (Chicago: University of Chicago Press, 1939).

32. Taylor Branch, *Parting the Waters: America in the King Years, 1954-63* (New York: Simon and Schuster, 1988).

33. Jo Ann Gibson Robinson, *The Montgomery Bus Boycott and the Women Who Started It: The Memoir of Jo Ann Gibson Robinson* (Knoxville, Tenn.: The University of Tennessee Press, 1987).

34. King, "Multiple Jeopardy, Multiple Consciousness."

35. Paula S. Rothenberg, *Racism and Sexism: An Integrated Study* (New York: St. Martin's Press, 1988).

36. For fuller discussions of the role of Nannie Helen Burroughs within and outside of the National Baptist Convention, see also Evelyn Brooks, "Religion, Politics, and Gender: The Leadership of Nannie Helen Burroughs," *Journal of Religious Thought* 44 (Winter/Spring 1988): 7-22; and Evelyn Brooks Barnett, "Nannie Burroughs and the Education of Black Women," in *The Afro-American Woman: Struggles and Images,* ed. Sharon Harley and Rosalyn Terborg-Penn, 97-108 (Port Washington, N.Y.: Kennikat Press, 1978).

37. Charles V. Hamilton, *The Black Preacher in America* (New York: William Morrow and Company, 1972).

38. Marilyn Richardson, ed., *Maria W. Stewart, America's First Black Woman Political Writer* (Bloomington, Ind.: Indiana University Press, 1987).

39. Joanne Grant, "Fundi: The Story of Ella Baker" (New York: Icarus Films, 1986).

40. Kay Mills, *This Little Light of Mine: The Life of Fannie Lou Hamer* (New York: Dutton, 1993).

41. Mary King, *Freedom Song; A Personal Story of the 1960s Civil Rights Movement* (New York: William Morrow and Company, 1987).

42. I provide more extended discussion of community workers and church mothers in Cheryl Townsend Gilkes, "'Together and in Harness': Women's Traditions in the Sanctified Church," *Signs: Journal of Women in Culture and Society* 11/4 (1985): 80-130; and idem, "The Roles of Church and Community Mothers: Ambivalent

American Sexism or Fragmented African Familyhood?," *Journal of Feminist Studies in Religion* 2 (Spring 1986): 41-59.

43. Edwin Schur, *Labeling Women Deviant: Gender, Stigma and Social Control* (New York: Random House, 1984).

44. Walker, *In Search of Our Mother's Gardens*, 290.

45. One of the most helpful discussions of this I have experienced was at a black feminist panel discussion on racism and self-hatred held at Simmons College in Boston, Massachusetts, in the early 1980s. The exact date and conference escape me now.

46. Michelle Wallace, *Black Macho and the Myth of the Superwoman* (New York: The Dial Press, 1979).

47. Giddings, *When and Where I Enter*.

48. Barbara Andolsen, *"Daughters of Jefferson, Daughters of Bootblacks": Racism and American Feminism* (Macon, Ga.: Mercer University Press, 1986).

49. Walker, *In Search of Our Mother's Gardens*, xii.

50. Theressa Hoover, "Black Women and the Churches: Triple Jeopardy," in *Black Theology: A Documentary History, 1966-1979*, ed. Gayraud S. Wilmore and James H. Cone, 377-388 (Maryknoll, N.Y.: Orbis Books, 1980).

51. Although left out of many of the current discussions of the underclass, I think that Sydney Wilhelm's volume *Who Needs the Negro* (Garden City, N.Y.: Doubleday and Company, 1971) provides an important and provocative context that needs re-examination. He argued that any group that became economically useless became prime targets for genocide. He used the Native American experience as a historical example. He also pointed to the fact that "equality" could now be asserted since economic discrimination would maintain the same essential state of white over black.

52. Cooper, *A Voice from the South*, 32.

# Acknowledgments

When a book of essays is written over the better part of two decades, the author owes tremendous debts of gratitude to many, many people. First of all, my gratitude begins with my father who, after being persuaded of the wisdom of my choice to study sociology, made the pivotal suggestion that started all of this: "Maybe you should talk to those ladies who worked so hard to keep the community together and raise scholarship money and things like that." After he read my study of community workers, he suggested that the Sanctified Church needed the attention of qualitative sociological research. Mommy and Daddy are still reading my stuff and asking questions and making suggestions that constantly enrich my thinking and my writing. My pastor, Jeffrey L. Brown, was quite assertive in ordering me to finish the book.

I am particularly grateful to James H. Cone, John Cartwright, Delores Williams, Marie Augusta Neal, Renita Weems, Thomas Hoyt, and Prathia Hall for opening doors, helping me through them, and constantly reading and encouraging over the past twenty years. Sharon and Walter Fluker, Constantine Hriskos, David Nugent, Thomas Longstaff, and Thomas Koenig have been very special friends, intellectually and practically, over the years.

Several collaborative groups have provided me with insights, criticisms, friendship, and tremendous affirmation. First the Inter-University Working Group on Gender, Race, and Class consisting of Bonnie Thornton Dill, Elizabeth Higginbotham, Maxine Baca Zinn, Evelyn Nakano Glenn, and Ruth Zambrana provided critical reflection on specific essays and on the larger theoretical issues pertinent to women of color in the United States. Through the Center for Research on Women, I met many new colleagues such as Deborah King, Lynn Weber, and Patricia Hill Collins who challenged and encouraged and criticized and affirmed. Through Howard University School of Divinity, I was privileged to collaborate with Cheryl Sanders and Delores Carpenter. Critical reflections on early drafts of several of these essays came from Clarence Newsome and the late Pearl Williams-Jones at conferences at Howard and the Society for the Study of Black Religion. Colleagues in the American Academy of Religion both in the Afro-American Religious History Group and the Womanist Approaches to Religion and Society Group have provided significant critical insights and encouragement, especially Bettye Collier-Thomas, Evelyn Brooks Higginbotham, Marcia Y. Riggs, Emilie M. Townes, Katie G. Cannon, Karen Baker-Fletcher, Jacqueline Grant, and Susan Brooks Thistlethwaite. Colleagues at various institutes have been absolutely tremendous, especially Deborah MacDowell, Skip Gates, Nick Salvatore, and Judith Weisenfeld. The theme, "If It Wasn't for the Women . . . " would never have come together if Robert Franklin had not invited me to try a draft of an early essay at Colgate-Rochester Divinity School's Mordecai Wyatt Johnson Institute in front of a large group of seminarians and clergy*men*.

Over the years many colleagues, either as friends, discussants at scholarly meetings, or both, have read and commented on various drafts of these essays. Some are specifically mentioned in the notes of each essay. However, several bear special mention: Lesley A. Brown, Arlene Kaplan Daniels, Margaret Andersen, Melvin G. Brown, Nancy Ammerman, and James Geschwender.

Last, but not least, the following institutions have provided support for research and writing of specific essays: Boston University, Colby College, the Center for the Study of African American History and Culture at Temple University, the American Sociological Association, the Center for Research on Women at Memphis State University, the Women's Convention of the Church of God in Christ, the Bunting Institute of Radcliffe College, the Women and Religion Program of the Divinity School at Harvard University, the W. E. B. Du Bois Institute of Harvard University, and the Institute for the Advanced Study of Religion at Yale University. Robert Ellsberg, my editor at Orbis, has believed in this project from the beginning and helped in every way possible. Finally, there are hundreds of women in churches and community organizations who allowed me to intrude, observe, and ask seemingly very dumb questions. I am sure I have left out many who have helped and influenced the works contained in this volume. Please charge it to my head and not my heart.

# Publication History

"'If It Wasn't for the Women . . . ': Community Work and Social Change" was originally published as "'If It Wasn't for the Women . . . ': Social Change, Racial-Ethnic Women, and Their Community Work," in *Women of Color in U.S. Society*, ed. Maxine Baca Zinn and Bonnie Thornton Dill (Philadelphia: Temple University Press, 1994).

"Exploring the Community Connection: Race, Class, and Women's Agency" was originally published as "A Case Study: Race-Ethnicity, Class, and African-American Women: Exploring the Community Connection," in *Revolutions in Knowledge: Feminism in the Social Sciences,* ed. Sue Rosenberg Zalk and Janice Gordon-Kelter, 63-78 (Boulder, Colo.: Westview Press, 1992).

"'Together and in Harness': Women's Traditions in the Sanctified Church" was originally published in *Signs: Journal of Women in Culture and Society* 10/4 (Summer 1985): 678-699.

"The Roles of Church and Community Mothers: Ambivalent American Sexism or Fragmented African Familyhood?" was originally published in *Journal of Feminist Studies in Religion* 2/2 (Fall, 1986): 41-59.

"The Role of Women in the Sanctified Church" was originally published in *Journal of Religious Thought* 43/1 (1986): 24-41.

"The Politics of 'Silence': Dual-Sex Political Systems and Women's Traditions of Conflict" was originally published as "The Politics of 'Silence': Dual-Sex Political Systems and Women's Traditions of Conflict in African American Religion," in *African American Christianity: Essays in History*, ed. Paul E. Johnson, 80-110 (Berkeley and Los Angeles: University of California Press, 1994).

"'Some Mother's Son and Some Father's Daughter': Issues of Gender, Biblical Language, and Worship" was originally published as "'Some Mother's Son and Some Father's Daughter': Gender and Biblical Language in Afro-Christian Worship Tradition," in *Shaping New Vision: Gender and Values in American Culture*, ed. Clarissa Atkinson, Constance H. Buchanan, and Margaret Miles, 73-99 (Ann Arbor, Mich.: University of Michigan Research Press, 1987).

A portion of the chapter "Sisters Who Can Lift a Community: Nannie Helen Burroughs, 'The Slabtown District Convention,' and the Cultural Production of Community and Social Change" was published as "Keeping Faith with the People: Reflections on Ethics, Leadership, and African-American Women's Historical Experience," in *The Stones That the Builders Rejected: The Development of Ethical Leadership from the Black Church Tradition*, ed. Walter E. Fluker, 73-81 (Harrisburg, Pa.: Trinity Press International, 1998).

"'Liberated to Work Like Dogs': Labeling Black Women and Their Work" was originally published in *The Experience and Meaning of Work for Women*, ed. Nia Lane Chester and Hildy Grossman, 165-188 (Hillsdale, N.J.: Lawrence Erlbaum Associates, 1990).

"The 'Loves' and 'Troubles' of African-American Women's Bodies" was originally published in *A Troubling in My Soul: Womanist Perspectives on Evil and Suffering*, ed. Emilie Townes (Maryknoll, N.Y.: Orbis Books, 1993).

"Ministry to Women: Hearing and Empowering 'Poor' Black Women" was originally published in *One Third of a Nation*, ed. Lorenzo Morris (Washington, D.C.: Howard University Press, 1997).

# Index

Smith, Willie Mae Ford, 137
sociology: on black women's traditions, 43-44; critical, 143; of knowledge, 121-23; on religion, 6-7, 84-85; and social change movements, 15-17; on urbanization, 84, 197-98, 203-4
"Something Within" (Campbell), 128, 201
Southern Baptist Convention, 210
*Southern Workman, The*, 149
stereotypes of black women, 38-39, 161-80, 191
Steward, Theophilus, 106
Stewart, Maria, 20, 109-10, 127-28
Student Non-Violent Coordinating Committee (SNCC), 19
"Surely Our God Is Able" (Brewster), 135-36

Talbert, Mary B., 148
Terrell, Mary Church, 20, 31, 182, 187, 201
testimony tradition, 131-33, 137-38
*Their Eyes Were Watching God* (Hurston), 127
Till, Emmett, 87-88
Truth, Sojourner, 110, 123, 128
Tubman, Harriet, 30, 110, 123, 187, 196, 211
Turner, Debbie, 195
Turner, Nat, 200
Tyson, Mike, 181, 195

Underground Railway, 30
United Holy Church of America, 70
Urban League, 18, 19, 21

Vincent, Marjorie, 195
Vodun, 97-98

Walker, Alice: and *Color Purple*, 187, 196, 211; on self-love, 182, 188-95; and "womanist" term, 10, 30-31, 76, 156-57, 186-88, 201-2
Walker, Madame C. J., 203
Walker, Maggie Lena, 148, 203
Wallace, Michelle, 207-8
Ward, Clara, 135-36
Washington, Desiree, 181, 195
Watkins, Gloria, 36
Wells [Barnett], Ida B., 20, 38, 140, 174, 187
West, Cornel, 145-46
White, Deborah Gray, 20, 34-35, 95, 100-101
Williams, Jasper, 134-35
Williams, Vanessa, 181, 195
Wilson, William Julius, 197-98
Winfrey, Oprah, 196-97
womanist culture, 10, 30-31, 76, 155-57, 186-88, 201-2
Women's Convention, COGIC, 124
Women's Day, 5-6, 8, 33, 35-36, 53, 114-15, 147
*Women's Work as Gleaned from the Women of the Bible* (Broughton), 111
Woodson, Carter, 21, 148
work by women: community, 15-27, 163-80; domestic, 37-38, 46, 127, 174-75, 203-4; factory, 166-67; farm, 80; and motherhood, 204; professional, 44-46, 163-80; urbanization of, 83-85
Wyatt, Addie, 173

Yaa Asantewaa, Queen Mother, 65
Young Women's Christian Association (YWCA), 19, 175

*Of Related Interest*

## Sexuality and the Black Church
*A Womanist Perspective*
### Kelly Brown Douglas
ISBN 1-57075-242-7

"Both a challenge and a gift. It challenges the Black church to
begin a long overdue analysis and critique of Black sexuality . . .
It is a gift in that Douglas reaches into the spirituality of the Black
faith tradition to develop a sexual discourse of resistance that can
give voice to its members about the wonders of the fullness and
uniqueness of who we are called to be—female and male."
*–Emilie M. Townes*

## Power in the Blood?
*The Cross in the African-American Experience*
### JoAnne Marie Terrell
ISBN 1-57075-216-8

"A major contribution to black and womanist theologies. It is
both critical and constructive. A must read for all students and
teachers of theology and religion."
*–James H. Cone*

## Can I Get a Witness?
*Prophetic Religious Voices of African American Women*
*An Anthology*
### Marcia Y. Riggs, editor
ISBN 1-57075-113-7

"An heirloom left by our mothers of many past generations."
*–Gayraud S. Wilmore*

Please support your local bookstore, or call 1-800-258-5838.
For a free catalogue, please write us at
Orbis Books, Box 308
Maryknoll NY 10545-0308
Or visit our website at www.orbisbooks.com

Thank you for reading *If It Wasn't for the Women ...*
We hope you enjoyed it.